P9-CEP-083

essays on PRICE THEORY and INDUSTRIAL ORGANIZATION

Joe S. Bain

Essays on Price Theory and Industrial Organization

Joe S. Bain

University of California, Berkeley

Little, Brown and Company *Boston*

To Beatrice

Library of Congress Catalog Card No. 72-186059

First Printing

Printed simultaneously in Canada by
Little, Brown & Company (Canada) Limited

Printed in the United States of America

Foreword

Do industries dominated by a few sellers earn more than normal profits, and distort the allocation of resources? Do we need larger firms in order to gain the benefits of economies of scale? Considering that United States law forbids a firm's taking predatory action against its rivals, how can a giant firm continue to dominate a market other than by its progressiveness and efficiency?

Around 1940, few if any economists could have given well-reasoned theoretical answers to these questions. None could have documented his replies with factual evidence. Today, the economists specializing in industrial organization agree fairly broadly on the answers. More important, many share a common approach to framing such questions and testing theoretical answers against economic facts. No economist has contributed more to building this basis for understanding industrial organization than Joe S. Bain, and it is a pleasure to see his principal scientific papers collected in a single volume. They have served as building blocks for this widely used conceptual structure. They report pioneering applications of statistical techniques to test that structure against the facts. They include useful summaries of research results that he has reported more fully in book-length studies. They retain their freshness and vigor, not just for the professional economist casting an eye over the foundations of the present-day field of industrial organization, but also for the student or general reader seeking a grasp of the economics of industries.

Market structure determines the market conduct, or behavior, of firms in designing and pricing their products, and on this conduct depends the quality of their market performance. *Market structure* comprises the economically relevant and stable feature of the environment that the firms in a market must take into account in determining their price and the traits of the product they offer. The methods they use to set price and product and to reconcile their conflicting postures in the marketplace comprise their *market conduct. Market performance* consists of the allocations of resources that result from this market conduct, appraised by the criteria of welfare economics. This, in a few words, is the taxonomic framework that has evolved in Joe Bain's writings; its rudiments are evident in the first paper reprinted here, which originally appeared in 1942. (Bain recollects its relation to antecedent work by Edward H. Chamberlin and Edward S. Mason, in Chapters 14 and 12 respectively.)

The chief features and uses of this framework are mirrored in—indeed, usually sprang from—papers appearing in this volume. First, the framework is rooted in price theory, and amounts to a loose-knit, taxonomic form of oligopoly theory. As Bain notes (Chapter 1), builders of conventional theoretical models of the firm and the industry persistently found them upon assumptions that cannot be directly confirmed or refuted—assumptions about the firm's motivation and the way in which it perceives its economic environment. Theoretical models of this sort can serve to rationalize any form of economic behavior we observe, after the event. But because they can explain anything, they can tag no outcome as being more or less likely than another to follow from a given set of actual conditions. We can, for instance, infer little about what effects would flow from requiring dominant firms in an industry to license their patents, if our theoretical models require that we know at the outset whether the oligopolist assumes that his rival will keep constant his price or the quantity he sells. The framework pioneered by Bain avoids this preoccupation with nonoperational cognitive and motivational assumptions, and instead concentrates on the observable features of the industry's environment and their probable effect on price and output decisions. The point is not that untestable assumptions can be avoided, but rather that they can be used to connect visible traits of market structure with measurable aspects of market performance, rendering the model testable as a whole. This framework was developed most fully in Bain's textbook treatise, *Industrial Organization,* but an early statement in Chapter 3 of this volume (published in 1949) still offers a clear and useful summary of the approach.

Conventional theories of markets of course employ some structural assumptions, and indeed emphasize one—the number and size distribution of sellers—above all others. Picking up the lead of Chamberlin and Mason, Bain showed that an effective set of theoretical models of markets must specify a number of structural features—although not so many as to stumble into the trap of explaining anything but predicting nothing. Furthermore, he originated the concept of barriers to entry—factors creating a significant advantage for the going firm over the new entrant to an industry. It is hard to overstress the importance of this concept. First, it offers an explanation of why firms in a highly concentrated industry may settle for what are clearly less than maximum short-run profits, in order to deter entry and maximize their long-run advantage. (Bain developed this idea in a paper appearing as Chapter 5 of this volume.) Second, it helps to explain why levels of seller concentration should vary as they do from industry to industry. Some economists have carried Schumpeter's Olympian view that (in effect) no monopoly lasts a thousand years to its illogical conclusion that any profits in excess of normal will, with trivial delays, cause a horde of competitors to spring into action. The concept of entry barriers explains why profitable near-monopoly positions can persist, and tells us where to expect this outcome. Although Bain's work on entry barriers took fullest form in *Barriers to New Competition* (1956), several papers reprinted here develop the underlying theory or provide handy condensations of some of the empirical results. Chapters 5 through 7 (especially 6) established the concept and its implications, and set the scene for the ambitious empirical measurements reported in that book. These are summarized, and their implications explored, in the papers reprinted as Chapters 8 and 9.

One virtue of Joe Bain's approach to industrial organization is that it comprehends, easily if not precisely, the concept of the "second best." This term designates the theorem which holds that, if one of a set of interdependent marginal equivalences required for maximum welfare is ineluctably violated, we generally make the (second) best of the situation by turning the other marginal equalities into specific inequalities. Loosely translated into industrial organization, the theorem suggests that, e.g., when one of an industry's structural traits cannot be made conducive to best market performance, others should perhaps also be distorted away from their ideal states. Because Bain's framework treats each dimension of market performance as depending on a whole set of elements of market structure, the user is forced to keep this possibility in mind, even if he gains no neat procedure for applying it. A famous argument of the "second best" type was put forward in 1939 by J. M. Clark, who urged that in the absence of product differentiation unfettered price competition might prove undesirable. Bain recognized in "Workable Competition in Oligopoly" (Chapter 3, first published in 1950) that arguments of this type naturally led to a more searching examination in terms of the concepts of market structure, conduct, and performance.

As Bain pushed the analysis of markets toward correct emphasis on their structural determinants, he was led to a critical view of the approaches to market behavior taken by both theorists and applied workers in industrial economics. Economists theorizing about oligopoly behavior have always shown an affinity for extreme but formally tractable assumptions, which allow them to derive precise formal conclusions about the consequences of indisputably simple-minded patterns of behavior. Unlike the theory specialists, Bain recognized the importance of uncertainty, information costs, and communication constraints upon rival sellers. He early noted (Chapter 2, 1948) the weighty degree of consensus required for oligopolistic sellers to achieve full monopolistic collusion, and went on to stress the identification of feasible patterns of market behavior among rival sellers. This work anticipated to an important degree the notion of focal bargaining points, advanced more recently in general theoretical treatments of bargaining situations. Bain's study of feasible patterns of market conduct also convinced him that, however engaging the cut and thrust of oligopolistic rivalry might prove for the onlooker, it provides a wobbly base for predicting anything about the resulting market performance. His engaging critique of "Price Leaders, Barometers, and Kinks" (Chapter 10) depicts the perils of leaping from descriptions of market conduct to conclusions about market performance if they occur in industries with unlike structures.

A popular and highly productive form of research in the field of industrial organization during the past few years has used statistical techniques to search for the sorts of associations that Bain hypothesized between the elements of market structure and the quality of performance. His general approach to industrial organization proves a natural foundation for cross-industry statistical testing, emphasizing as it does the comparative long-run consequences of alternative market structures. His 1951 study of the relation between industrial concentration and rates of profit (Chapter 4) is the ancestor of these statistical investigations, and still provides a model in its scrupulous care with the peculiarities of the available data and its disinclination to assume the simple linear relations between variables that prove so convenient in regression analysis. Later studies have explored additional hypotheses, with at least modest success. However, Bain grumbles aptly (Chapters 11 and 12) about their occasional lack of care in specifying relations correctly and their selection of statistical proxies for availability rather than aptness.

Industrial organization, as reflected in Joe Bain's papers and the considerable amount of related research by other scholars, has far from closed its frontiers of either conceptual or empirical development. As he notes, the question of the comparative stability and rate of change in the elements of market structure have been only partially studied (Chapter 12; compare his own research contribution in Chapter 13). The effect of shifts in the elements of market structure on performance—clearly an important question for anti-trust policy—has barely been touched. The way in which the elements of market structure interact and affect each other is poorly mapped, and the power of firms to choose conduct patterns that alter the market structure surrounding them is yet to be assessed. International trade and foreign direct investment should be integrated into both the conceptual and empirical structures of the subject, especially when it is exported from the United States to more open economies. One hopes that Joe Bain's work will prove as fruitful in guiding developments in these areas as it has in the past, and that scholars and students in the field can look forward to further guidance from him in the future.

Richard E. Caves

Harvard University

Preface

This volume collects a selection of my journal articles, contributions to Festschrifts and conference proceedings, and lectures, as well as an excerpt from one of my books, all in the related fields of price theory and industrial organization. It includes in a logical sequence the original presentations for a professional audience of my more prominent contributions to the literature of these fields—in large part reflecting my participation in the development of a distinctive approach to the study of industrial organization. This development emphasizes applying economic analysis to empirical data, the origination and elaboration of related theory, its restatement in forms susceptible to empirical refutation, the empirical testing of resultant theoretical hypotheses, and a "wedding" of theoretical and empirical approaches to the study of firms and markets.

Most of these essays present ideas and arguments that subsequently appeared in simplified form in my textbooks, *Industrial Organization* and *Price Theory*. Some are the original presentations of theory and applied analysis later incorporated in my monograph, *Barriers to New Competition*, or represent extensions of its analyses. Three pieces are essentially independent essays on controversial topics.

The collection should make more easily accessible to younger economists my original writings on price theory and industrial organization—a putative benefit if they have encountered the ideas developed there mainly in my textbooks, or in secondary treatments wherein these ideas were often incompletely and sometimes inaccurately characterized.

In the development of my work in the designated fields, I have been deeply in debt to many colleagues and students for the stimuli and criticisms they have provided. It would be impossible to overestimate the depth of my dependence on the work of Edward S. Mason, who in the 1930's and later developed the basic conceptual framework upon which the modern field of industrial organization has been built. He "invented" the field as we now know it. Similarly, I am very deeply indebted to the late Edward H. Chamberlin. The direct influence of his *Theory of Monopolistic Competition* is clearly apparent in my work. In addition, his writings had a powerful catalytic effect on my own thinking, particularly as my unsuccessful endeavors to reconcile various empirical findings with some of his predictions stimulated me to revise or elaborate some aspects of the theory of firms and markets.

Thanks for permitting me to reprint these essays are due to Macmillan & Co., John Wiley & Sons, Houghton Mifflin Company, the *American Economic Review,* the *Quarterly Journal of Economics,* the *Review of Economics and Statistics,* the *Journal of Marketing,* and the *Journal of Business.*

Joe S. Bain

Contents

Essays on Price Theory and Industrial Organization

Chapter One

Market Classifications in Modern Price Theory

The function of price theory is, in general, to explain the determination, the behavior, and the significance of prices. To accomplish this end, theory undertakes several related tasks. Initially it adopts certain empirical generalizations—assumptions—concerning human behavior and its motivation and concerning physical or technical behavior, relevant to the determination of price. Generalizations concerning diminishing utility, desire of entrepreneurs to maximize profits, and variations of physical productivity with variations in proportions of factors fall in this category. Price theory further adopts certain empirical generalizations associating various aspects of market environment with price behavior, and differentiating sorts of price behavior on the basis of differences in associated market environment. Chamberlinian theory, for example, suggests a classification of markets on the basis of number of sellers (including many, few, and one) and on the basis of degree of differentiation of the product, and suggests the empirical generalization that price behavior will be different as among markets in pure competition, monopolistic competition, oligopoly, and monopoly.[1] A third, and often the most explicitly emphasized function of price theory, is that of deducing precisely (usually with the aid of additional generalizations explicit or implied) the manner in which the preceding empirical generalizations hold. The complexity of this stage depends, in part, on the complexity of the assumptions which have been made. In a simple case this may amount merely to demonstrating that with a negatively sloped demand curve and a positively sloped supply curve, price is determinate at the intersection. Contemporary price theory, however, demonstrates in detail the manner in which numbers in the market and differentiation of the product are reflected in conditions of demand for the individual seller, and ultimately therefore in price. It is, of course, true that the process of eliciting the

Reprinted from *Quarterly Journal of Economics*, 56, August 1942, pp. 560-574, courtesy of the publisher.

[1]Edward Chamberlin, *The Theory of Monopolistic Competition*, Cambridge, 1933, especially Ch. 3 and 4.

implications of certain assumptions may suggest corollary generalizations which may themselves have empirical relevance.

All price theory necessarily embodies all of these elements, but that phase of it—whether empirical generalization or logical deduction—which receives major attention is likely to depend on the preference of the individual theorist and also on the prevailing customs of his class. It is perfectly possible for the theorist, *qua* theorist, to be primarily interested in assembling an adequate group of empirical generalizations concerning behavior, and relatively less preoccupied with the logical demonstration that they should hold. Or he may be primarily interested, as has been the fashion of late in many cases, with a skillful and ingenious elaboration of the logical possibilities of a few simple factual generalizations.[2]

It is probably true that contemporary price theory, as represented (to take a sample) in Chamberlin, Mrs. Robinson, and Hicks, excels particularly in the detail and ingenuity of its logic, but is based upon a rather sketchy and incomplete group of genuine empirical generalizations. It may therefore be charged in a good many cases with selecting for definitive rationalization a much simpler sort of behavior than occurs in fact, or alternatively with rationalizing observed behavior in terms of an inadequate sample of the variables and environmental factors which condition price making. The shortcomings of contemporary price theory seem to lie (1) in an oversimplification of real behavior for the purposes of theorizing, exemplified in a failure to differentiate between apparently different sorts of prices and markets, and (2) in a type of explanation which, though logically correct, seems to lack empirical content in the sense of having the possibility of factual verification. Both difficulties, as we shall see, stem from the inadequacy of the basic empirical generalizations (in the sense that these difficulties could be eliminated by seeking out a more adequate group of such generalizations).

Although the preceding criticisms apply to all contemporary price theory in a broad sense, they need to be made specific with respect to any of several different formulations which modern price theorists have adopted. Here we shall select for examination the two most prominent formulations—that suggested by Joan Robinson in *The Economics of Imperfect Competition,*[3] and carried out in the work of such writers as Lerner,[4] and that suggested by Chamberlin in his *Theory of Monopolistic Competition.*[5]

CHAMBERLIN AND ROBINSON: COMPARATIVE METHODOLOGY

What might be characterized as the Robinsonian theory of prices consists almost entirely of an account of how the firm adjusts its costs to the demand curve for

[2]J. R. Hicks, *Value and Capital,* Oxford, 1939, especially Parts I and II, devoted largely to an extended elaboration of the possibilities of a perfectly competitive world.

[3]London, 1933.

[4]A. P. Lerner, "The Concept of Monopoly and the Measurement of Monopoly Power," *Review of Economic Studies,* Vol. I, pp. 157-175.

[5]Chamberlinian ideas have also been elaborated on a formal level in Robert Triffin, *Monopolistic Competition and General Equilibrium Theory,* Cambridge, 1940.

its product.[6] Short-run equilibrium output for any firm is defined as that for which marginal cost (assumed known) is equal to marginal revenue (assumed known). The characteristics of short-run price equilibrium are then differentiated as between firms with horizontal and with variously sloping demand curves. The theory is next extended to explain long-run price equilibrium (potentially with the introduction of some assumption about entry) and to differentiate between situations with various conditions of return to scale in the long run. Other elaborations along the same line may be introduced. In any case, however, the nature of the explanation of pricing offered has one major characteristic—it is an explanation basically in terms of given demand curves and cost curves. It says that prices are determined by adjusting "known" costs to a "known" demand schedule. The basic empirical assertions seem to be that every firm has a demand curve, that every firm has cost curves obeying certain physical laws, and that every firm tries to maximize its profit. The theory then merely describes the equilibrium conditions for profit maximization.

One obvious shortcoming of such a theory is that it is purely two dimensional in character, emphasizing only the functional relationships of price to output and cost to output, but since such a difficulty is easily remedied we will not labor it here. It is most pertinent to inquire, first, whether such a theory has empirical content, in the sense that it permits the investigator to explain an observed price as being associated with some other observable thing or things. Does the theory add to our knowledge of markets and prices in the sense that it tells us when in the real world we may expect one sort of behavior and when another? Or does it merely furnish a pure rationalization of what happens, assuring us that there is a sufficient (and complicated) reason for any behavior, but giving us no empirical basis for anticipating different sorts of behavior?

The answer to this question seems to depend upon whether or not the theoretical "price determinants" (i.e., the demand curves and the cost curves) are ascertainable independently of the prices they determine. If the demand and cost curves which presumably determine prices are in fact *ascertained,* then a theory which explains prices in terms of them has an available empirical content, since it allows us to associate certain observed things (cost and demand curves) with certain observed results (prices). If the demand curves are not ascertained in fact, because of statistical or other difficulties, but are *practically ascertainable,* then the theory has a potential but unrealized empirical content. If, finally, the curves either are *not practically ascertainable,* or at the extreme are *not even conceivably ascertainable,* then the theory is without empirical content and furnishes nothing more than pure rationalization of observed behavior.

In which category does the Robinsonian formulation of price theory fall? If the case were to be judged in terms of cost curves alone, it would fall largely in the second, since cost curves seem practically susceptible of ascertainment, even though statistical computation has been undertaken in only a few cases. The

[6]Such a characterization cannot be wholly correct, since Mrs. Robinson's work is in effect merely a close approach to the type of theory indicated, paying so little attention to that which "lies behind" the demand curve that we may for the purpose of argument neglect it.

crux of the matter, however, concerns demand curves. On the surface, since some statistical demand curves have been computed, and other similar ones could be, the "demand side" of price analysis would seem also likely to put price theory in the second category. A close examination of the nature of the demand curves with which price theory is concerned, however, indicates that because of them this sort of price theory will fall in the third category–totally lacking in empirical content.

The primary and most general reason for this is that the theoretical demand curve is always an ex ante demand curve which exists in the expectations of a producer. An *ex post* demand curve, no matter how adequate the statistical technique which prepared it, is not the same thing, nor does it bear any specific or necessarily close relationship to it. Not only have those demand curves which exist in the minds of producers not been ascertained, but it is very questionable whether they are practically susceptible of ascertainment. Insofar as this is true, a price theory stemming from "given" demand curves is devoid of empirical content, on the ground that the curves are practically non-ascertainable.

The same difficulty is reinforced in any case where conceptually the demand curve for the individual seller is contingent as regards its shape and position upon reactions of rival sellers which are likely to be induced by movements along it–i.e., in every case of oligopoly. Here the demand curve is doubly a matter of the subjective of the seller–as regards not only his expectations concerning the demand for the product, but also his expectations regarding the probable reactions of his rivals. The demand schedule for the individual oligopolist is hardly susceptible of practical ascertainment. It is such a highly tenuous concept that one might question its explicit existence in the mind of the producer and therefore whether it is even conceivably ascertainable.[7] As applied to oligopolistic situations in particular, but to all others as well, then, it is questionable whether the Robinsonian formulation of price theory has any empirical content.[8] This holds even though we refrain from criticizing a two-dimensional analysis as applied to what is in fact very evidently a multi-dimensional market adjustment.

This criticism is occasionally phrased in polemic terms by charging this sort of theory with *implicit definition* of the alleged determinants of price behavior. If it is assumed that producers always maximize their profits, and if the demand and supply curves in terms of which profit maximization is calculated are unknown, then in explaining any actual price or price movement the theory may be taken to imply that this price is sufficiently explained by demand and supply curves (implicitly defined as) consistent with its existence. This is merely another way of saying that a theory without empirical content (in the sense that it offers no practical possibility of ascertaining the determinants of behavior) can

[7]One reader comments, "(In this) situation no two points on a demand curve can be simultaneously valid, *even if the given seller can foresee his rivals' reactions to a given price change.* If, selling at a particular price, a firm estimated how much a given reduction would increase its sales, taking account of the reaction of rivals, it does not follow that having made the reduction it could then return to its former position on the 'demand curve.' "

[8]An exception might be made in the single case of pure competition, where the seller's demand curve is derived solely from known market price.

offer only pure rationalization of behavior. This limitation is, in fact, common to all economic theory which relates behavior to magnitudes which exist primarily in the subjectives of individuals, and in general merely indicates a limitation on the content of such theory. Such "implicit definition" is misleading only if the non-ascertained or non-ascertainable character of the so-called determinants of behavior is not sufficiently emphasized, or if the determinants implicitly defined are "forced," in the sense that people could hardly be expected to think in the terms indicated. Without judging Robinsonian theory on the first count, it might be indicated that the idea of adjustment to an individual demand curve in an oligopoly situation seems far from directly representative of the calculations actually made in such a case.

The main limitation of Robinsonian price theory, however, is apparently an absence of empirical content, stemming from the fact that the entire explanation hinges on price determinants (demand curves in particular) which are the property of the subjectives of individuals, and which are practically non-ascertainable. Such a theory is meaningful, but it is no help if we wish to be able to identify in the real world various situations where various sorts of price behavior may be expected. Is it not possible for a theory to fulfill this latter task?

The Chamberlinian theory, although employing the same tools of analysis, seems by contrast to possess greater empirical content. Instead of beginning largely with "given" demand and cost curves, the non-ascertainability of the former of which has been emphasized, it starts "one step further back" with certain direct empirical generalizations, all elements of which are susceptible of easy practical ascertainment. These are generalizations concerning the effect upon associated price behavior of the number of sellers in a "market" and of the degree of differentiation of the product within a "market." Chamberlin makes the direct empirical observation that as markets differ with respect to these characteristics, so their price behavior will differ (although to be sure these generalizations are of the most simplified and rudimentary sort).[9] From these generalizations it is in fact possible to derive a simple classification of markets, with the suggestion that each category has peculiar elements of behavior. Machlup has suggested the following:[10]

1. Markets with many sellers.
   a. Undifferentiated product–(pure competition)
   b. Differentiated product–(monopolistic competition)
2. Markets with few sellers.
   a. Undifferentiated product (pure oligopoly)
   b. Differentiated product (differentiated oligopoly)
3. Markets with one seller (monopoly).

[9]See also, Triffin, op. cit., p. 143, for some terminological suggestions.

[10]Fritz Machlup, "Monopoly and Competition," *American Economic Review,* XXXVII September 1937, pp. 445-451. The following classification paraphrases the original. See also R. L. Hall and C. J. Hitch, "Price Theory and Business Behavior," *Oxford Economic Papers,* No. 2, pp. 12-45, for the treatment of market classification and certain empirical investigations therein.

Without investigating for the moment the adequacy of this framework of empirical generalization, it is apparent that, when considered with relation to it, the demand-cost analysis gains a new orientation. Instead of standing alone, it now fulfills the task of rationalizing in terms of assumed human motives the implications of certain observed "laws of behavior" which themselves do not directly concern human motivation. Thus Chamberlin shows how each observed market situation will presumably be reflected in the position, shape, and behavior of demand curves, and deduces the implications of the situation in terms of assumed entrepreneurial reaction to these curves. But he has first added a compartment to price theory which Mrs. Robinson largely neglects, but which nevertheless is a meaningful and necessary part of price analysis in general. A price theory which includes first direct empirical generalizations and second rationalization of these generalizations in terms of human motivation is a great deal more useful than one which begins only with the second half of this procedure.

INADEQUACY OF CHAMBERLIN'S ASSUMPTIONS

As soon as a price theory attempts this important first step, however, it at once invites criticism of the adequacy and relevance of its empirical generalizations. The Chamberlinian theory suggests only the most incomplete and sketchy range of such generalizations, and allows only an extremely condensed classification of markets. Of the shortcomings of this classification there are two sorts of evidence. In the first place, there is a good deal of *prima facie* evidence both that markets differ according to characteristics other than numbers and degree of differentiation of the product, and that these other differences are associated with significant differences in price and market behavior. The facts cry for a more adequate classification, recognizing more market characteristics. In the second place, rationalization of behavior within certain of the very broad categories established—for both sorts of oligopoly—has failed to yield as definitive results as might reasonably be expected. If all markets falling within the oligopoly category are lumped together (or perhaps subdivided once, on the basis of differentiation of the product) Chamberlinian theory disappoints us twice. It suggests that the pricing results are indeterminate, depending upon what *A* assumes about *B*, etc.; and it fails to suggest any systematic fashion in which the behavior of one oligopoly will differ from that of another. This is a fairly serious shortcoming, in view of the fact (1) that most oligopolistic industries exhibit patterns of behavior as systematic and regular as any others, and (2) that systematic differences in behavior exist among different sorts of oligopolies. Nor is the oligopoly category to be lightly dismissed, since a high proportion of all industries in the real world fall within its limits.

These shortcomings are obviously not shortcomings of logic. The dilemma of logically indeterminate behavior in the face of observed systematic behavior is attributable to one of two things. First, Chamberlinian theory elicits, in terms of assumed human motivation, the type of price logically implied for markets with a few sellers. It is true that for oligopolies, either with or without differentiated product, no uniquely determinate price is implied. But Chamberlin has left out of account market characteristics other than numbers and differentiation. If they were recognized and used as a basis for further subdividing the broad oligopoly category, it is possible that the pricing logically implied for the smaller and more definitely defined market types might square better with observed fact. Thus for markets with a few sellers, differentiated product, plus characteristic *X*, plus characteristic *Y*, a uniquely determinate price might be logically implied. The implications in terms of human motivation of hitherto neglected market characteristics might be the solution.

On the other hand, even though certain regularities of behavior and their systematic association with market conditions may be observed, it may be that their rational necessity in terms of human motivation cannot be established, and that they will have to be accepted *a priori.* In either case, theory should explore the possibility fully, both by looking for empirical regularities and their association with observable market characteristics, and by attempting to rationalize the observed tendencies.

Roughly the same argument applies to the difficulty of the observed differences among the behavior of oligopolies which are not accounted for by Chamberlinian theory. Oligopoly is an extremely broad category, and within it numerous important differences with respect to characteristics of market structure other than numbers may exist. The difficulty indicated may be attacked first by deriving a more adequate set of empirical generalizations concerning market behavior, and second by attempting to rationalize the observed tendencies by the use of traditional techniques. Failure in the second attempt does not necessarily vitiate the meaningfulness of the first.

It is thus apparent that, although the Chamberlinian theory has a broader orientation than the Robinsonian and begins explicitly with certain generalizations possessing definite empirical content, it fails to offer an adequate body of such generalizations as a basis for further theorizing. Presuming that the potentialities of the Robinsonian approach have been rather fully exploited, it seems reasonable that further effort in contemporary price theory should be directed largely toward deriving a really adequate body of empirical generalizations.

DIRECTIONS FOR EXPANDING CHAMBERLINIAN THEORY

Some examples of neglected market characteristics behavioristically associated with differences in the attributes of pricing are: the number of and the degree of concentration among buyers; the durability of the good in question; whether the good is purchased by producers or by consumers; the adaptability of the good to variation over time, including the importance of style elements; the geographical dispersion of the market and the importance of transport costs. All of these and other market characteristics are very probably associated in one fashion or another with the price behavior which emerges from a particular market. It is not at all impossible that this association is regular and systematic. If it is, it is the task of theory to elicit this association and to propound an adequate system of hypotheses describing it.

It is therefore suggested that theorists should attempt to arrive at a much more comprehensive set of empirical generalizations concerning price behavior. From this might emerge a classification of industrial markets considerably more detailed than the Chamberlinian.[11] For example, on the basis of such significant market characteristics[12] as number of sellers, differentiation of product, durability of good, importance of product-variation, number of buyers, and consumer's or producer's good, we might obtain the following classification:

I. Markets with few sellers (oligopoly)
  A. Producers' goods
    1. Durable goods
      a. Differentiated
        (i) Product variation important
          (*a*) Few buyers
          (*b*) Many buyers
        (ii) Product variation unimportant
          (*a*) Few buyers
          (*b*) Many buyers
      b. Undifferentiated
        (i) Product variation unimportant
          (*a*) Few buyers
          (*b*) Many buyers
        (ii) Product variation important
          (*a*) Few buyers
          (*b*) Many buyers
    2. Non-durable goods
      a. Differentiated
        (i) Product variation important
          (*a*) Few buyers
          (*b*) Many buyers
        (ii) Product variation unimportant
          (*a*) Few buyers
          (*b*) Many buyers

[11] To the suggestions herein contained concerning the need for an adequate body of empirical generalizations, and to the conception of price theory as beginning with a broad, inductively derived classification of markets associating price behavior with market characteristics, I heartily subscribe, but for them I refuse any credit for original authorship. An approach of this character in well articulated form has been suggested by Professor E. S. Mason in seminars in Industrial Organization and Price Policy at Harvard University. These suggestions include a tentative classification of markets more comprehensive than any suggested here, but which to my knowledge has not yet been published. The general character of this approach, however, is certainly significant enough to demand exposition, and is therefore included as an integral part of the present argument.

[12] This list is suggested only as a sample.

b. Undifferentiated
(i) Product variation unimportant
(*a*) Few buyers
(*b*) Many buyers
(ii) Product variation important
(*a*) Few buyers
(*b*) Many buyers

B. Consumers' goods
1. Durable goods
a. Differentiated
(i) Product variation important
(*a*) Few buyers
(*b*) Many buyers
(ii) Product variation unimportant
(*a*) Few buyers
(*b*) Many buyers
b. Undifferentiated
(i) Product variation unimportant
(*a*) Few buyers
(*b*) Many buyers
(ii) Product variation important
(*a*) Few buyers
(*b*) Many buyers
2. Non-durable goods
a. Differentiated
(i) Product variation important
(*a*) Few buyers
(*b*) Many buyers
(ii) Product variation unimportant
(*a*) Few buyers
(*b*) Many buyers
b. Undifferentiated
(i) Product variation unimportant
(*a*) Few buyers
(*b*) Many buyers
(ii) Product variation important
(*a*) Few buyers
(*b*) Many buyers

II. Markets with many sellers
A. Producers' goods
1. Durable goods
a. Differentiated
(i) Product variation important
(*a*) Few buyers
(*b*) Many buyers

- (ii) Product variation unimportant
  - (*a*) Few buyers
  - (*b*) Many buyers
- *b.* Undifferentiated
  - (i) Product variation unimportant
    - (*a*) Few buyers
    - (*b*) Many buyers
  - (ii) Product variation important
    - (*a*) Few buyers
    - (*b*) Many buyers
- 2. Non-durable goods
  - *a.* Differentiated
    - (i) Product variation important
      - (*a*) Few buyers
      - (*b*) Many buyers
    - (ii) Product variation unimportant
      - (*a*) Few buyers
      - (*b*) Many buyers
  - *b.* Undifferentiated
    - (i) Product variation unimportant
      - (*a*) Few buyers
      - (*b*) Many buyers
    - (ii) Product variation important
      - (*a*) Few buyers
      - (*b*) Many buyers
- *B.* Consumers' goods
  - 1. Durable goods
    - *a.* Differentiated
      - (i) Product variation important
        - (*a*) Few buyers
        - (*b*) Many buyers
      - (ii) Product variation unimportant
        - (*a*) Few buyers
        - (*b*) Many buyers
    - *b.* Undifferentiated
      - (i) Product variation unimportant
        - (*a*) Few buyers
        - (*b*) Many buyers
      - (ii) Product variation important
        - (*a*) Few buyers
        - (*b*) Many buyers
  - 2. Non-durable goods
    - *a.* Differentiated
      - (i) Product variation important
        - (*a*) Few buyers
        - (*b*) Many buyers

(ii) Product variation unimportant

(*a*) Few buyers

(*b*) Many buyers

b. Undifferentiated

(i) Product variation unimportant

(*a*) Few buyers

(*b*) Many buyers

(ii) Product variation important

(*a*) Few buyers

(*b*) Many buyers

(Markets with one seller are neglected for purposes of brevity.) Other market characteristics might be added to elaborate this classification.

About such classifications, of which this is only a part of a tentative example, the following should be noted. First, they of course represent tentative hypotheses, the relevance of which requires both inductive verification and, if possible, analytical demonstration of some sort. Second, because they are primarily empirical in their reference, only those logically available categories need be explored which have empirical counterparts in sufficient number and importance to justify generalization. Not every possible sub-category of the above sixty-four, for example, need take a real place in the proposed theory. The actual number of real categories in any such classification may be further reduced below the total possible number, insofar as various of the relevant market characteristics are systematically associated. If in nearly all cases, for example, non-durable producers' goods have no important degree of differentiation within markets, then the non-durable producers' goods category need not be subdivided on the basis of differentiation. For this, as well as for the previous reason, we may expect that the real working classification will not be as unwieldy as its logical counterpart.

In the preceding model, for example, we might expect to find the following condensation possible (subject of course to detailed verification):

I. Few sellers

A. Producers' goods; product variation unimportant

1. Durable

a. Differentiated in important degree

(i) Many buyers

(ii) Few buyers

b. Undifferentiated or only slightly differentiated

(i) Many buyers

(ii) Few buyers

2. Non-durable; only slightly differentiated

a. Many buyers

b. Few buyers

B. Consumer's goods; many buyers

1. Differentiated

a. Durable
   (i) Product variation important
   (ii) Product variation unimportant
b. Non-durable; product variation unimportant
2. Non-differentiated; non-durable; product variation unimportant

II. Many sellers
   A. Producers' goods; slightly differentiated; product variation unimportant; non-durable
      1. Many buyers
      2. Few buyers
   B. Consumers' goods; many buyers; differentiated in important degree
      1. Durable; product variation important
      2. Non-durable; product variation unimportant

This decreases the number of terminal classifications from sixty-four to fourteen, and seems by and large to be empirically justifiable.[13] Of course, further market characteristics (e.g., the degree of concentration) seem worthy of inclusion in any experimental classification. Proceeding only so far and so tentatively as we have in the above example, however, there seems to be an inherent reasonableness for looking for a similarity in the market behavior of firms which, for example, sell highly differentiated, durable, style-variable consumers' goods in oligopolistic markets, and for expecting a different behavior for firms which sell, for example, standardized, non-durable producers' goods in an oligopolistic market with a few dominant buyers.

The present writer has not approached the point of articulating such a theory, and must be content to suggest it. The lines along which such a development might proceed, however, are fairly clear. First, it should by a process of trial and error arrive at a reasonable and adequate system of empirical generalizations concerning those things associated with price and market behavior, and at a corresponding market classification, which should be reduced to the simplest amenable terms. Second, it should assemble an adequate empirical description of the sort of behavior associated with each category. Finally, it should, if possible, offer some analytical explanation of the association observed. In so doing, it may find it convenient to revert in some degree to the conventional toolbox, and in some degree necessary to employ other expedients. Associated with this much broader body of empirical generalization, however, the conventional process of rationalization should proceed on a much more secure and meaningful foundation, and might then form a part of a system of price theory with greater explanatory value.

[13] Detailed empirical justification is, of course, required for the grouping together of associated characteristics, and for the elimination of certain possible categories. Preliminary investigation justifies the above grouping.

Chapter Two

Output Quotas in Imperfect Cartels

In his recent article on pricing by multi-plant monopolies and by cartels, Mr. D. Patinkin has devised an ingenious formal model for cartel price and output policy.[1] He has also suggested that the model may furnish predictions of price policy, not only in cartels, but also in oligopolistic industries with collusive arrangements less complete than "full" cartels and in multi-firm industries subject to governmental regulation of price and output. This note indicates why the cartel model may be legitimately employed to interpret pricing in such cases only after one very basic amendment.

The cartel model concerns an industry of firms selling presumably identical products, subject to free entry of added firms, and with an effective cartel which at every juncture makes the price and output decisions for the industry. It shows how the cartel office, in order to maximize industry profits, should determine industry price, industry output, and the allocation of that output among the several firms. Among the more novel formal conclusions stated or implied are the following (pp. 194-198 of the article): (1) that the cartel will assign output quotas to the member firms so as to minimize the aggregate cost of any chosen industry output, (2) that in order to accomplish this the cartel may, except in limiting cases, assign different quotas to different firms and may even order one or more firms to shut down, and (3) that all firms may be expected to accept their "rational" quotas, or even to shut down, in the interest of getting an absolute maximum aggregate industry profit. These formal conclusions are qualified by the statements that there may be bickering over prices and quotas, especially if different firms have different costs, and that individual firms may be tempted to "cheat" on their quotas, but it is not indicated that these tendencies will really destroy the rational output allocation so long as the cartel holds

Reprinted from *Quarterly Journal of Economics,* 62, August 1948, pp. 617-622, courtesy of the publisher.

[1] "Multi-Plant Forms, Cartels, and Imperfect Competition," *Quarterly Journal of Economics,* LXI, February 1947, pp. 173-205.

together. These are the principal elaborations on the familiar theme that a cartel will have a price-output policy "like that of a monopoly."

These conclusions are potentially acceptable, but only on certain side assumptions which Mr. Patinkin recognizes but may not emphasize sufficiently. The strategic question is under what conditions all the member firms of a cartel may be expected to agree to anything like their Patinkin quotas. *On the supposition that each firm receives as earnings only the revenue from its own output,* there is no reason to suppose that the Patinkin quota system will ever be deliberately approximated in any cartel agreement. The cartel always contains divergent and essentially antagonistic ownership interests—this is its main difference from a multi-plant monopoly—and each interest wants its own profit. The firm's output quota being the prime determinant of its own profit, it can hardly be expected to adjust its share of any cartel output simply so as to maximize the aggregate cartel profit, especially if it thereby reduces its own earnings. This is seen most clearly in the case of the plant which should "rationally" shut down under a Patinkin quota system, but applies equally as well to any firm which under such a system would receive a smaller share of a given industry output than it could otherwise get. The fact is that *with earnings following output,*[2] the presumptive rationale of output *allocation* by the cartel (as distinct from the rationale of industry output determination) will not be one of maximization of industry profit at all. It will be rather one of straight power-politics negotiation, in which each participant goes after as big a quota as he can get (up to the level where his marginal cost equals price).[3] Any approach to minimized aggregate cost of a given industry output will be strictly accidental, and no firm will ever voluntarily shut down when some production would be profitable. It may be argued that in limiting cases, with firms having similar costs and their number not being excessive, a Patinkin quota system might incidentally satisfy all in terms of profit. But even here, the true motif of output allocation would be a balancing of antagonistic ownership interests, rather than a calculation of minimal aggregate costs for a given output. Old-fashioned market-sharing or some equivalent is the general pattern so long as earnings follow outputs.[4]

The crucial assumption underlying Mr. Patinkin's particular model thus must be that the cartel arrangement includes a workable mechanism for distributing cartel revenues on a basis other than that of assigned production quotas. Until the firm's share of cartel earnings is made effectively independent of its

[2]I.e., each firm receives revenue only from the output it produces and sells itself.

[3]Cf. George J. Stigler, *The Theory of Price,* New York, 1946, p. 238, on the idea of *Quotenkampf.*

[4]With earnings following output, a tentative solution might be outlined thus: (*a*) market shares are established for all firms by a negotiation in which relative costs are only one of several considerations; (*b*) given its resultant "share" of the industry demand curve, each firm identifies a corresponding monopoly price which suits it best, but different firms want different prices and none is necessarily the rational cartel price; (*c*) the actual industry price is found within the range of those desired by individual firms, by negotiation or otherwise; (*d*) industry price and output and its allocation will differ in an *a priori* unpredictable manner from those predicted by Patinkin.

production quota, it cannot be expected to agree to having its share of cartel output determined simply so as to maximize cartel profits. But when the cartel includes a workable device for pooling and redistributing either revenues or outputs—whether by a central sales agency or by intercompany payments or by intercompany purchase arrangements—then adoption of a rational Patinkin quota system is believable. Then quotas can be determined without reference to profit allocation, and the antagonistic interests seeking earnings can be reconciled separately, without influencing quota allocations. The only further condition then necessary is that some producers trust others enough to curtail or shut down their own production, if necessary, in the interest of overall efficiency, and thus to depend upon the revenues from the outputs of others for their own earnings. The unique characteristics of the Patinkin model have general application only if earnings do not follow outputs.

The preceding is emphasized because of its bearing upon the suggested applications of Patinkin's model to industries with collusive agreement not so comprehensive as that just described—i.e., to the case of the "imperfect" cartel or "imperfect" collusion. He suggests (page 201) that oligopolistic price policies under effective price leadership and with some market-sharing arrangement give "results identical with our cartel model."[5] Later he remarks (page 205) that in regulated multi-firm industries—milk, coal, and crude petroleum—"the cartel model is an exact, and not merely an approximate, description, in the sense that there is an actual body making and enforcing decisions from the viewpoint of the industry as a whole." Now, if these statements mean more than that some approximation to over-all monopoly price may be reached in such industries (a routine conclusion)—in effect if they suggest the pursuit of Patinkin's principle of output allocation—they are potentially valid *only* on the supposition that the industries in question have workable devices for distributing earnings on a basis other than that of firm outputs. Lacking these, there is every reason to suppose that individual quota determination at any chosen industry output will be dominated by individual profit considerations and will not be oriented to minimizing aggregate costs of that output. If profits or outputs cannot be pooled and shared, we revert to some model of old-fashioned market sharing, with collusive agreement (tacit or otherwise) on price but implicit rivalry either at the conference table or in the market for shares of any industry output. In this case, the principlal *novel* conclusions of Patinkin's model are not applicable.

The cooperative arrangements in most American industries unfortunately appear to be such that profit-pooling is not possible and that the Patinkin rationale is therefore not observed in fixing market shares. In many American oligopolies with price leadership, there is probably tacit collusion on price and a general movement of the price toward some "monopoly" level. To this routine inference there is no objection. But the conditions are not ordinarily such as to encourage the determination of output shares on a "rational" or cost-minimizing

[5]Such results are alternately characterized as "approximate cartel results," but the implication is that they are more closely approximate, for example, than Chamberlin's oligopoly analysis would make them.

basis. In most such industries there are no profit or output pools to facilitate the redistribution of earnings; intercompany purchase arrangements are seldom used to supply shut-down firms with output to sell; and individual firms typically depend on their own outputs for whatever profits they are to earn. This is possibly because the Sherman Act discourages the formal cartels which might implement such profit-pooling; but whatever the reason, the conditions are not consistent with the crucial assumption of the Patinkin model. Individual firms thus appear to strive for as large shares of a given industry output as they can profitably produce, and the resulting allocations are often clearly inconsistent with minimizing aggregate industry costs for a given output. Output "quotas" seem most frequently to be determined by non-price competition, collusion on price remaining effective, or by power negotiations within the collusive group. American industry is replete with examples of apparent collusion on price but evident non-price rivalry for market shares, and the N. R. A. code experience offers adequate evidence of negotiation of output quotas on bases not primarily related to costs. It may be concluded in the typical American case of "imperfectly collusive" oligopoly, the allocation of outputs among member firms follows a pattern systematically other than that set forth in the Patinkin model.

Nor is it true that this model furnishes even an approximate description of price-output determination in regulated multi-firm industries like coal and petroleum. Perhaps it should, but it doesn't. The writer bases his statement primarily on a knowledge of proration of petroleum by state authorities—a case which Mr. Patinkin cites—but believes the behavior observed there occurs elsewhere. The overall quota for oil under proration (or for coal under the Guffey act) has evidently not been set to maximize the industry profits. Output has been restricted and price rasied, but the monopoly level has hardly been approached. This is in part because there has been an element of public representation on the controlling authorities which discourages unduly high prices. But it is also because the oil proration system typically provides no means for transferring earnings to firms which would probably have to shut down if rational monopoly restriction were practiced. *Earnings still follow output*—there is no complete cartel—and ordinarily each firm can earn only by what it produces and sells. A prime requisite of politically workable proration is thus that practically every firm be allowed to produce something. With a multitude of small firms with discrete minimum operation rates, this requirement alone severely limits the ability of the proration authority to reduce industry output toward a monopoly level.

The same "earnings follow output" principle also dominates the allocation of the aggregate output among various firms exploiting a single oil pool. Conservationists wish to determine individual quotas according to engineering considerations, so as to maximize the yield from an entire pool. But considerations of "equity"—i.e., the assumed right of each firm to produce and sell an "equitable" share of the output drawn from the common pool—dominate the allocation. So long as each firm is left dependent for earnings on its own output, as it is in the absence of "unitization," output allocation must be dominated by "equity" and pay only secondary heed to considerations of conservation and of aggregate cost.[6]

Even with regulated multi-firm industries, we frequently have a cartel so comprehensive as to permit application of Patinkin's rational allocation principles. If there is no mechanism for redistributing earnings, so-called equity considerations will probably dominate output allocation and the resulting allocation pattern will depart willy-nilly from the rational one. We conclude that output allocations in oligopolies with "imperfect" collusion and in most regulated industries as presently regulated are likely to bear no systematic relation to those described in Patinkin's cartel model.

[6]See Northcutt Ely, "The Conservation of Oil," *Readings in the Social Control of Industry,* Philadelphia, 1942, pp. 338-343. "Equity" in oil proration ordinarily is served by allowing a flat minimum daily output per well, and by apportioning additional output according to "potential" production, surface acreage over the pool, etc. The result bears no predictable relation to marginal or average costs. See also D. R. McKeitham, "Present Allocation Practices," American Petroleum Institute, *Drilling and Production Practices,* 1942.

Chapter Three

Workable Competition in Oligopoly: Theoretical Considerations and Some Empirical Evidence

Since Professor Clark presented a paper on "workable competition"[1] ten years ago . . . , the concept therein emphasized has deservedly received a good deal of attention. In an economy where technological and other factors make any close approximation to pure and perfect competition substantially unattainable, it is important for purposes of policy to know in what kinds of imperfect markets competitive behavior will be reasonably compatible with a viable capitalism and will reasonably enhance general economic welfare. Clark made a noteworthy beginning in the analysis of this issue. At this time it may be appropriate to reconsider his suggestions, and also to inquire to what extent these may be revised and extended in the light of progress in theory and empirical study during the last decade. To abbreviate the discussion, I will confine myself entirely to the issue of workable competition within markets of oligopolistic structure—where at least some individual sellers control enough of the market that a recognized interdependence may reasonably be inferred.

According to Clark, the main considerations which influence competitive behavior in a market are the number and size distribution of sellers, the degree of product differentiation, the geographical market structure, the conditions of entry and exit, the long- and short-run cost conditions of firms, and the character of market information; also the degree of current output control by firms, the channels of distribution, and the method of price making—whether price is "quoted" or "supply-governed." In the derived classification of market situations, Clark establishes two major categories of oligopoly—pure oligopoly and monopolistic competition—the latter category including large-number cases

Reprinted from *American Economic Review*, 40 (Proceedings), May 1950, pp. 35-47, courtesy of the American Economic Association.

[1] J. M. Clark, "Toward a Concept of Workable Competition," *American Economic Review*, XXX, June 1940, pp. 241-256.

as well as differentiated oligopoly. The monopolistic-competition category is not essentially subdivided, except to set aside the evidently rare case of supply-governed price from the common one of quoted price. Pure oligopoly, however, has several subcategories: (1) with supply-governed prices; (2) with quoted prices which are either open and perfectly conformed to, or imperfectly known and subject to chaotic discrimination, or open with limited departures and secret concessions; and (3) with quoted prices and significant spatial differentiation with or without freight absorption. Distinctions were not drawn within the oligopoly categories upon the basis of concentration among sellers, conditions of entry, etc. Except for setting aside differentiated-product cases, the major distinctions run in terms of price-making methods, degree of market information, and evident direction of competitive behavior.

Clark's major argument as related to this classification is that given the imperfection imposed by fewness of sellers, some additional remedial imperfection is needed as an antidote to the first in order to preserve workable competition. Thus he believes that differentiated oligopoly, if product differentiation is not extreme, gives rise to "some of the healthiest cases of workable competition in large-scale industry." Perfectly conformed-to open prices in pure oligopoly are suspect, although they are more likely to be sticky than fully monopolistic. Chaotic price competition with imperfect knowledge is likely to be ruinous to sellers, especially if there is cyclical or stand-by excess capacity. Open price with limited departures "contains no guarantee of ideal prices; but it is something intermediate between [effective tacit collusion] and the ruinously low prices likely to result from unlimited market chaos; more strongly competitive than the first, and more workable than the second." No definite conclusions are reached as to workability of oligopolistic competition with supply-governed prices or with important spatial differentiation. To this Clark adds that in the long run the threat of entry of competitors and the horizontality of the long-run cost curves of firms serve as useful checks against extreme departures from competitive results.

There is obviously much of merit in this essay, briefly and inadequately reviewed here, including a rather effective answer to those who would hold that all oligopoly tends to approximate pure monopoly behavior, or that reasonably satisfactory results are possible only if all oligopolists price independently on a price-equals-marginal-cost basis. Fairly satisfactory competitive results may emerge from imperfect collusion or because of the long-run threat of entry. Taking Clark's argument as a beginning, however, let us see if further progress is possible. I will abbreviate the discussion by first offering two suggestions, mainly in the form of constructive criticism of Clark's essay.

First, as regards the concept of workable competition, the economist seems reasonably obliged to define it other than by the citation of examples, and more explicitly than as somewhere between full collusive monopoly and apparently destructive market warfare. The evident criteria of workable competition are the results emergent from the market process; competition is workable if productive efficiency reasonably approaches the best attainable, if industry output is not much restricted below and does not much exceed a level generally consistent with good allocation of resources, if an excessive proportion of resources is not devoted to sales promotion effort, if the income share going to profit is not substantially higher than required but high enough to reward investment and to induce socially desirable innovation, if opportunities for such innovations are not grossly neglected, and if prices respond to cyclical changes in a way which does not demonstrably intensify the cyclical problem. The definition thus implies the determination first of certain ideals or goals of performance and second of tolerable degrees of deviation from these goals. Unfortunately, economic theory to date does not supply precise, meaningful, and unquestioned norms for all of of the essential dimensions of behavior; no certain norm for price flexibility is available, for example, and evaluations of desirable amounts of selling cost are at least operationally quite ambiguous. In addition, assessment of actual behavior in terms of such norms is impeded by difficulties of measurement and because static equilibrium norms are applied to dynamic process situations. And finally, for criteria of tolerable deviations, we have little more than the ad hoc judgments of the observer concerning what might be had and how serious the adverse impact of a given deviation is. In view of all this, any economist's assessment of the workability of competition is likely to have a highly provisional and even personal character and is likely to rest heavily on the ad hoc assessment of obvious alternatives in given situations.

The actual assessment of workability of competition in particular situations—to be made presumably in the teeth of the serious difficulties just enumerated—will consist in the appraisal of certain measurable results of the market process. On a highly provisional level I would suggest the following general signs of nonworkable competition in oligopoly: a profit rate averaging quasi-perpetually well above an established normal return on investment (or falling persistently below it);[2] scale of many firms seriously outside the optimal range;[3] considerable chronic excess capacity not justified by secular change or reasonable stand-by provision; competitive selling costs exceeding a stated proportion of total cost; persistent lag in adoption of cost-reducing technical changes or persistent suppression of product changes which would advantage buyers. In each case one might establish objective standards by reference to which results could be classified as clearly unworkable, clearly workable, or in a borderline range. A market could be considered a case of unworkable competition if it had an extremely bad rating in any direction or moderately bad or suspicious ratings in several.

Given some such definition of workable and unworkable competition, in terms of results, we may still wish to probe for an association between such results and their possible determinants, to the end of establishing and classifying the

[2]A long-run tendency to subnormal profits seems unlikely in oligopoly, since the tendency should be self-correcting in a number of ways.

[3]Low or negligible excess profits plus reasonable efficiency of scale and capacity would imply a reasonably good relation of price to long-run marginal cost, and the absence of any serious degree of monopolistic output restriction.

underlying and potentially controllable conditions which may determine the workability of results.

Such determinants of price and other market results might be sought primarily either at the level of characteristics of market structure (number of sellers, etc.) or at the level of characteristics of competitive behavior (collusive, price quoting, etc.).[4] My second point is that the potential association of price results to market structure deserves primary emphasis. Whatever the degree of association within oligopolies between competitive behavior and results, it seems quite likely that such behavior may be in turn either influenced or determined by certain characteristics of the underlying market structure. If so, a demonstrated association between market structure and results would establish the more fundamental determinants of workability of competition (and, also, determinants more easily influenced by conventional public policy measures). Moreover, it seems unlikely a priori that the results emergent from a given pattern of competitive behavior are substantially independent of the underlying market structure. Certain structural chracteristics of markets—perhaps other than those which influence the pattern of competitive behavior—may exert a definite influence on results emergent from a given pricing pattern, and there may thus be no determinate simple association between character of competitive behavior and emergent results. It would thus seem preferable to explore first the possible association of workability of competition to market structure, and in the process also to appraise the complex role evidently played by apparent competitive behavior as a resultant and a determinant. As the association of market structure to results is explored, moreover, a priori analysis would suggest attention not only to product differentiation (emphasized by Clark) but also to any other potentially important characteristics of structure, certainly including the number and size distribution of sellers and of buyers and the condition of entry to the market.

Granted, however, that it would be convenient to establish an association between oligopoly market structure and the workability of competition, does such an association actually exist? This question, like many others in economics, can finally be answered only by detailed empirical investigation, but it may be useful to inquire whether, on a priori grounds, any such association is to be expected. By arguing from a very few simple premises and declining to pursue the argument beyond the point at which the introduction of further premises would be required, some theorists have concluded that all oligopoly price, cost, and output results are in strict logic indeterminate within a considerable range, and that, so long as the number of sellers is few, no determinate association between market structure and such results can be predicted. Although their caution may be commendable, I would suggest that by pursuing the usual arguments further, and adopting added assumptions, as required, based on our

[4]Clark examines both levels, although within the oligopoly category he emphasizes the latter. But he poses the principal problem which interests us here: can we associate workable and unworkable results for oligopolies with certain characteristics of market structure or of competitive behavior?

best judgment of the probable character of the strategic facts, we may escape the conclusion of a sort of "blanket indeterminacy" for oligopoly and may arrive at hypotheses concerning the systematic association of oligopolistic market structure and results. The development of such hypotheses, even though the assumptions on which they must rest may be tentative, is an obvious and useful step in the setting of empirical tests. As a beginning along this line, I should like to advance a few such hypotheses for trial, indicating as time permits the particular "added assumptions" and elaborations of conventional argument upon which they rest. These will concern mainly the association of market structure to long-run results in four principal dimensions: degree of monopolistic output restriction, profits, selling costs, and the level, relative to the ideal, of the long-run average costs of producing given industry output.

As a setting for these hypotheses, let us recognize first that oligopoly markets in general can conceivably develop any of several variant patterns of competitive behavior, of which some principal types might be:

1. Effective and closely observed collusion on price and/or output quotas; or its equivalent through tacit collusion or mutually recognized interdependence.
2. Imperfect collusion, subject to serious internal dissension, defections, secret price shading, etc.; or its equivalent through mutually recognized interdependence.
3. The conventional kinked demand curve pattern, resulting from a certain pattern of sellers' conjectures about their rivals' reactions.
4. "Chaotic" competition or relatively active price rivalry, potentially emergent from unrecognized interdependence, inconsistent conjectures by rivals, etc. (If chaotic to the point of persistent losses, it may be argued that this pattern would be temporary, or transitional to another.)

The choice among such patterns will presumably have some impact on results–in particular on the degree of monopolistic output restriction and possibly on the size of selling costs. Thus the first case should permit of some approximation to monopoly price and output (if these values are appropriately defined under various conditions of entry); in the second and third cases, price should, *ceteris paribus*, tend to be lower and outputs larger, though by an indeterminate amount; the last case should tend to yield lower prices than any of the others, and might conceivably yield "destructively" low prices.[5] It might also be predicted tentatively that with collusion imperfect or absent, selling costs would tend more systematically to exceed the rational monopoly level.

One obvious issue is whether the character of market structure may influence the choice among such patterns–whether there is an association of market structure to pattern of competitive behavior. But this is not the only question, since the character of certain significant results would appear not to be determined by the pattern of competitive behavior, but to be subject, given such

[5]"Destructive" prices here refer to those persistently insufficient to yield a normal return on investment; in the long run they should certainly be self-eliminating, and even over moderate time intervals do not promise to be a major threat in oligopoly, since the incentive and the means for avoiding them are generally at hand.

pattern, to the influence of certain characteristics of market structure. We must thus inquire (1) if certain characteristics of market structure potentially influence the choice of competitive pattern and (2) if these or other such characteristics influence the results which a given pattern may yield.

Beginning with the latter question, it first appears that the condition of entry to an oligopolistic market may be strategic to the determination of the long-run efficiency of production—of the level, relative to the best attainable, reached by the long-run average cost for any given industry output through the adjustment of the number and scale of firms. My hypothesis in general is that under conditions of very or moderately difficult entry, reasonable long-run efficiency in scale and capacity should develop, whereas under easy entry (if this is found in oligopoly) the prospect is much less certain and substantial inefficiency may result.

First, it seems highly probable that oligopoly firms will, in the interest of profit, systematically attempt to rationalize their operations so as to avoid gross discrepancies from efficient scale and gross amounts of continually redundant capacity, at least unless the continual influx of new entry makes such attempts futile. Situations in which the bulk of output would be produced under substantial diseconomies of scale or capacity, for example, will otherwise tend to be eliminated by expansion, combination, etc. Such a result is potentially uncertain, in view of the problem of finding terms of agreement (and perfect rationalization seems quite unlikely), but I will postulate that the balance between the joint profit maximizing motive and the conflicts potentially forestalling agreements is generally such that, law permitting, approximate rationalization will develop unless there is a persistent disruptive force.

Second, the conditions for initial attainment and the stable maintenance of a rationalized situation should be found largely in certain conditions of entry to industries. In general it may be argued that established oligopolists, collusive or otherwise, will recognize and react to threats of entry; that the existence of impediments to entry will make it possible for them to charge prices high enough to be profitable but low enough to discourage further entry; and that established firms, provided competition does not drag price even lower, will follow such a price policy whenever the long-run profits offered by this course exceed the sum of the potentially larger short-run gains which would induce entry and the reduced future returns after entry occurs.[6] In such cases, rationalization of scale and capacity with forestalled entry should result regardless of competitive pattern. On the other hand, where entry is easy enough that short-run monopoly pricing offers a better total prospect, excessive entry may be attracted, provided that price rivalry does not keep price below the entry-attracting level.[7] Here the impetus to rationalization is lessened and maintenance of long-run efficiency is only one of several possibilities.

[6]See J. S. Bain, "A Note on Pricing in Monopoly and Oligopoly," *American Economic Review,* March 1949, pp. 448-464 (Ch. 5, this book).

[7]Even if it does, there will presumably be a tendency to regroup, as by merger, to obtain short-run monopoly profits, so that there is a considerable prospect of the waste either of inefficiently small firms or of a dynamically unstable market structure.

This gives us a distinction between two long-run efficiency cases, essentially in terms of the comparative attractiveness, under various conditions of entry, of the alternative time sequences of future demand (as discounted) between which established sellers may choose. Since the net superiority of one over the other sequence should depend not only upon the height of barriers to entry and the lags involved in accomplishing it, but also upon the established seller's time preference and his prognosis of market rivalry after entry, a simple unique relation between objectively ascertainable conditions of entry to a market and long-run efficiency does not necessarily exist.[8] But we may, on the basis of certain empirical generalizations about the usual seller's expectations and time preferences,[9] advance a tentative hypothesis concerning the average relation of apparent condition of entry to long-run efficiency.

Let us distinguish three principal cases of entry:

1. Blockaded or very difficult entry, where there is an absolute institutional blockage (as through patent or resource control), or where established firms enjoy very substantial cost advantages over potential entrants,[10] or where the scale of an optimum firm is very large relative to the market and the economies of scale are great. In such cases, entry could presumably be forestalled by established firms at prices yielding substantial long-run excess profits.

2. Moderately difficult (or moderately easy) entry, where established firms enjoy only moderate cost advantages over potential entrants, or where there are substantial economies of scale but where a firm producing a moderate portion of industry output can attain them.[11] In such cases, entry could presumably be forestalled at prices yielding only moderate or small long-run excess profits.

3. Easy entry, where the established firms enjoy small or negligible advantages of cost and where economies of scale are not important. Here an entry-forestalling price policy would presumably yield very small or negligible excess profits. (Simple implicit definition of these categories is not intended; in particular the lower limit of the middle class is tentatively placed where conditions of entry would permit no more than 3 or 4 per cent of excess profit on investment.)

Assuming that in general only moderate lags would be experienced in attracting new entry (and that the relevant time preferences generally are low), I

[8]The elasticity of industry demand should also be a determining factor; for a simple first approximation I will neglect it and pursue the argument on the provisional assumption that differences in elasticity among industry demands will not be of decisive importance.

[9]Here I would postulate (1) that large corporate firms of indefinite existence will in general probably not discount future profits very heavily and (2) that the uncertainty concerning market rivalry, and hence profits, after entry is attracted will weigh heavily against the short-run monopoly profit maximization course whenever entry can be forestalled with some regular long-run profit. These two conditions would imply that a rather moderate barrier to entry would suffice to swing the balance in favor of an entry-forestalling price policy, provided that established sellers are not protected by very long lags in effecting new entry.

[10]Cost advantages should presumably include those not only of production cost but also of selling cost, such as might arise from established product preferences for going firms, although the latter would be difficult to ascertain or measure empirically.

[11]Or where there are moderate advantages of cost to very large scale, etc.

advance the tentative hypothesis that in the first and the second cases, under any competitive pattern, established sellers will set price low enough[12] to forestall entry and will establish and maintain reasonable efficiency in scale and capacity, since in such cases the discounted long-run profit offered by this course is likely to be the greatest obtainable. Under easy entry, on the other hand, we may contemplate as alternative possibilities (1) long-run inefficiency with an excessive number of excessively small firms, (2) dynamically unstable market structure, with resultant inefficiencies, and (3) relatively good efficiency if price rivalry imposes it—and thus predict that in a significant proportion of such cases long-run inefficiency may be found. This hypothesis (which obviously rests upon a number of assumptions derived from casual observation) is itself conceivably verifiable if some measurement and rough quantitative classification of entry conditions are established, and I submit it for test.

A second hypothesis, derived from the preceding argument, is that there should be some association between the condition of entry and the price, profit, and degree of monopolistic output restriction within an oligopoly. This association is not necessarily a simple one, since such results depend not only upon the condition of entry but also upon the pattern of competitive behavior, which would not appear to be directly associated to the condition of entry. For given competitive patterns, however, certain conclusions emerge. With effective collusion throughout, very difficult entry should lead to high prices and profits and substantial monopolistic output restriction as sellers set that relatively high price which will maximize long-run profits while forestalling entry. By the same token, under moderately difficult entry collusive sellers must set a lower price and larger output and receive a lower profit to forestall entry. Easy entry, however, with the threat of entry presumably disregarded, should under persistent collusion give high price and restricted output, though with limited profits. Other competitive patterns, such as imperfect collusion and the kinked demand pattern, should lead on the average to lower than the collusive price in each case; so far as such lower prices are also systematically related to the respective collusive prices (as might be argued on certain assumptions) the preceding general comparisons should hold more broadly. Otherwise, the relation of condition of entry to price and profit is not clear, except that with only moderately difficult entry there is a relatively low top limit on such prices and profts. Under unmitigated price rivalry, of course, an approximation to competitive price and output, or even "destructive" pricing, could result regardless of entry conditions. The general comparison would indicate that within oligopolies the moderately difficult entry category should have the best workability rating, and the other two categories at least highly doubtful ratings.

Let us now return to the impact of market structure on the pattern of competitive behavior. A potentially significant—and not altogether unfamiliar—hypothesis here is that the degree of concentration of industry output among

[12]That is, collusive price should go no higher and under other competitive patterns this limit will not be exceeded and may not be reached or maintained.

sellers will affect this pattern. Let us begin with a qualitative distinction between very high and moderate concentration in oligopoly—the first where a very high proportion of the market is controlled by a very few large sellers and where smaller firms are absent or quite few; the second where a more moderate proportion of the market is controlled by a similar number of large sellers and where small- or medium-sized firms may be more numerous and control a moderate fraction of the market.[13] Moderate concentration, it may be argued, should tend to give rise to quasi-competitive market behavior—imperfect collusion, kinked demand curve conformations, and the sporadic appearance of chaotic competition—whereas high concentration should provide an environment conducive to effect collusion or its equivalent. This hypothesis essentially rests on the premise and argument that given the incentive to joint profit maximization, the impediments to express or tacit agreement increase, while the restraint of recognized interdependence on independent price cutting should decrease (with ordinary frictions and imperfections) as concentration decreases, and at such a rate that a shift in competitive pattern results over a certain concentration zone within oligopoly. If this is so, then under given entry conditions industries of moderate concentration should have relatively lower average prices and profits and less output restriction than those of high concentration. Higher excess profits and more severe output restriction should tend to center more largely on the highly concentrated sphere, conditions of entry permitting. The preceding qualitative distinction, however, requires implementation in quantitative terms. Since a priori logic applied to available assumptions is of little help on this point, the crucial definitions can best emerge from statistical investigations. Here I will propose, on the basis of preliminary investigations, something like control of from 65 to 75 per cent of the market by eight or fewer sellers as a tentative dividing line.

The number and size distribution of buyers may also have some impact on the pattern of competitive behavior. The principal issue posed here is whether there will be significant differences among pricing in oligopolistic industries selling to many small buyers, a few large buyers, a few large and some or many small, etc. Although the a priori indications for bilateral oligopoly are not strictly determinate, it may be argued that high buyer concentration will tend to put pressure on the sellers of a sort which makes effective collusion among them more difficult, or otherwise reduces prices, especially if the seller ologopoly is not very highly concentrated.[14] A substantial concentration among buyers may

[13]It should be noted that the existence of some relatively small sellers is not necessarily inconsistent with conditions of very difficult or moderately difficult entry, nor with the forestalling of entry by going price policies. The impediments to entry may consist in absolute cost advantages over outsiders (as through patent or resource control) shared by smaller and larger established firms, rather than in dominant economies of scale. Even where such economies are dominant, small firms may survive on the starvation margin at a price which attracts no further entry, or geographical and other market imperfections may make a place for a limited number of smaller firms. Finally, it is always important to inquire to what extent the smaller firms in a "census industry" are actually producing in competition with the larger ones.

[14]For example, the individual large buyer may be able to make price concessions in

therefore tend to be associated with lower prices and profit rates to the sellers, and conceivably with "destructively" low prices.

The remaining characteristic of market structure to be considered here is product differentiation, which may obviously influence the character of results emergent from a given competitive pattern. Posing a rough dichotomy between standardized products in the choice among which buyers are unresponsive to sales appeals (large producers' goods) and products which can be effectively differentiated by some means, it may be suggested (1) that with differentiated products selling costs will tend to be larger under any competitive pattern that they would be with standardized products, (2) that although with differentiation significant selling costs may be expected even under non-price collusion, such costs will tend to be relatively larger in any pattern where collusion does not extend to the non-price level, and (3) that as we progress from difficult toward easy entry, selling costs may tend to increase, since they may be systematically employed to discourage entry. The potentially beneficial effects on price and output of a moderate threat of entry or of a noncollusive competitive pattern may thus be offset in some degree by an accentuated emphasis on selling costs. A priori appraisal of the seriousness of this adverse effect, however, is substantially impossible in our present state of knowledge.

The influence of product differentiation upon the pattern of competitive behavior emergent from an industry seems doubtful; it might be argued on certain premises that the outlet for rivalry on the non-price level may dampen any tendency toward severe price competition and may enhance the prospect for effective collusion on price. But I would hesitate to propose that differentiation should have a dominant influence on pricing; its principal concealed effect may be in heightening the barriers to entry.

The various hypotheses which I have tentatively advanced suggest that there may be some significant associations between market structure and the relative workability of results emergent from oligopolistic markets. In view of the nature of the underlying assumptions, they should evidently be viewed as setting forth general average tendencies rather than rigid rules. Although we have considered only a limited range of market structure characteristics and of significant results and although the only substantial defense of the hypotheses advanced must emerge from empirical test, it may be useful to inquire in terms of these predictions what composite market structures (combining various conditions of entry, number of sellers, etc.) would be relatively workable under oligopoly. Rather than developing a full market classification, I will simply summarize these predictions as they apply to what seem to be the most common categories in fact:

1. Oligopolies with blockaded or very difficult entry and a high concentration of sellers—not a rare case. In general these do not promise workability. Although

violation of explicit or tacit collusive understanding very attractive to the individual seller; or collusion among buyers may be effective in breaking interseller collusion and even in imposing a more or less monopsonistic price.

reasonable efficiency may be expected, high prices and profits and substantial output restriction are forecast. If products are differentiated, selling costs may be excessive. Fewness of buyers, if present, may have a beneficial effect. (I will neglect moderate concentration with difficult entry on the ground that the case is evidently unusual, but in this case workability should still be definitely suspect.)

2. Oligopolies with moderately difficult entry and moderate concentration—probably a common case. In general, markets of this sort promise the closest approximations to workability among oligopolies, provided that there is not persistently "destructive" pricing, which seems theoretically unlikely as a long-run tendency. Efficiency should be reasonably good and prices and profits low or moderate. With product differentiation, however, selling costs may be excessive; thus standardized-product industries within this category get the best rating. Fewness of buyers may help, provided buyer power is not overwhelming. (If seller concentration is high, as seems less common, the rating is not substantially changed.)

3. Oligopolies with easy entry, high or moderate concentration. This category can give satisfactory results, but in general the prognosis is for at least equal possibility of unworkable efficiency, price, and output results, so long as the industry remains an oligopoly. (I have substantial doubts that easy entry is very common within oligopolies.)

In terms of these predictions, workability should perhaps be most strongly associated with the condition of entry to markets (although in a complex fashion); product differentiation per se does not promise to be an ameliorating factor, although fewness of buyers may be; workability may increase as concentration declines, but with obvious exceptions for selling costs, and subject to the dominant importance of entry.

The preceding hypotheses concerning the association of oligopoly market structure to workability of competition are of course tentative and rather speculative, but aside from their specific content, I believe that in attempting to develop them one becomes convinced that there may be in fact some such systematic and logically explicable association. In view of the variety of assumptions upon which one could proceed in a priori analysis, however, it is likely to be usefully established only by empirical investigation. The only test which I have so far carried through is between concentration and profit rate, and this for forty-seven census industries selected on the basis of theoretical significance of concentration ratio and availability of profit data. Associating 1935 concentration ratio with 1936-40 average industry profit rate on equity (before taxes, from SEC data), it appears that whereas in twenty-two industries where 70 per cent or more of value product was controlled by eight firms, the mean annual profit rate was about 15 per cent, in seventeen industries where the concentration ratio was from 30 to 70 per cent, the mean profit rate was about 8 per cent. Although there is a considerable dispersion of profit rates within any concentration class, the interclass variation is dominant, and average figures show a break at about the 70 per cent line; below this, profits averaged substantially lower for all subgroups. This tcst is for a limited time interval, of course, and profits per se are hardly an adequate measure of workability. But it is possible that, if vigorous effort is given to the development of other essential data, we may establish the nature of practicable market environment most conducive to workable competition.

Chapter Four

Relation of Profit Rate to Industry Concentration: American Manufacturing, 1936-1940

Students of industrial price behavior have recently shown much interest in the concept of workable competition and in the potential association between the workability of competition and the structure of the industry.[1] Their evident uncertainty about the nature of such a relationship suggests the need for detailed empirical studies which would formulate specific hypotheses on the relations of market structure to market performance and would then test such hypotheses with available evidence. In another place,[2] I have advanced some hypotheses concerning such relationships, emphasizing those of seller concentration, buyer concentration, condition of entry, and degree of product differentiation to profits, selling costs, and relative efficiency of scale and capacity. This paper reports on the results of a statistical study of one of the relationships in this complex, as found in American manufacturing industries from 1936 through 1940—namely that of the size of profits or profit rates to the degree of seller concentration within industries.[3]

Reprinted from *Quarterly Journal of Economics,* 65, August 1951, pp. 293-324, courtesy of the publisher.

[1]Cf. E. S. Mason, "The Current Status of the Monopoly Problem in the United States," *Harvard Law Review,* LXII, June 1949, pp. 1265-85; M. A. Adelman, "Effective Competition and the Anti-Trust Laws," ibid., LXI, September 1948, pp. 1289-1350; Corwin Edwards, *Maintaining Competition,* New York, 1949.

[2]J. S. Bain, "Workable Competition in Oligopoly," *American Economic Review,* XL, May 1950, pp. 35-47 (Ch. 3, this book).

[3]I am indebted to the Bureau of Business and Economic Research, University of California, Berkeley, for extensive assistance in this study throughout the academic year 1949-50, and to Mr. Allan Muir, who undertook substantially all the work of statistical compilation and calculation and who contributed measurably to the development of statistical analysis.

Statement of the hypothesis to be tested[4] involves an initial distinction among industries according to the degree of seller concentration, recognizing (1) highly concentrated oligopolies, where a very few firms control a high proportion of industry output, (2) less concentrated oligopolies, where the proportion of industry output controlled by a given number of firms is smaller but where oligopolistic interdependence must still be presumed to exist, and (3) industries of atomistic structure. *The hypothesis in brief is that the average profit rate of firms in oligopolistic industries of a high concentration will tend to be significantly larger than that of firms in less concentrated oligopolies or in industries of atomistic structure.* Firms in oligopolies of high seller concentration will tend to earn higher profit rates than all others.[5] This hypothesis is essentially developed from conventional price theory, and the manner of its development may be briefly traced.

A single firm monopolist or a group of oligopolists operating with effective express or tacit collusion should approach a conventional maximization solution and realize in long-run equilibrium the maximum excess profit[6] aggregate which is permitted by the relation of the industry demand curve to the costs of production and selling and by the conditions of entry.[7] Sellers in industries of atomistic structure, or oligopolists who cannot reach or maintain fully effective collusion will not tend to maximize this excess profit aggregate, and with (1) identical entry conditions and (2) an identical industry demand and cost situation, will tend to sell at a lower price and receive a smaller profit.[8] In short,

[4]Before examining the hypothesis to be tested, let us note that the size of the profit rate for a firm or industry should not be regarded as a sole or an infallible index of the workability of competition. Clearly it is one of several dimensions of market performance which must be interpreted as a complex in evaluating the workability of competition. Low or normal profits are ordinarily associated with certain model types of competitive equilibrium, and profits chronically much in excess of some normal rate with undesirable restriction of output and adverse income distribution effects. But the existence of a low profit rate may be associated with adverse results on other levels (such as chronic excess capacity) and any profit performance must be read in the light of the rate of technical progress, the trend of demand, and so forth. We are thus essentially unable here to discover any net relation of concentration to the workability of competition; we seek simply the relation of concentration to the profit rate, whatever its ultimate significance.

[5]The major distinction, it may be emphasized, is not between industries of oligopolistic and atomistic structure, but between the more highly concentrated oligopolies and all other industries.

[6]The term excess profit is used here throughout to refer to a return in excess of all costs, including imputed interest costs on equity capital, and not to the concept as defined in tax laws.

[7]The conventional maximization solution must be construed to include either one where marginal cost equals industry marginal revenue (as where entry is blockaded or alternatively cannot be advantageously forestalled) or one where price is enough lower to forestall entry and thus to maximize the long-run profits of the established firms. See J. S. Bain, "A Note on Pricing in Monopoly and Oligopoly," *American Economic Review*, March 1949, pp. 448-64 (Ch. 5, this book).

[8]Except in the circumstance where entry must in either case force profits to or below the competitive level.

if we hold demand and cost conditions and entry conditions constant, monopoly or effectively collusive oligopoly tends to yield higher profit aggregates and prices in long-run equilibrium than competition or imperfectly or non-collusive oligopoly.

Retaining suppositions (1) and (2) above, monopoly or effectively collusive oligopoly will also bring forth a higher excess profit rate on sales. This will be true even where cost and demand conditions are not identical, so long as the opportunity for aggregate profit relative to aggregate sales is the same. The excess profit rate on sales (after deducting all costs, including all paid and imputed interest) should average higher in long-run equilibrium among industries with monopoly or effectively collusive oligopoly than among others, so far as on the average the relation of industry demand to cost and the conditions of entry are about the same.

This association should actually hold even in long-run equilibrium only on the average and not in each case. Similarity of demand-cost relations should be found only on the average, as should any similarity of entry conditions. When we leave the static model, the same association should tend to hold on the average through time, but a considerable dispersion of individual profit rates for particular intervals could be caused by difference in trends and fluctuations of demand, in the rate of innovation, and so forth. Thus individual industries in the more "competitive" category may have as high as or higher profit rates than individuals in the "monopoly" category, but on the assumption that all other influences on the profit rate "average-out" within groups, the group averages over time of excess profit rates on sales should differ in the manner indicated.[9]

Average excess profit rates on sales should thus be higher with than without monopoly or effective oligopolistic collusion. This prediction evolves into one that there will be larger profit rates with high seller concentration than with moderate or low seller concentration if we posit a systematic association between the probability of effective collusion and the degree of seller concentration within an industry. A tentative hypothesis is herewith advanced to that effect.[10] Given this, we arrive at the hypothesis that there will be a systematic difference in average excess profit rates on sales between highly concentrated oligopolies and other industries. This difference should be found, strictly, even if there are on the average identical entry conditions in the two groups. So far as entry tends to be more difficult in highly concentrated industries, as seems probable, there is a second reason for larger profit rates with higher concentration.

[9]This "averaging-out" should also presumably apply to any effects of any other differences in market structure which may have an independent influence on profit rates.

[10]That is, in highly concentrated oligopolistic industries, there will on the average be found more effective express or tacit collusion, and in oligopolistic industries of lower concentration, as in industries of relatively unconcentrated structure, there will be found on the average less effective or more imperfect collusion, more profit-destructive rivalry of either an open or secret sort, and thus a significantly closer approach to the results of competitive pricing. Cf. J. S. Bain, "Workable Competition in Oligopoly," loc. cit., pp. 43-44 (Ch. 3, this book).

As the hypothesis is developed to this point, the predicted profit-rate differences are explicitly differences in ratios of excess profit to sales. Because data on profit rates on equity are more readily available, let us inquire whether the predicted relationship should also hold for the ratios of profit to equity. The rate of excess profit on sales may be expressed (non-operating costs and revenues being neglected) as:[11]

$$\frac{\text{sales revenue minus contractual costs minus imputed interest}^{12}}{\text{sales revenue}}$$

Readily available profit-rate data are largely in the form of rates of return on investment or on equity before deducting imputed interest. The relevant equity rate is:

$$\frac{\text{sales revenue minus contractual costs}}{\text{stockholders' equity}^{13}}$$

This may also be stated as:

$$\frac{\text{sales revenue minus contractual costs minus imputed interest}}{\text{stockholders' equity}} \text{ plus interest rate}$$

(These are of course all *average* rather than *marginal* rates.) As between firms or groups of firms, should the same relation hold among their rates of return on equity, either gross or net of the interest rate, as between their sales rates? For comparisons of individual cases the answer is no, since the ratio of equity to sales will vary among cases.[14] However, so far as there is on the average among groups of firms or industries being compared about the same ratio of equity to sales, their average equity rates should stand in about the same relation as their sales rates. Then, assuming the sales-equity ratio averages the same for industries of different concentration, the postulated relation of industry concentration to profit rate should hold for rates of return on equity, net or gross of imputed interest, as well as for sales rates. An additional source of profit-rate variation within groups has been introduced if equity rates are used, but the average relation should be roughly the same.

The validity of this assumption and of the derived conclusion has been tested by experimental calculations for groups of industries of the relationship of profit

[11]It is postulated throughout at this point that there is a theoretically correct measurement of all magnitudes which appear in these ratios; the character of such measurement and the possible aberrations in accounting measures are discussed below.

[12]Imputed interest equals stockholders' equity (at the appropriate cost valuation) times an interest rate.

[13]At the same appropriate cost valuation used in calculating imputed interest.

[14]The assumed motive, it may be noted, is to maximize aggregate profits and not average equity rates. Higher aggregate profits, in a given demand and cost situation, give a higher (but not maximal) excess profit rate on sales than lower aggregate profits associated with lower prices, but not necessarily a higher equity rate if the equity-sales ratio is sufficiently lower in the low-aggregate-profit case.

rate to concentration, using first the equity rate, second the rate of excess profits on sales, and third the rate of earning before all interest on total investment. There is no significant difference in the findings on group-average relationships by the three methods. The crucial ratios appear to be similar enough so that for statistical purposes the measures are effectively interchangeable; hence, subsequent to the experiment, equity rates have been used in all calculations as the only measure of profit.

In the most convenient form for testing, therefore, the central hypothesis is that there will be higher average profit rates on equity in industries of high concentration than in less concentrated oligopolies or in industries of atomistic structure. The hypothesis does not suggest the exact degree of concentration which will separate highly concentrated oligopolies from other industries; it is a purpose of this study to determine where such a line, if any, falls. Similarly, no finer distinction is tentatively drawn than between highly concentrated and other industries, although evidences of associations which might justify finer distinctions must be sought and evaluated.

THE INDUSTRY DEFINITION, THE MEASURE OF CONCENTRATION, AND THE SELECTION OF AN INDUSTRY SAMPLE

Given the hypothesis for test, we must first make explicit the definitions of certain terms it employs and see to what extent corresponding categories and measures found in the available statistical data are congruent with them. The first such concepts for definition are the industry and the degree of industry concentration. For the purpose of such an hypothesis at least, the industry appears to be primarily a concept of demand–it is a group of outputs which to all (or most) of the buyers of each are generally close substitutes for each other and distant substitutes for all other outputs.[15] The industry may be viewed in derivative fashion as a group of firms or divisions thereof, so far as the firms or divisions thereof all produce entirely (or, for rough purposes, almost entirely) within the close-substitute output group.[16] The degree of industry concentration to which our hypothesis refers is the degree of concentration within an industry so defined–e.g., the proportion of the combined production volume of such a group of close substitute outputs supplied by one, four, eight, or twenty firms.

To test our hypothesis, we need to identify a number of such industries, obtain a measure of concentration within each of them, and obtain also a measure of profit rates earned in producing their outputs. Ideally we might wish to make up theoretically significant industries de novo from the most basic data,

[15]Cross elasticities of demand, in other words, define the industry; it is a group of outputs tied together by high cross elasticities of demand inter se, which have low cross elasticities of demand with any other outputs. Cross elasticties of supply alone do not link outputs into a single industry.

[16]But it is quite possible for a firm or even a plant to produce simultaneously in several theoretical industries.

and to calculate concentration measures for them, but the magnitude of such a task has made this impossible for the present. As a result, we are forced to refer to already available groupings of firms or outputs and available measures of concentration within them, and to decide which of these groupings correspond approximately to theoretical industries as defined, or more generally for which groupings the received concentration measures represent the true theoretical concentration affecting the outputs included. We may then select a sample of such groupings and related concentration measures in terms of which our hypothesis may validly be tested.

For the time interval to be studied, 1936-40, the most comprehensive available data identifying industries and measuring their concentration refer to about 340 manufacturing "industries" identified in the Census of Manufacturers for 1935. In addition, there are concentration measures available for 1937 for about half of the 3600-odd manufactured "products" which the Census recognizes as making up its "industries." Our general problem involves first deciding for which such "industries" or "products" the received concentration measures are theoretically significant. Since profit-rate data are seldom available for firms operating within a sphere so narrow as a Census "product," however, we must, if we are even roughly to match profit data with concentration measures, confine ourselves to seeking "significant" Census industries.

To what extent do Census "industries" correspond to theoretical industries as defined? So far as they tend to represent different groups of outputs serving different needs of users—like firearms or fertilizers—they may tend to correspond, but they may also deviate in important respects from theoretical industries. First, although the Census industry occasionally includes only a single group of close substitute outputs—as in the cigarette industry—it commonly includes several technologically related output groups, identifiable as Census products, within each of which there is evidently close substitution but between which there is or may be slight inter-group substitutability for buyers. "The steel industry," which includes armor plate, axles, concrete reinforcing bars, etc., is a case in point; several or many theoretical industries are potentially included in this Census industry. Second, the Census industry may be so defined as to exclude entirely close substitutes for the outputs which it includes. When the cane sugar industry is defined so as to exclude beet sugar, this is very obviously the case. Third, the Census industry, because it always includes the entire national supply of the products it contains, frequently may lump together several local or regional industries producing a given commodity, i.e., several output groups which have poor intergroup substitutability at going prices because of transport costs. This is evidently true of bakery products or common brick. If a Census industry is not guilty of any of these deviations from the theoretical norm, of course, it will tend to approximate a theoretical industry in that it will include a single group of close substitute outputs and exclude no close substitutes for them.

Remembering these potential discrepancies between theoretical and Census industries, we have analyzed the 340 Census industries in search of the answers to two questions. First, which of them correspond closely to theoretical industries, so that their concentration measures obviously qualify as theoretically significant? Second, since there are few of these, for which *other* Census industries are the received concentration measures theoretically significant in that the Census industry concentration is representative of the true concentrations for the several theoretical industries which the Census industry may contain?

Obviously suspect is the Census industry which includes several potentially close-substitute output groups which are actually poor substitutes because of geographical market segmentation. The Census industry then includes several theoretical industries, and its concentration measure will tend to represent that in each of the local industries only in the event that each of the principal firms is diversified among all areas so as to control roughly the same proportion of each local market. If the various firms specialize in given areas, as must be assumed in the absence of information on the point, the Census industry concentration figure will tend to understate the true concentrations for the component theoretical industries. Thus we have rejected out of hand Census industries (and related concentration measures) for which the data have revealed significant geographical market segmentation but no evidence of balanced inter-area diversification by firms. Our sample has thus been drawn only from industries where all principal sellers tend to reach all major market areas alike.

Geographical difficulties aside, however, which Census industries have appropriate scope in terms of the potential substitutability of included and excluded outputs? This is a difficult decision to make. Lacking the crucial data on cross-elasticities of demand, we may either make a large number of horseback judgments, or accept either the Census "industry" or the Census "product" definition as an approximation to what we seek. To avoid reliance on personal judgment in selecting a sample, we have assumed in general that, geographical factors aside, a theoretical industry is found in the case of each Census industry *either* in this "industry" *or* in the individual Census products which it includes. Thus with the firearms industry, which includes the Census products pistols, rifles, and shotguns, we assume that either there is a firearms industry in the theoretical sense, or there are pistol, rifle, and shotgun industries in the theoretical sense. Geographical difficulties aside, the theoretical industry we seek is assumed to be no broader than the Census industry—which is thus presumed to exclude no close substitutes—and no narrower than the Census product. We have avoided making a decision as to whether the true industry is the Census "industry" or the Census "product." Each Census industry is thus generally viewed as comprising either a theoretical industry or a complex of several theoretical industries.

This last judgment has been modified only in a very few cases where there was conclusive evidence that close-substitute outputs were excluded from the Census industry—for example, the Census classification establishing three sugar industries was not honored. In such cases, the Census industry has been rejected from the sample on the ground that its concentration measure would tend seriously to overstate the true concentration for the theoretical industry within which the outputs in question fell. The same policy has been followed where there was evidence of a significant supply of imports of close substitute outputs, automatically excluded from Census data.

For almost all Census industries, however, we have followed the assumption that, geographical difficulties aside, either the industries or their component products represent theoretical industries, but that we do not know which do. We thus do not specifically identify the theoretical industry in most instances. If this is the case, how can we decide whether or not a Census industry concentration measure, computed for the aggregate output of such an industry, will tend to represent the concentration measure for the theoretical industry or industries putatively contained? This question may be analyzed on the assumption, which will not be reiterated throughout, that we are dealing only with industries which are free of geographical market segmentation and have not been found overly narrow in definition.

Occasionally, of course, we find a Census industry with but a single product, and thus by assumption a simple theoretical industry for which the concentration measure may be accepted at face value. This is the case, for example, with matches, locomotives, and cigarettes. In most cases, however, we have a number of products within the Census industry, and the issue must be faced. Its resolution is quite simple—we need only to identify those Census industries for which the concentration measure is roughly the same both for the Census industry and for each of its principal products. For in these the industry concentration measure will tend to represent the true theoretical concentration for the industry or component industries in question regardless of whether Census product or Census industry is the theoretical entity. The Census industry concentration measure will in effect be interchangeable with the component product concentration measures when, and only when, there is within the Census industry a sort of symmetrically balanced diversification among all products by all firms, instead of narrower product specialization by firms. If there is specialization by firms among products, the aggregate concentration measure for the Census industry will generally be lower than the concentration measures for the individual products.[17] It follows that where within a Census industry there is a roughly balanced diversification of all principal firms among all principal products, the industry concentration measure tends to represent true theoretical concentration for included outputs regardless of whether Census industry or product is a theoretical industry, provided that one or the other is. On the other hand, if there is distinct specialization of firms among products, the industry concentration measure will be theoretically valid only if all the

[17]Thus if in industry *X* there are three products, *a, b,* and *c,* and of each of these firm 1 produces 60 per cent, firm 2, 30 per cent and firm 3, 10 per cent, the concentration figure for the aggregated output of the industry will be the same as for each component. But if firm 1 produces 80 per cent of *a,* firm 2, 80 per cent of *b,* and firm 3, 80 per cent of *c,* such an aggregate figure will generally misrepresent concentration for one or more of the component products.

included products are close substitutes; if they are not, it will misrepresent the true concentration for the component theoretical industries. Assuming indecision as to whether products within a Census industry are close substitutes, we may thus accept as valid for testing our hypothesis only Census industries and related concentration measures where there is either only a single Census product or a roughly balanced diversification of firms among several products. We must reject the others as potentially invalid. This criterion of selection has been applied along with others previously mentioned.[18]

The joint application of the various criteria described above has resulted in a selection of an industry sample by the progressive elimination of Census industries for which (1) geographical market segmentation may destroy the significance of the concentration measure, (2) there is conclusive evidence that the Census industry excludes close substitutes for included outputs, or (3) there are several Census products, with a significant degree of specialization by principal firms among products. This has left a residual sample of Census industries which are cleared on the three preceding counts and which include a few single-product Census industries and a good many multi-product industries wherein product and industry concentration measures tend to be very similar. If we assume that for these either the Census product or the Census industry corresponds to a theoretical industry, their concentration measures should be significant for testing our hypothesis.

The mechanical procedure employed in selecting the sample, and the results of this procedure, may be described as follows. From 340 industries in the 1935 Census of Manufacturers,[19] we first selected those for which some profit data were available from S.E.C. publications[20] for 1936-40, and eliminated the remainder. This left 152 industries, for 149 of which there were also available concentration data. These 149 were then screened to determine which should be rejected on the ground either of geographical market segmentation or of

[18]As this criterion has been applied, it has appeared that there is a large number of industries—for example chemicals n.e.c. or electrical machinery, apparatus, and supplies—which include several Census products which may be poor substitutes for each other, and within which the various firms are largely specialized in only one or a part of these products. Such industries have been rejected from our sample on the ground that if the products were poor substitutes the aggregate industry concentration figure would be grossly lower than that for the appropriate theoretical industry groups in the complex. On the other hand, there is a very considerable number of census industries which include several substitute output groups or Census products, and within which each of the principal firms is relatively unspecialized and has roughly the same standing in each or most of the major Census products. In these cases, the aggregate concentration tends to be roughly representative of concentration for each of the major component output groups. These Census industries and corresponding concentration ratios, in the absence of geographical difficulties and of a peremptory rejection on grounds the Census industry is obviously too narrow, are thus acceptable for purposes of testing our hypothesis, since the industry concentration figure will on our assumptions be theoretically significant whether or not the component products are close substitutes.

[19]See National Resources Committee, *Structure of the American Economy*, Washington, 1939, Part I, Appendix 7.

[20]The industry was obviously useless in the sample unless profit data could be obtained. Reliance on S.E.C. profit data was decided upon since the S.E.C. provided the most adequate and reliable uniform source of the requisite firm by firm profits for this interval.

specialization of firms among products within the Census industry. In this procedure we first followed the classification of industries developed in *Structure of the American Economy,*[21] which segregates Census industries first into those having "national," "regional," and "local" markets and second into those which are "straight" and "mixed." Industries with "national" markets evidently represent those which are little affected by geographical market segmentation. "Straight" and "mixed" industries correspond in a rough way respectively to industries with "diversified" and "specialized" firms as identified above—a "straight" industry is one "in which each manufacturer as a rule engages in the production of all commodities covered by the industry classification," and a "mixed" industry one "in which manufacturers confine themselves to the production of only part of the commodities included in the industry."[22] Following this classification we then selected only those industries which were classified by the *Structure of the American Economy* (hereafter referred to as the NRC) as having "national" markets and as being also "straight." A total of 83 industries were thus selected, and the remainder rejected.

The reduced sample of industries was now examined to determine the adequacy of the corresponding profit data. In 34 cases it was found that S.E.C. profit data were available for less than three firms and generally did not cover a large proportion of industry output. Such industries were thus eliminated, and 49 represented by profit data for three or more firms remained.[23] Because communications from those who developed and supervised the development of the "straight-mixed" classification in the NRC study suggest that the standards used were rather general and the procedures employed rather rough and ready, these 49 industries were then rescreened as data permitted; the component Census product concentration ratios shown in T.N.E.C. Monograph No. 27[24] were examined, and six industries were rejected for which the industry concentration measure did not correspond closely to the concentration measures shown for the principal component products.[25] In addition, three industries were reentered on the list, as having been erroneously classified[26] by NRC; also, three were rejected as obviously too narrow in definition, and one because of large imports excluded from the Census industry output. There then remained a residual sample of 42 industries upon which subsequent investigations have centered.

[21] Op. cit., pp. 264-69.

[22] Ibid., p. 264.

[23] In about 30 per cent of the industries finally retained in our sample there were data for only three firms, and the average number of firms per industry was about eight. In most of the industries retained with only three firms, however, the concentration was moderate to high and the proportion of industry output represented, so far as could be ascertained, moderate to large.

[24] Pp. 418 ff.

[25] From available data on product concentration such a rescreening was possible for about three-fourths of these industries; the others could not be rescreened in this fashion, but for nearly all of them available information from other sources indicated roughly balanced diversification of firms among products.

[26] I.e., where the industry concentration measure would approximate those of any component theoretical industries.

This sample includes all manufacturing industries in the 1935 Census for which (1) a certain minimum of profit data were available in the selected source, and (2) the industry concentration measure would tend to give a reasonable approximation to the true concentration for the theoretical industry or industries within which the included outputs fell. There is an obvious probability of some deviation of such industry concentration measures from the appropriate theoretical measures, so far as our assumptions concerning industry identity are not exactly fulfilled and so far as many such measures may potentially represent several component measures of slightly different value. But we have developed a sample relatively free from dependence on personal guesswork, the concentration measures for which seem to give as reliable an approximation to theoretical concentration as is obtainable with available data.

CHARACTER AND LIMITATIONS OF THE PROFIT DATA

A second step is to survey the available profit data and see to what extent they provide measures of the theoretical profits to which the hypothesis refers. Reference has been made to dependence on profit data published by the S.E.C. We selected the Securities and Exchange Commission's *Survey of American Listed Corporations, 1936-40* as the source of profit data because for the period in question this represents the most reliable comprehensive and uniform available source of income information for both narrow industry divisions and firms.[27] This source covers 1106 registered companies placed in 75 manufacturing groups for this interval. Profit data therefrom provided a measure of profits for the industries in our selected sample.

Since the S.E.C. industry classification is not strictly parallel to the 1935 Census classification, and since the latter had to be followed as the only one with reference to which concentration data were available, it was necessary to reclassify S.E.C. firms as to industry whenever the S.E.C. industry definition did not correspond very closely to a Census definition. In a substantial majority of cases, therefore, the S.E.C. industries were "torn down" and the individual firms were allocated one by one to the appropriate Census industry.[28]

[27]Data by firms are essential if the acceptability of industry classifications in the profit data is to be evaluated, and if such classifications are to be rectified when unsatisfactory.

[28]The allocation was made on the basis of a study of each firm, primarily in Moody's Industrials, to determine its principal line of business as indicated by principal products, value of products, capacity of plants, etc.

As firm profits are allocated to a Census industry and associated with a concentration ratio for that industry, it should be noted that there is frequently a somewhat imperfect fit. The Census industry is built up by classifying establishments or plants, thus occasionally (and appropriately) splitting multi-plant firms among different Census industries, and the Census industry concentration measure refers to the proportion of the aggregate output of a group of such plants controlled by a given number of firms. Profit data, on the other hand, are generally available only for complete firms, which in numerous cases may derive their earnings from the operations of plants in two or more Census industries. Although firm profits have been uniformly allocated to the Census industry within which the firm is primarily occupied, and have been rejected from the sample when the firm did not apparently derive a substantial majority of its earnings from a single Census industry, it is thus true that the firm profits associated with a given Census industry, while they

The next question concerns the significance of these profit data for testing our major hypothesis. An initial problem involves the adequacy and general character of the sample of firms supplied by S.E.C. sources. It is obviously small, including only a fraction of the total number of firms operating in most of the industries. In the sample of 42 industries there are 335 firms represented—an average of about eight per industry—and in about half of the industries the number of firms included is three, four, or five. The S.E.C. sample is made up dominantly of the larger firms—55 of our 335 had a net worth above 50 million dollars and 133 were above 10 million in net worth. One result of this is that in general the profit data tend to include enough of each industry output to give a representative showing for the industry. By the same token, however, the sample of firms is potentially biased in that it gives much fuller representation to large than to small firms,[29] and in that the average earning rates of smaller and larger firms *may* differ. If the latter were true, the sample could give a distorted picture of the relative profitability of the less concentrated industries.[30] Findings relative to the gross relation of profit rate to concentration are likely to be distorted, however, only if there is some systematic and significant variation of profit rates with size of firm among size classes that contribute significantly to total industry earnings. An analysis of the relation of profit rate to size within the selected sample finds no statistically significant general relation of size to profits and does not suggest the likelihood of any major distortion of findings because of the size bias in the sample. The possibility, however, will be discussed in more detail below.

A second issue involves the extent to which accounting profits as reflected in S.E.C. reports are a measure of the theoretical profits to which our major hypothesis refers. The a priori model from which the concentration-profits hypothesis is drawn really refers to firms and industries in long-run static equilibrium. In such a situation, moreover, the revenues and costs which determine profits as defined are strictly instantaneous magnitudes having generally an identical price-level reference and time reference. The predictions drawn from this model may be extended to actual time-process situations by arguing that what would hold for long-run static equilibrium should also tend to hold for average performance over time, although with numerous sources of dispersion from the central tendency thus identified. It should then hold strictly, however, for profits as measured after an adjustment in past costs for any price level change. And it is of course subject to a correct statement generally of the

---

dominantly represent earnings in that industry, often include some earnings derived from operations in other Census industries. The profit rates associated with a given Census industry therefore often may represent rather crude approximations to the profit rates earned on the products which are included in the industry and to which the industry concentration ratio refers.

[29]Only 51 firms with less than one million net worth are included in our sample.

[30]That is, smaller firms, which may in general contribute large proportions of industry output in less concentrated industries, are less frequently included, so that we tend to cover smaller fractions of the outputs of such industries; if smaller firms should tend to earn at a different rate than large, the comparative profitability of less concentrated industries would be misstated.

costs of operation. On the other hand, the recorded costs and revenues which determine the accounting profit of the usual firm will not in general have the same price level and general time reference; and in addition, the costs and revenues shown in accounts may otherwise not be accurately representative of the corresponding magnitudes to which the underlying theory implicitly refers. If accounting profits are to be used in testing our hypothesis, the significance of the resulting aberrations in the measurement of theoretical profits requires examination.

If price levels are changing over time, the "true" profits or theoretical excess profits to which our hypothesis refers are defined as if measured for each time interval after some adjustment, because of price level changes, of depreciation, of all other past-dated cost elements, and of the original-cost valuation of assets. A firm "breaks even" for a period if it recovers in current revenues all currently incurred, currently allocable costs, plus the original cost of all previously acquired assets legitimately amortized, adjusted for price level change since acquisition, plus a current market interest return on original cost value of owners' equity, similarly adjusted for price level change.[31] This identifies the theoretical zero-profit level with capital maintenance in the sense of maintenance of "assets of constant purchasing power" in the hands of owners.[32] True profits are found in earnings above this level.

If we select this adapted definition of true theoretical profits, then company accounts will tend to show such profits accurately so far as they make the requisite price level adjustments. Evidently such adjustments are not made as a general rule or systematically. Under the general rule of original-cost valuation, subject only to occasional or special readjustments, the tendency is not to revalue for price change. Thus accounts tend to exaggerate or understate true profits and profit rates according to the relation of the going price level to some average of the levels which held at the date of acquisition of past-acquired assets.

For any interval under study, therefore, we should not expect the absolute level of accounting profit rates to be theoretically significant unless the present-past price-level relations can be ascertained to be of a given order. For purposes of this study, however, it is the comparison of profit rates of different firms or industries which is essential rather than the absolute level of rates. So far as firms or industries compared experienced different average price levels as of the date of acquisition of fixed and other amortizable assets, their relative accounting profit rates will of course give a distorted picture of their relative theoretical profit rates, to which our hypothesis refers. However, for relatively large groups of firms and industries, we may suppose that on the average the price-change effects on accounting profit rates will be similar, and that for such groups the sort of potential aberrations referred to will "average out," with any

[31] Or if the positive difference between revenues and all items but the last, divided by the adjusted cost value of equity, gives a gross equity rate equal to the interest rate.

[32] This definition of profit should be viewed as a first approximation subject to the assumption that no loan capital is used. If it is, true profit would be that stated plus or minus a windfall to owners essentially equivalent to the windfall loss or gain of principal by creditors because of price level change.

true net relation of theoretical rates surviving in group averages. A significant source of dispersion or random variation in individual profit-rate showings is of course introduced.

A second source of aberration in measurement is to be found in the fact that accounting valuations and depreciation charges do not always follow a strict single rule, and that there thus may be significant differences in profit-calculation procedures followed by different firms in the same or different industries. It is not evident, however, that accounting profit showings are simply arbitrary and unsystematic numbers bearing no relation to theoretical profits as defined. In relatively recent intervals, such as the period 1936-40 under examination, the influence of "accepted accounting procedures" established by certified accountants for income tax and general auditing purposes appears to have become such that original-cost valuations and regularized depreciation and amortization practices have been made the rule. Thus in general the accounting profit showings of different firms should have at least roughly similar significance and bear a fairly systematic and similar relation to theoretical profits, subject to qualifications mentioned above concerning price-level changes. Still, we have discovered another source of random variation in individual profit showings. A further consideration of similar import is that so far as the company in question not only operates in production but also acts as an investor in securities, its over-all earning rate may not accurately reflect the earning on operations to which our hypothesis implicitly refers.

The preceding refers to potential aberrations in the measurement by accounts of theoretical profits on operations. Such true profits, however, even if accurately measured, will seldom in individual cases exactly average through time to a long-run equilibrium level, but will be influenced by lagging response to, and faulty anticipation of, a never-ending succession of dynamic changes. Our hypothesis refers to profit results which should occur in long-run equilibrium, or on the average over time for many cases so far as results on the average tend to approximate those of long-run equilibrium. So far as in individual cases demand and cost are not accurately anticipated or fully adjusted to—or so far as "risk" is miscalculated—profit differences will emerge among firms and industries which are explicable only as windfalls and not by our hypothesis. Thus we should expect our predicted relation to hold strictly only "plus or minus windfalls," which windfalls however should tend largely to cancel out in group averages.[33] Finally, of course, the predicted relation is a partial one, neglecting any concurrent influence on profit rates of other characteristics of market structure. So far as comparative profits are independently influenced by

[33]Further, individual profit rates on equity (or sales) may be variously influenced by windfalls to owners due to the use of borrowed capital with varying price levels, as the extent of such use varies. Also, as indicated above, the whole hypothesis concerning the relation of equity profit rates to concentration rests on the assumption that on the average among groups the relation of cost to demand is similar and the ratio of equity to sales is similar. Individual variations around the central tendency may result from differences in the equity-sales ratio (whatever the cause) and from differences in the relation of cost to demand.

other differences in market structure, a further potential source of deviations from the predicted tendency is identified.

In summary, how accurate a representation of the theoretical long-run tendency of profit rates of firms and industries is given by S.E.C. accounting data? Although such data should give a rough guide to the comparative long-run average profitability of various sizeable groups of firms and industries, there are numerous sources of deviation of individual accounting profit rates from their theoretical long-run tendency. These are of sufficient weight that we should judge it quite improbable that the major hypothesis, even if true, would be verified by every pair of individual firms or industries.

From this analysis, two requirements for the subsequent analytical procedure clearly emerge. First, major reliance will have to be placed upon group averaging and upon comparison of group average profit rates at different levels of concentration. Correspondingly, conventional simple correlation procedures do not promise to be especially fruitful. Second, in view of the large number of "random" elements in the picture (many of which cannot be evaluated sufficiently to permit use of multiple correlation techniques), major attention will have to be given to tests for the statistical significance of any difference found in group averages. It is essential in this setting to know whether intragroup variance is of such magnitude as to obliterate the significance of any difference discovered between group averages. Subject to these strictures, the S.E.C. profit data have been accepted as rough measures of the theoretical profit tendencies relevant to our hypothesis.

CALCULATION OF ACCOUNTING PROFIT RATES

For our finally selected sample of 42 industries and 335 firms (and also for larger unrectified samples used for certain test purposes), S.E.C. profit data were tabulated for the calendar years 1936 through 1940. The year 1936 was the first for which S.E.C. data were presented for a sufficient sample of firms; the terminal year was the last in an unbroken series, substantially unaffected by wartime changes in market conformations. Thus we have a period of five years of relatively "normal peacetime," the cyclical characteristics of which are familiar to all.[34] The S.E.C. conversion of fiscal to calendar years, which classified the profits of any fiscal year as belonging to the calendar year in which the fiscal year ended, was accepted as relatively satisfactory for our purposes.[35] Similarly we followed S.E.C. in its acceptance of consolidated statements where presented, and in all other technical matters except the assignment of firms to industries, discussed above. The profit measure chosen was the ratio of annual net profit after income taxes[36] to net worth as of the beginning of the year,[37]

[34]Data for postwar peacetime are as yet not available for enough years to permit extension of the test into recent years.

[35]*Survey of American Listed Corporations,* p. viii.

[36]Ibid., p. ix.

[37]Ibid., loc. cit.

both conventionally defined by S.E.C.[38] This was calculated for each firm for each of the years under examination; we will refer to it as the *firm annual profit rate.*[39] From the firms' annual profit rates, two sorts of average rate were calculated. First, we derived for each firm a simple unweighted average of annual profit rates for the five years in question; this average will be referred to as the *firm average profit rate.* Second, we calculated for each industry an *industry average profit rate* for the five years, derived by calculating for each year a weighted average profit rate for the firms in the industry (sum of firm profits divided by sum of firm net worths) and then taking a simple unweighted average of the annual weighted average rates.[40] The primary profit measures employed in testing our major hypothesis are thus *industry average profit rates* (1936-40) for each of the 42 industries in our selected sample, and *firm average profit rates* (1936-40) for each of the component firms.

The measure of industry concentration chosen, to be associated either with the industry average rate or with the average rates of the member firms of the industry, is the proportion of value product of the Census industry contributed by the first eight firms in 1935, as calculated in *Structure of the American Economy,* Part 1, Appendix 7. Results using the eight-firm measure show no significant statistical differences from those using proportion of value product contributed by four; the 1935 date was used necessarily as the only proximate year for which industry concentration data were available. Ideally, further measures of the size distribution of firms within an industry would be desirable, but we must accept those available for purposes of an initial test. Also, of course, the linking of 1935 concentration data with 1936-40 profits is not done through choice. Recent data on postwar concentration, however, suggest that our industry concentration ratios are in general fairly stable through time, so that the error attributable to use of the available concentration data should ordinarily be small.

ASSOCIATION OF INDUSTRY PROFIT RATES AND CONCENTRATION

The major hypothesis is that on the average higher profit rates will be earned in industries of high concentration than in industries of lower concentration. In testing this hypothesis, however, it has seemed pertinent to test also for the

[38]Since our interest was primarily in comparison of rates rather than determination of absolute level, it was felt that the use of first-of-the-year net worth figures would not result in any serious aberrations in our findings. Some distortion in individual firm profit rates may of course result.

[39]The ratio of net profits before income taxes to net worth was also calculated and used for certain test calculations; no significant difference in statistical results appeared.

[40]In deriving an industry average rate for any year, it seems obviously appropriate to weight the individual firm rates according to firm size, since our interest is in the profitability of total investment in the industry. For either firms or industries, however, it seems inappropriate to assign weights to the rates of different years, since each year's rate becomes in a sense a pure number having a status equal to that of any other annual rate, regardless of the movement of net worth through time. At least as good a theoretical case can be made for this logic as for any other.

association of profit rates with other potential determinants, and of such determinants with concentration. Thus we have also tested for the association of profit rate and of industry concentration with the size of firm, the proportion of overhead costs, the relative importance of capital assets, the durability of the good, and the character of buyers. Other attractive possibilities were not explored because of lack of data.

Attention centers critically, however, on the concentration-profits relationships, and we may turn first to the association of the industry profit rate with industry concentration in our sample of 42 industries. Table 4.1 lists these industries in order of concentration, together with 1935 concentration ratios and 1936-40 industry average profit rates.

In analyzing these data, we have wished (1) to see if profit rates on the average decline with decreasing concentration, and (2) to ascertain the shape of any such relationship. If it exists, is it a simple linear relationship, or is it of some different sort? With only 42 industries in our sample, we are obviously hampered in developing conclusive answers to these and similar questions. However, certain tentative findings may be set forth.

First, there is no conclusive indication of any closely observed linear relationship of industry concentration to profit rates. Table 4.2 shows the simple average of industry average profit rates (1936-40) within each concentration decile for the 42 industries of our sample. A regression line fitted to the data shows a decided downward slope for profit rates as concentration decreases, but the correlation is poor ($r = .33$) and the fit to any such line is obviously so poor that the inference of a rectilinear or other simple relationship of concentration to profits is not warranted. The general showing is that of a fairly high average level of profit rates down to the 70 per cent concentration line, a much lower average level down to the 30 per cent line, and (based on a very small sample) a higher level again below the 30 per cent line. But no steady linear downward progression of profit rates with declining concentration is evident.

Second, the positive conclusion which does emerge is that there is a rather distinct break in average profit-rate showing at the 70 per cent concentration line, and that there is a significant difference in the average of industry average profit rates above and below this line. In the selected sample, the simple average of 22 industry average profit rates for industries wherein 70 per cent or more of value product was controlled by eight firms was 12.1 per cent; for 20 industries below the 70 per cent line it was 6.9 per cent. Applying the Fisher *z* test[41] to this dichotomy, with the individual industry average profit rate as the unit observation, we find less than a one-tenth of one per cent chance that this difference could be accounted for by random factors. A tentative conclusion is thus that industries with an eight-firm concentration ratio above 70 per cent tended, in 1936-40 at least, to have significantly higher average profits rates than

[41]The *z* test, as here applied, judges the significance of the difference in two group means by determining the probability that random variation, as evidenced by the dispersion of observations within each group around the group mean, could account for the observed difference between the means.

Table 4.1 Concentration Ratios and 1936-40 Average Profit Rates for a Sample of 42 Industries

Census number	*Industry designation (abbreviated)*	*Proportion of value product supplied by first eight firms in 1935*	*1936-40 industry average profit rate after income taxes* [a]
222	Asphalt-felt-base floor covering; linoleum	100.0	9.0
1652	Cigarettes	99.4	14.4
1314	Typewriters and parts	99.3	15.8
108	Chewing gum	97.3	16.9
113	Corn syrup, sugar, oil and starch	95.0	9.3
1408	Motor vehicles	94.2	16.3
803	Rubber tires and tubes	90.4	8.2
629	Rayon and allied products	90.2	12.1
1301	Agricultural implements	87.7	9.1
1022	Gypsum products	86.4	10.1
1123	Tin cans and other tinware	85.6	9.1
1636	Photographic apparatus and materials	84.9	12.9
1647	Tobacco, chewing and smoking	84.3	11.7
1405	Cars, railroad	84.0	2.8
1201	Aluminum products	83.7	9.7
631	Soap	83.1	15.2
1634	Pens, fountain, etc.	82.8	12.3
1218	Smelting and refining, zinc	82.2	4.7
1315	Washing machines	79.7	14.0
1401	Aircraft and parts	72.8	20.8
133	Liquors, distilled	71.4	14.2
1638	Roofing	68.2	7.4
201	Carpets and rugs	68.2	4.7
1112	Steel works and rolling mills	63.8	4.9
123	Meat packing	63.5	3.6
1102	Cast iron pipe	63.0	8.6
705	Petroleum refining	58.9	6.8
1126	Wire	54.0	7.5
115	Flavoring extracts	54.0	1.8
1608	Cigars	50.7	6.9
1104	Doors and shutters, metal	49.0	18.3
1325	Printer's machinery	47.4	2.2
1002	Cement	44.7	5.4
116	Flour	37.0	7.6
907	Leather	34.3	0.8
1117	Screw machine products	32.9	8.2
904	Boots and shoes	30.8	7.5
105	Canned fruits and vegetables	30.4	7.4
209	Rayon manufactures	27.1	8.4
408	Paper goods	23.7	12.4
112	Confectionery	19.9	17.0
311	Lumber and timber products	7.6	9.1

[a]Net profit after income taxes as a percentage of net worth.

Table 4.2 Average of Industry Average Profit Rates within Concentration Deciles, 1936-1940, for 42 Selected Industries

Concentration range (per cent of value product supplied by eight firms)	*Number of industries*	*Average of industry average profit rates*[a]
90-100	8	12.7
80-89.9	11	10.5
70-79.9	3	16.3
60-69.9	5	5.8
50-59.9	4	5.8
40-49.9	2	3.8
30-39.9	5	6.3
20-29.9	2	10.4
10-19.9	1	17.0
0- 9.9	1	9.1

[a]Average of net profits after income taxes as percentages of net worth.

those with a ratio below 70 per cent. The evidence available does not seem to warrant other than this dichotomous distinction.

Since this finding might conceivably be judged an important one, it is essential to examine its derivation in some greater detail. In the first place, it emerges from a selected sample the selection of which has been described above. In choosing the final sample of 42 Census industries from the 149 for which both profit and concentration data were available, two eliminations and one revision were made. First, we eliminated all industries for which profit data were available for fewer than three firms; second, we eliminated all industries classified by NRC[42] as either "local" or "regional" as to markets or "mixed" (with component firms specializing in only part of the products included); third, we rectified the resultant remainder sample of 49 industries, eliminating ten and adding three. As a back-check we have therefore calculated the simple average of industry average profit rates below and above the 70 per cent line for the larger unrectified samples of industries. The general finding has been that although in all cases the average of industry profit rates for the higher concentration group remains higher, the difference is not statistically significant by the z test until industries represented by fewer than three firms have been eliminated and until the "local-regional" and "mixed" industries have been eliminated according to the NRC definitions. The "NRC sample" of 49 industries (before our final rectification), all of which are represented by three or more firms, shows a difference in group average profit rates which has less than a five per cent chance of being due to random factors. The elimination of industries represented by only one or two firms was thus crucial to our major finding, as was the application of the NRC classification hitherto described. Our final sample gives the same result as the three-or-more-firm NRC sample, but raises the significance of the observed difference in group means. Table 4.3 summarizes the findings on group means above and below the 70 per cent concentration line for various samples tested.

[42]*Structure of the American Economy*, Part 1.

Table 4.3 Group Average Profit Rates, 1936-1940, for Concentration Classes of Industries, as Computed for Various Samples, and Statistical Significance Thereof by "Z" Test

Sample	*Number of industries*	*Average profit rate of industries above 70 per cent concentration*	*Average profit rate of industries below 70 per cent concentration*	*Probability, by z test that difference in means is not significant*
Final selected sample	42	12.1	6.9	Less than 1/10 of 1 per cent
NRC sample – industries with three or more firms	49	11.2	7.6	Less than 5 per cent
NRC sample – all industries	83	10.3	8.7	More than 5 per cent
Total sample – industries with three or more firms	88	11.5	9.7	More than 5 per cent
Total sample – all industries	149	10.6	9.6	More than 5 per cent

In judging the meaningfulness of the major finding to this point, the reader must assess the theoretical validity of the crucial elimination processes which gave rise to it. The only arbitrary operation was that of eliminating all industries for which profit data were available for less than three firms. This procedure was solely responsible for the removal of 34 of the 100 industries which were eliminated in moving from the total original sample to the NRC sample of industries with more than three firms.[43] Most of the industries eliminated on the ground of numbers alone were small and the indication was that a small proportion of industry volume would have been represented—only 43 firms were present in these 34 industries as a whole, so that 25 were represented by a single firm. Thus the procedure is supported as a means of seeking as good a statistical representation of the profits of an industry as possible. On the other hand, it must be emphasized that the 43 firms in these 34 industries evidenced a profit-concentration relationship inconsistent with that of the selected sample.[44]

Other cautions must also be advised. The rejection of the "mixed" industries and of those with geographically segmented markets seems to have been clearly justified on theoretical grounds, and the small difference between group means in the unrectified "total sample" would seem correspondingly to have no especial import. In the residual sample, however, the industry concentration ratios can, in view of the industry definition applied, at best give only approximations to the true theoretical concentrations for the outputs to which they refer; there is potentially an unascertained margin of error in these ratios. As the z test has been applied, these ratios are implicitly taken as a definitive basis for grouping, and the test does not allow for potential errors in grouping which might result from aberrations in these ratios. Second, the profits associated with given industries are in some cases affected by earnings in other industries, although this may possibly be viewed as one source of the random variation which has been evaluated. Third, the bias of the sample in the direction of large firms may result in some distortion of our findings, so far as small firms earn at different rates than large and so far as a greater proportion of output in less concentrated industries is supplied by small firms. Findings described below do not make this seem especially probable, but we are not in a position conclusively to reject the possibility. Finally, the "proof of significance" of the difference in group means would seem to rest on the assumption that certain influences on accounting

[43] Application of the NRC criteria alone would remove the other 66, although removal was demanded by both criteria in 27 cases.

[44] Averages of industry profit rates above and below the 70 per cent concentration line in these 34 industries were 9.1 and 10.5 per cent respectively. Industries eliminated alone on grounds of representation in profit data by less than three firms were cottonseed oil and meal, linseed oil and meal, matches, wood preserving, firearms, children's carriages, and sleds, waste, surgical appliances, house furnishings, lace goods, malt, oleomargarine, baking powder, silk manufacturing, dyeing and finishing, sewing machines, miscellaneous tools, abrasive products, plumbers' supplies, asbestos products, nails not made in wire mills, bolts and nuts not made in rolling mills, wirework n.e.c., smelting and refining non-ferrous metals not from ore, explosives, glue and gelatin, tanning materials and dyestuffs, wood distillation, pianos, graphite, converted paper products, wall paper, miscellaneous engraving, and drug grinding.

profit rates other than concentration, such as price level changes, aberrations in measurement, dynamical departures from long-run equilibrium, etc. together result in a random variation of the rates in each group around their long-run tendency. Subject to these and similar reservations the findings may be placed on file for whatever tentative indications they provide.

ASSOCIATION OF FIRM PROFIT RATES AND INDUSTRY CONCENTRATION

If results based upon our rectified sample are provisionally accepted, however, there remains a further question at least, concerning the extent to which total variance has been taken into account in applying the *z* test to the difference between the two group averages of industry profit rates when each industry average profit rate is taken as a unit observation. The procedure followed in deriving an average of industry profit rates above and below the 70 per cent concentration line was to derive for each industry a simple average for the years 1936 through 1940 of the weighted average annual profit rates of the firms in the industry, and then for each concentration category to take a simple average of the industry average rates thus derived. The *z* test for significance of the difference in the group means thus derived, as so far applied, essentially compares this difference between the two means with the variance of the individual industry profit rates around the group means–i.e., with the dispersion of such profit rates within each concentration category. The intragroup variance measured is thus a variance of industry profit rates around an average of such rates. In this calculation, one component of total variance within groups may actually have been concealed or suppressed–namely the variance of individual firm profit rates around the individual industry mean. In other terms, the total variance is that of the firm profit rates around the group mean, and we have recognized only part of it in taking the deviations of industry average profit rates from group means as our initial measure of variance.

To meet this potential objection, we have made two additional tests of the significance of the difference in group average profit rates, where all ascertainable elements of variance are recognized. First, we have calculated a simple unweighted average of firm average profit rates (1936-40) for each of the two industry concentration groups[45] and have applied the *z* test to the resulting difference in group averages, using the unweighted difference of each firm profit rate from its group average as the basic measure of intragroup variance. Second, we have calculated a weighted average of all firm average profit rates for each of the two concentration groups, and have applied a similar significance test which takes as the basic measure of intragroup variance the weighted difference of the firm's profit rate from the weighted group mean rate.[46] The difference between weighted group means is then compared with an appropriate measure of

[45]That is, for firms in industries with concentration above and below our 70 per cent line.
[46]The weights are the net worths of firms.

weighted intragroup variation.[47] Although the first test is more conventional, the latter seems somewhat more meaningful in terms of the hypothesis being tested.[48]

The first test for significance—using unweighted firm profit rates as unit observations and unweighted group means and deviations—found that for the selected sample the 143 firms in industries in the above-70-per-cent concentration group had a simple average profit rate of 9.0 per cent whereas 192 firms in industries in the lower concentration group had an average rate of 7.7 per cent. The difference in group averages, by the *z* test, had a greater than five per cent chance of being due to random variation. However, the difference in group averages and the showing on significance were greatly influenced by two extreme observations for relatively small firms in the above-70-per-cent group, showing loss rates of about 140 and 215 per cent respectively;[49] when these were eliminated the group averages for the remaining 333 firms were 11.7 and 7.7 respectively and the difference was significant beyond the one-tenth of one per cent level. Subject to the rejection of two extreme observations of a total of 335, therefore, our tentative finding of a significant relation of profit-rate concentration is sustained. This finding, incidentally, would appear unlikely to be upset by the inclusion of the 43 firms excluded from our sample because of less than three firms representing an industry.

The second test, involving the difference between the weighted group averages of firm profit rates and the weighted variance within groups, showed the weighted group mean profit rates to be 12.6 per cent and 5.9 per cent and the difference to be significant beyond the one-tenth of one per cent level.

Some interest may attach to the fact that the difference between the weighted group means for firms (12.6 and 5.9 per cent, all 335 firms included) is larger than the difference between simple group means for firms (9.0 to 7.7 per cent when all firms are included). This discrepancy is due in part to the fact that the two extreme cases alluded to above are low-weighted and affect the weighted group mean for the high concentration class less than they do the unweighted mean. But even after we eliminate these two cases, the difference between the unweighted group means is substantially smaller than the corresponding difference between weighted means. The discrepancy is evidently also due to the fact that the observed association of concentration to profit rate is much more evident among the larger firms than among the smaller. If we stratify the 333 firms in the selected sample (the two extreme cases omitted) according to net

[47] I am indebted to Professor George Kuznets, of the Giannini Foundation, University of California, for showing me the character of a significance test wherein the weighted deviations of the various observations are taken as measures of variance, and where random variation in both the observations and their weights is postulated. The test is based on an approximation to the variance of the ratio of two random variables, from the linear terms of the Taylor expansion. Cf. Frank Yates, *Sampling Methods for Censuses and Surveys,* 1945, p. 212; also W. E. Deming, *Some Theory of Sampling,* 1950, pp. 165 ff.

[48] We are concerned more, that is, with the aggregate profitability of a group of firms of given concentration rating than with the individual firm rating, which is also affected by the unpredicted sharing of profit among firms within an industry.

[49] These were Graham-Paige Motor Co. and Seversky Aircraft Corp.

worth in 1936, it appears that for firms with net worth above five million dollars the response of firm profit rate to concentration of the industry is clear, whereas below the five million net worth line such a response is by no means evident. Table 4.4 shows the simple average of firm profit rates (1936-40) in two concentration groups for each of nine net worth classes for 333 firms (two extreme observations omitted) of our selected sample.

Table 4.4 Simple Averages of Firm Profit Rates (1936-1940) for Two Concentration Classes and Nine Net-Worth Classes for 333 Firms of the Selected Sample

	Number of firms		*Average profit rate of firms 1936-40*	
Net worth of firm in 1936	*Above 70 per cent industry concentration*	*Below 70 per cent industry concentration*	*Firms above 70 per cent concentration*	*Firms below 70 per cent concentration*
Above 50 million	23	32	10.4	6.0
10-50 million	37	41	9.7	5.3
5-10 million	19	24	17.9	8.2
1- 5 million	33	73	6.3	8.6
0.5-1 million	16	14	14.9	8.3
250-500 thousand	6	5	(16.8)	5.8
100-250 thousand	7	2	3.6	22.7
50-100 thousand	0	0	–	–
0- 50 thousand	0	1	–	41.8
Total	141	192		

If a tentative hypothesis were to be drawn from this showing, it would be that for firms with net worth greater than five million dollars, 1936-40 profit rates were on the average significantly higher if the firm was a member of an industry where eight firms controlled 70 per cent or more of value product; for firms with less than five million net worth, the average firm profit rate does not seem to have been significantly associated with industry concentration. Smaller firms tended to fare about the same regardless of industry concentration; the dominant firms in general had earning rates which were influenced by such concentration. This statistical significance of this apparent complex association, however, has not been tested and is definitely open to doubt.

The evidence presented in Table 4.4 may also cast some light on the potentiality, previously referred to, that a sample unduly weighted in the direction of large firms may give a distorted picture of the gross relation of profits to concentration. In effect, has the scanty representation of small firms, which generally supply a larger portion of the output of less concentrated industries, probably distorted the comparison of the average profit rates of industries of high and low concentration? We are really in no position with our data to answer this question as far as it involves firms with less than one-half million net worth, since the sample for them is so small. However, firms so small do not ordinarily contribute the bulk of output even in the less concentrated manufacturing industries. As regards firms above the half-million net worth line, there is not a *statistically significant* relation of the size of firm to profits for all firms, and it appears unlikely that one would be found separately within the two concentration classes. This argues that the poor representation of small firms will not result in distortion of the relative values of average profits for high and low concentration groups. On the other hand, it does appear from this sample that there *could* be some tendency for firms below the five million net worth line to earn less than larger firms in the highly concentrated industries, and more than the larger firms in the less concentrated industries. A better representation of small firms *might* have brought the group mean profit rates somewhat closer together, although it appears very unlikely that it would have obliterated the difference. Tests for the significance of the overall relation of profits to size do not support this conclusion, but the possibility is open. Here the matter must rest for the time being.

Without repeating them, it should be noted that the reservations stated with respect to the findings on the relation of industry profit rates to concentration in general apply equally to the findings above on the relation of firm profit rates to industry concentration.

ASSOCIATION OF PROFIT RATES WITH OTHER DETERMINANTS

Given these tentative findings on the association of industry concentration to profit rates, the question naturally arises whether such profit rates may have also been significantly associated with potential determinants other than concentration, and also, if this is so, whether there may be any association between concentration and such determinants which would give rise to a complex explanation of the association established so far. Available data do not permit us to explore many of the interesting possibilities along this line. So far as readily measurable potential determinants are concerned, we have tentatively concluded that the answer to both of these questions is no, but it may be useful to review briefly our findings in this regard.

An obvious potential determinant of profit rate, especially in view of various studies centered on it, is the absolute size of the firm, as measured either by assets or by net worth. Our finding has been that for firms in our sample as a whole there is no statistically significant association of firm profit rate to firm size. The possibility of a significant association of size to profits for firms within given concentration classes has not been tested, but an inspection of the data suggests that one probably would not be found. For larger firms there is an association between concentration and firm profit rate which is evidently stronger than any visible association of profit rate to firm size, although within our sample this does not hold for smaller firms. This finding is of course based on a sample much smaller than that used in some previous studies of firm size and profits, and one which gives disproportionate emphasis to larger firms. Such other studies, however, have not tested for the statistical significance of observed differences in profit-rate averages among size groups.

In more detail, our findings on the relation of firm size to profit rate for our selected sample are as follows. (1) When firms are split into six asset-size classes (two extreme profit-rate showings omitted) the observed differences in average profit rates by classes are not statistically significant by the *z* test. (2) The same result appears when firms are grouped into two size classes, divided at the five million dollar asset line.[50] (3) When firms are divided into two concentration classes, there is within our sample no significant association of the firm's net worth to industry concentration. The average net worth is larger in the lower concentration group, although not significantly so.[51] Our general conclusion, from a more extended analysis which will not be reproduced here, is that for our selected sample there is no significant simple association of firm size with profit rate, and no simple association of firm size with industry concentration such as could evidently account for the observed association of concentration to profit rate. The possibility of some association of net worth to concentration in larger samples has been discussed above, but if established this would not revise this conclusion unless a significant association of size to profits could be established.

The further tests for potential determinants or co-determinants of the profit rate which we have made may be reviewed briefly. Additional characteristics of firms and industries within our selected sample which were measured include ratio of capital to total assets, ratio of overhead to total costs, ratio of net worth to sales, composition of purchasers as between producers and consumers, and durability of output. In general we have explored for a relationship of these potential determinants to the profit rate, to concentration, to firm size, and to each other. Substantially no positive findings emerged. Although there were very slight initial indications of association in some cases, practically none appeared to be statistically significant and none contributed perceptibly to the further explanation of the major findings previously described.

SUMMARY

The major hypothesis to be tested was that the profit rates of firms in industries of high seller concentration should on the average be larger than those of firms in industries of lower concentration, although subject to a considerable dispersion of the profit rates of individual firms and industries. Our statistical study has suggested that this was very probably the case in the interval 1936 through 1940 in American manufacturing industry, and that the association of concentration to profits was such that there was a rough dichotomy of industries into those with more and less than 70 per cent of value product controlled by eight firms. Association of concentration to other potential determinants

[50]The number of firms was reduced from 333 to 280 because of lack of asset data wherever asset measures were used. Average profit rates above and below the five million asset line are respectively 9.6 and 9.3.

[51]Further examination of the relation of firm net worth to industry concentration shows the largest average net worth of firms in the industry concentration deciles of 50 to 60 per cent and 60 to 70 per cent. This segment was shown by Table 4.1 to be one of relatively low profit rates.

measured was not found, nor were other such determinants significantly related to profit rates. Absolute size of firm did not appear to be significantly related to profit rates in any simple fashion.

These findings should be accepted subject to a number of reservations, enumerated above, which stem from the character of definitions employed, the limitations of the data, the character of the sample, and so forth. To the extent that there remains suspicion of resultant bias in findings, the present findings should of course be viewed as tentative. Furthermore, even if the findings are accepted for the interval 1936-40, the conclusion is not necessarily warranted that the hypothesis is thus conclusively verified as a general tendency for all periods. Testing for earlier and later periods is clearly indicated. Unfortunately, lack of data makes tests prior to 1936 difficult, and we must wait for the accumulation of postwar data for tests for more recent periods. Finally, we have been unable with available data to test for the relation of profit rates to certain potential determinants–especially other characteristics of market structure–which in theory seem likely to influence profits and also perhaps to be associated systematically with industry concentration. The condition of entry to the industry is perhaps the most prominent of these. Exploration of the effect of such potential determinants on profits would add greatly to our present knowledge of the determinants of profitability.

At the moment we have a very provisional and tentative hypothesis for further testing. Should it be further verified, we may be on the road to an answer to the question of what is an "appreciable" or "considerable" or "workable" number and size distribution of sellers or to a knowledge of above what critical concentration level an industry is likely to earn exceptional profits.

CORRIGENDUM[52]

The following revisions should be noted in the group-average profit rates shown for groups of industries and firms with various concentration ratios (pp. 45 ff.), for the selected sample only. In the calculation of these averages, industry 1104 (Metal Doors and Shutters), the concentration ratio for which is correctly shown as 49.0 in Table 4.1, was through a clerical error entered as having a concentration ratio between 80 and 89.9

Rectifying this error, the following slightly revised averages should be substituted:

1. In Table 4.2, average profit rate of industries in the 80-89.9 category, 9.8; of industries in the 40-49.9 category, 8.6.
2. In Table 4.3 (row one), average profit rate of industries of above 70 per cent concentration, 11.8; of below 70 per cent concentration, 7.5.
3. On page 52, line 7, simple average profit rate of 143 (now 139) firms in industries of above 70 per cent concentration, 8.8; on line 14, of 141 (now 137)

[52]Reprinted from *Quarterly Journal of Economics,* 65, November 1951, p. 602, courtesy of the publisher.

firms in industries of above 70 per cent concentration, 11.6; on lines 27 and 28, of 192 (now 196) firms in industries of below 70 per cent concentration, 7.8. No perceptible change in weighted averages of firm profit rates.

4. In Table 4.4, for firms of 1-5 million net worth, average profit rate in the above-70-per-cent concentration class, 5.2; in the below-70-per-cent concentration class, 9.0. For firms of 0.5-1 million net worth, average profit rate in the above-70-per-cent concentration class, 15.5; in the below-70-per-cent concentration class, 8.2.

The significance of differences in group averages previously found evidently remains, and no revision of general findings results.

Chapter Five

Pricing in Monopoly and Oligopoly

The conventional versions of *a priori* price analysis apparently suggest that a single-firm monopoly or a collusive oligopoly will choose a price-output combination such as to maximize *the industry profit.* Product differentiation and selling cost being neglected, the currently established firm or firms are supposed to equate their marginal costs to the marginal revenue drawn from the industry demand curve for the commodity which they produce in common. This balance should presumably be struck over any long period between long-run marginal cost and the marginal revenue from the long-run industry demand, and in any short period between short-run marginal cost and the marginal revenue from the short-run industry demand. Price in either period should be set to maximize the difference between the aggregate revenue from the sale of the given commodity and the aggregate cost of its production by any established group of firms. Empirical studies of price policy by monopolists or by oligopolists with *apparently* effective collusion on price, however, frequently fail to sustain these predictions. In many such industries, short-run outputs at which short-run marginal costs plainly exceed short-run industry marginal revenue are apparently common. But more striking is the evidence in some of these industries of prices held persistently over many years within a range where the industry demand curve is evidently inelastic, the corresponding marginal revenue thus being negative and necessarily below long-run marginal cost.[1] This indicates a prolonged tendency (potentially for a theoretical "long-run") to hold price well below the level which would maximize the difference between aggregate revenue from the sale of the industry's commodity and the aggregate cost of producing it,[2] and apparently contradicts the basic a priori predictions of a theory of collusive pricing.

Reprinted from *American Economic Review,* 39, March 1949, pp. 448-464, courtesy of the American Economic Association.

[1]Two fairly convincing examples of this are the cigarette and steel industries.

[2]Of producing it, explicitly, with the "given" number of firms, but also with any other conceivable number of firms if industry marginal revenue is negative.

This apparent impasse has been variously resolved by students of industry with suggestions: (1) that sellers do not try to maximize monetary profit; (2) that they err in their attempt to maximize profits; (3) that in the face of great uncertainty concerning demand they simply add some markup to normal average cost and hope for the best; (4) that they fear government interference and public ill will if they exploit their monopoly positions fully; (5) that the apparently collusive oligopoly is not fully or successfully collusive, so that rivalry keeps price down; (6) that sellers set low prices for very considerable time periods in order to raise the level of future industry demand; and (7) that *established sellers* persistently or "in the long run" *forego prices high enough to maximize the industry profit* for fear of thereby attracting new entry to the industry and thus *reducing the demands for their outputs and their own profits.*

Although each of these explanations may contain an element of truth as applied to particular cases, they proceed on somewhat different levels in their implied criticisms of conventional theory. The rejection of profit-maximization as a goal suggests a corresponding rejection of conventional price theory; the thesis that either errors or uncertainties are dominant suggests that if such theory is basically valid in its assumptions it nevertheless has little genuine value for predicting actual price results. The suggestion that oligopolistic rivalry reduces prices below the monopoly level leaves theory unscathed, simply implying that the model for monopoly pricing has been misapplied. On the other hand, the hypotheses concerning fear of interference, threat of entry, and pricing to stimulate future demand do not deny that the observed results may be explicable in terms of a theory of monopoly or collusive oligopoly price which assumes profit maximization, effective collusion, and approximately given data, but suggest that the industry or seller demand curves employed in that theory must be redrawn to reflect explicitly the effects of the phenomena in question.

Until the results of such a redrafting are explored, we cannot properly assess the potential explanatory value of conventional price theory. In this paper, we examine two possible modifications of the theory of monopoly price, to take account first of the relation of present price to future profit and second of the impact of the threat of entry;[3] in the latter case we suggest certain possibly novel conclusions concerning the unit for which profit may be maximized and the relation of marginal cost to marginal revenue.

INTERPERIOD DEMAND RELATIONSHIPS

An elaboration of conventional theory to recognize the relation of current price to future demand has been suggested by M. W. Reder; it may deserve re-emphasis in connection with the present issue.[4]

[3]Although the threat of government interference will not be treated explicitly, it could be handled in about the same manner as entry.

[4]"Intertemporal Relations of Demand and Supply within the Firm," *Canadian Journal of Economics and Political Science, VII,* February 1941, pp. 25-38, and especially pp. 32-35.

The monopolistic firm (or group of collusive oligopolists[5]) may be provisionally viewed as dealing with an entire industry demand curve in a succession of time intervals, in each of which it can freely select a price-output combination for the industry. It will thus logically take account of the effect of any current price-output decision on the position of the industry demand curve in future periods. A lower price now may mean a larger (or smaller) demand later, and any such anticipated relationship should affect any current pricing policy. If it does, a single long-run industry demand curve cannot be viewed as an independent determinant even of the long-run tendency of price. Such a relation is then not given independently of the prices which the seller(s) charge at various times during the future, but will assume various levels according to the behavior of a series of short-run prices. Instead the seller(s) necessarily refer to a series of short-period demand curves for each of a succession of future intervals; these fully replace any long-run demand curve for the purposes of making all output adjustments. And we must now speak not of a single long-run tendency for price, but rather of a price-pattern through time.

A simple model can be constructed in which a single-firm monopolist is conceived of as pricing solely in a current Period I and a future Period II. There is an industry demand curve for each such period and a corresponding pair of marginal revenue curves. Monopoly price for the first period in isolation would be set to equate the marginal cost of that period to the marginal revenue of that period. But demand in Period II may be supposed to depend upon Period I price; for example, the Period II demand curve may shift outward as Period I price falls. Viewing this relation in prospect from the beginning of the first period, the monopolist may be supposed to adjust Period I price so as to allow maximization of the sum of the profits of the two periods. This procedure may result in setting Period I price below the level for which the marginal cost and marginal revenue of that period are equated, so long as the resulting decrement to Period I profits is more than offset by a resulting increment in Period II profits (as appropriately discounted for interest and risk).

Use of the demand-supply technique in such a sequence analysis permits precise formal treatment of the effects of anticipated relations between current price and future demand. To employ the analysis for purposes of prediction, we should attempt to determine the sign and value of the cross-elasticity between Period I price and Period II quantity for the monopolist—

$$\frac{\delta q_{(t=2)}}{\delta p_{(t=1)}} \cdot \frac{p_{(t=1)}}{q_{(t=2)}}$$

One can identify actual cases where this elasticity might be alternatively positive or negative in sign, or zero. Where it is negative and significantly large, a current monopoly price below the current profit-maximizing level can be formally explained; where it is positive and large, current prices above this level could be

[5]For a simplified argument, we will suppose the collusive oligopoly in each case to be a "pure" oligopoly, in which the several firms sell identical products at a necessarily identical price (the possibility of discrimination being neglected).

predicted. This model of course does not have the monopoly doing other than to maximize the "long-run" difference between aggregate industry revenue and aggregate production cost, so long as these are measured as capital values of future revenue and cost streams to a time horizon. But it does indicate the rational possibility of deliberate departures from profit maximization for "short" periods longer than those required to permit every adaptation in scale of firm and plant.

THE THREAT OF ENTRY —GENERAL CONSIDERATIONS

Let us now turn to the effects of anticipated entry. Even a single-firm monopoly is not necessarily impregnable to entry if the industry is a very profitable one, and in oligopolistic industries the threat of entry is likely to be stronger. The monopolist or the group of collusive oligopolists might therefore be viewed as setting each of an indefinite succession of current prices or profits with an eye to their effect in attracting entry into the industry and thus in reducing the demand for the output of the now-established firm(s).[6] One possibility is that the initially established seller or collusive sellers will be faced with the choice of (a) setting each of a succession of short-run prices (and hence long-run average price) so as to maximize the *industry* profit, but with the result that added firms enter the industry and reduce the share of industry profit gained by the initially established firms, and (b) setting each short-run price (and hence long-run average prices) at a lower level, thus discouraging further entry, and keeping the smaller (and non-maximized) industry profit ali for themselves. Should the second course then offer larger long-run profits *to the initially established firms,* they would presumably follow it, and price could for the indefinitely long run lie below the level required to maximize the difference between the aggregate revenue from the sale of the given commodity and the aggregate cost of producing it. Long-run maximization of *industry profit* and of *the profit of a group of currently established firms* may not coincide. This is presumably a thesis implied by those who point to threat of entry as a factor holding price below the level which would maximize the long-run profits of the industry.

This hypothesis can easily be developed on a formal level if we accept two premises upon which it must implicitly be based. These are (1) that the established monopolist or group of collusive oligopolists are aware of any real threat of entry to their industry, and will adjust to it in such a way as to enhance their own (as distinguished from industry) profits, and (2) that potential entrants to such a monopoly or oligopoly are primarily influenced in deciding whether or not to enter by the prices charged and profits currently earned by the established firms. The first premise seems only reasonable,[7] but the merit of

[6]The threat of entry, and its relation to price, will of course depend upon the height and effectiveness of such institutional barriers as patent holdings, control of raw materials, etc.

[7]To argue that sellers in concentrated industries deliberately disregard the consequences of threatened entry would picture them as unbelievably stupid.

the second could be contested. A potential entrant to a purely competitive industry is presumably guided entirely by the expected long-run tendency of industry price as related to his contemplated costs. This is because his increment to the industry would neither perceptibly influence the price nor engender any direct reaction from any established seller. The potential entrant to a monopoly or oligopoly, on the other hand, who will typically make a substantial lump increment to the industry capacity (since economies of scale will ordinarily require a fairly large firm), may expect both to influence the pre-existing price and to elicit some reaction from the established seller(s). This holds whether or not he contemplates collusion with those sellers. In effect, there is a special sort of oligopolistic interdependence between the established seller(s) and the potential entrants in such instances, and it is not entirely plausible that the potential entrant should entirely neglect this interdependence and view the going industry price as the principal indicator of whether or not entry will be profitable.

At the extreme, it could even be argued that a potential entrant to an oligopoly should pay little regard to price or profit received by established firms, especially if he thought price was being held down in order to "bluff" him away from the industry. He should look at the industry demand, the current competitive or collusive conditions in the industry, the prospects for rivalry or collusion after his entry, the share of the market he expects to capture, and his projected costs of production. Paramount in his considerations, provided the industry demand under some conceivable arrangement could provide profits to an entrant, should be his appraisal of the sort of rivalry and the type of price policies he will encounter from the previously established seller(s) after he enters. In judging these determinants of his decision, current price or profit in the industry need play no *direct* role, since the anticipated industry price *after entry* and the entrant's anticipated market share are the strategic considerations. And if he knows the industry demand with reasonable certainty and makes calculations concerning the conditions of rivalry after his entry, upon which he is willing to act, he might look entirely past any current price set by the established firm(s). He then would be immune to bluffing, and the established firm(s) could never discourage entry by lowering prices and earning moderate profits.

The supposition that the potential entrant's judgment of industry demand and of the rivalry he will meet is entirely unrelated to current price or profit in the industry, however, probably goes too far. Even if he does not believe the observed price will remain there for him to exploit, he may nevertheless regard this price as an indicator both of the character of industry demand and of the probable character of rival policy after his entry. Industry demands are never certainly known, and they are probably known less fully by potential entrants than by established firms. The fact that the established firm(s) make only moderate profits may thus create in the mind of the potential entrant sufficient uncertainty concerning the elasticity of the industry demand curve at higher prices to deter him from entering. Moreover, he may view the price which the established firm(s) currently charge as a partial indicator of the rival price policy he will face after entry. Other considerations should influence his judgment of projected rivalry, but current pricing may be a crucial factor in evaluating it. It is thus possible that the potential entrant is influenced by current prices and profits and that there may be a critical price below which he will not enter and above which he will enter. This hypothesis seems plausible enough so long as the potential entrant regards the current pricing policy of established sellers as being probably a statement of intentions rather than a bluff. It is probably more plausible than otherwise when applied to oligopolies where product differentiation is not very great, and where the entry problem is thus not unduly complicated by the necessity of gaining buyer acceptance of a new product. We will speak here primarily of its application to oligopolies with relatively slight product differentiation.[8]

On the basis of the preceding argument, we may provisionally accept the second premise of the thesis concerning threat of entry, that the potential entrant to a monopoly or oligopoly is primarily influenced by the price charged (and profit earned) by the established seller(s)—influenced not because he expects this price to hold unchanged after entry, but because he regards it as "proving" the industry demand at a given level and as a critical indicator of the projected state of rivalry or price policy after entry. Accepting the first and second premises, we may now investigate their formal implications for the price policy of an established monopolist or group of collusive (pure) oligopolists faced with a threat of entry. What will happen in these cases if (a) the established seller(s) anticipate any threat of entry (highly probable), (b) potential entrants are influenced in their entry decisions by current price in the industry (a strong possibility), and (c) the established seller(s) know this and consider adjusting their prices to discourage entry.

A "LIMIT PRICE" ANALYSIS

For a formal treatment, two special concepts may be conveniently employed. The first is the "limit price," or highest common price which the established seller(s) believe they can charge without inducing at least one increment to entry—presumably a significant lump increment. This limit price depends ultimately upon the cost functions which potential entrants expect to have, upon their estimates of the industry demand and of the share of the market which they can capture if they enter, and upon their view of the degree of competition or collusion which will obtain in the industry after their entry. The subjective estimate of this limit price by the established seller(s), however, rather than the view of potential entrants, is the real determinant of the price policies

[8]It may be added that with imperfect market information, "potential entrants" may be made aware of the possibilities of an industry mainly by its profit record, and will never present an active threat if they are not alerted by high profits. In this case, low current prices and profits may serve as a deterrent to entry because they do not attract attention and thereby create actively potential entrants.

of the established seller(s). Since the limit price must be defined in terms of the guess of the established firm(s) concerning the anticipations of the potential rivals, it is especially subject to error as an *ex ante* magnitude, and it may be invalid if potential entrants read it as a bluff. But it is nevertheless potentially valid and determinate.[9] The second concept is the estimate by the established seller(s) of the conditions of demand for their outputs after entry occurs in response to their setting a price above the limit. This involves their estimate of the market share they will lose to an entrant, and also of the conditions of competition or collusion which will obtain after entry. If the established seller(s) formulate estimates on limit price, as defined, and on the position and character of the demand for their outputs after entry, these estimates can be recognized in an anticipated demand curve or sequence of demand curves for their outputs, and a formal solution developed.

This solution can follow the lines developed for the case of interdependence of prices through time. We can first construct a given industry demand curve for the current Period I and for Periods II, III, etc.[10] The demand for the output of the established seller(s) in the current Period I is the industry demand of that period. In any later period, however, it can be expected to be the same as the *industry* demand only so long as price in the preceding period has remained at or below a limit price, A, so that entry has been forestalled. If any given period price is set above A, the demand for the output of the established seller(s) in all later periods is expected to become less than the industry demand by the amount of a market share going to the new entrant, and it may be otherwise altered or made uncertain if effective collusion with the entrant is not contemplated or considered attainable. If entry will occur in discrete lumps, moreover, the demand for the output of the established seller(s) in later periods does not shift continuously in response to variations in Period I price. Instead it makes a discrete shift backward if A is surpassed in Period I, and the solution is affected by this discontinuity. Given these conditions, the established seller(s) will devise a price policy for Period I and in all later periods so as to maximize the discounted present value of profits for all future periods. With an effective threat of entry, it is potentially consistent with such profit maximization by the established seller(s) that price will be held at the limit level continually through time, even though this limit price may in every current period be lower than that for which the marginal cost of the established seller (or horizontally added marginal costs of the established sellers) equals the marginal revenue drawn from the industry demand curve for that period. Such a solution can be determinate and give stability without entry for the indefinitely long run (permitting all desired adjustments of scale by the existing firms) provided the limit price estimated by the established seller(s) is in fact low enough to exclude entry. If the established seller(s) set a "limit" price which turns out to be too high to

[9]Account must be taken, of course, of the consequences of erroneous as well as correct estimates of this price by the established seller(s).

[10]Each such industry demand curve is assumed to be independently given in the absence of inter-period price relationships.

exclude entry, of course, their error may result in an effectively irreversible change in the structure of the industry.

Because the sequence analysis is unnecessarily awkward for dealing with the threat of entry, the preceding solution is only sketched. Assuming no interdependence of the *industry* demands of successive time periods to be involved in the case, the impact of a threat of entry can be analyzed more easily by referring to the anticipated long-run demand conditions for the output of the established monopolist or collusive oligopolists–or to the expected response of their long-run average sales to changes in the average level of price they maintain over long periods. Following this course, two alternative models may be developed, one assuming that the established seller(s) anticipate rivalry and lack of agreement with any new entrant, and the other assuming that they anticipate collusion with any new entrant.

The first model postulates (1) a determinate long-run demand curve for industry output, which is unaffected by price adjustments or by entry; (2) occupation of the industry initially by a single-firm monopolist or group of effectively collusive pure oligopolists; (3) estimation by the established seller(s) of a limit price above which a "lump" of entry will be attracted; and (4) considerable uncertainty on the part of the established seller(s) concerning the conditions of demand for their outputs if entry is attracted. Given these conditions, the anticipated long-run demand for the output of the established seller(s) may be analyzed as follows. The long-run industry demand curve is supposed to be the line $DABD'$, as in Figure 5.1, and the marginal revenue drawn to it is *Dabm*. This demand is assumed to be unaffected by any adjustments sellers may make. Suppose now that the limit price above which the established seller(s) expect an increment of entry is Q_aA: If they charge more than this (or produce less output than OQ_a, thus causing the effective market price to exceed the limit), they expect to experience some indeterminate loss in sales volume to an entrant and some indeterminate change in price. The anticipated demand curve for the output of the established seller(s) above the price $Q_a A$ thus is *not* DA. They have the truncated demand curve AD' to exploit up to the price $Q_a A$, and the corresponding marginal revenue segment *am*. But if they raise or attempt to raise long-run price above Q_aA, the anticipated long-run demand curve for their output becomes indeterminate somewhere in the range to the left of A. They thus have the choice of the truncated industry demand curve AD' for exclusive exploitation up to the price Q_aA, and an indeterminate demand for their outputs if they once go above Q_aA. It should be especially noted that they are unable to sell less than the amount OQ_a at the price Q_aA and thus to exclude entry, since this would result in an effective market price higher than the limit, via resales, and thus presumably "reveal the bluff" and attract entry.[11]

The alternatives open to the established seller(s) are now (1) to sell more than OQ_a at a price below Q_aA, thus excluding entry, (2) to sell OQ_a at the price Q_aA,

[11] We exclude herewith the possibility of effective private rationing or price discrimination by the established seller(s), which might enable them to produce less than OQ_a and still hold the effective market price at $Q_a A$; this appears to be a special and unlikely case.

Figure 5.1

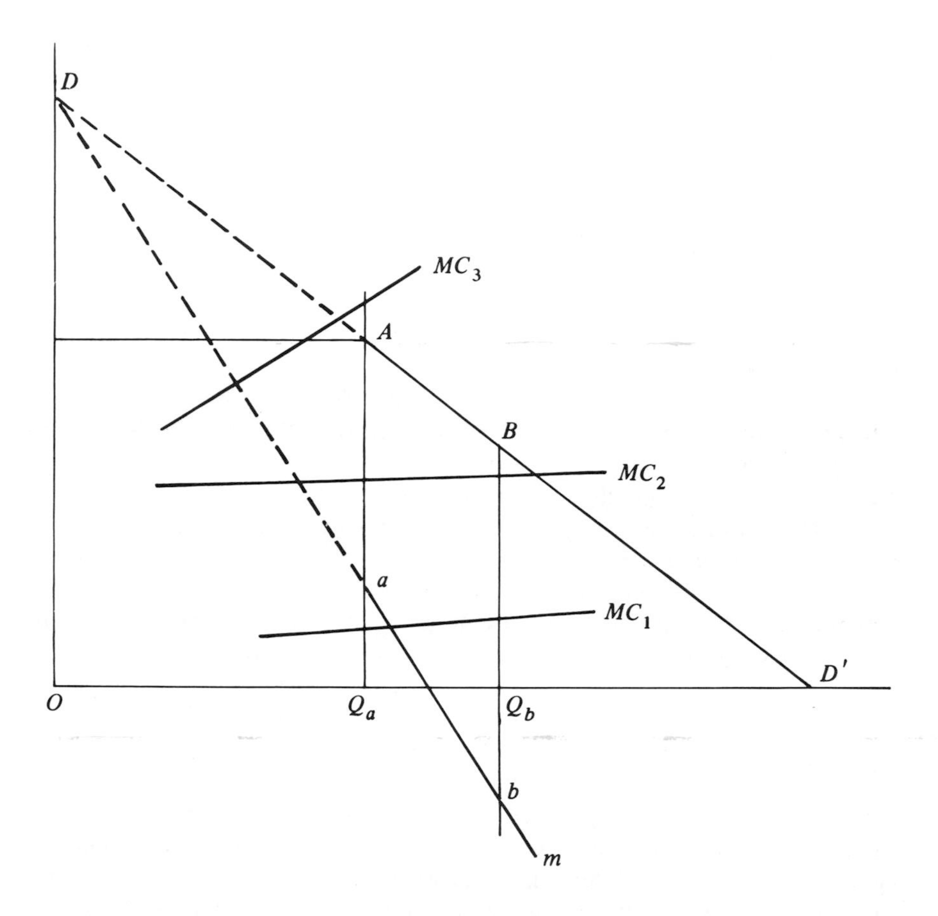

also excluding entry, and (3) to raise price above Q_aA, or reduce output below OQ_a, thus attracting entry and taking chances on profits and prices in the ensuing indeterminate situation. They will presumably pursue the course that promises to be most profitable, taking account of the fact that profits under courses (1) and (2) are relatively determinate whereas profits under course (3) are indeterminate and hence highly uncertain. The established seller(s) will follow the first or second course in preference to the third wherever the relatively certain profits offered by those courses exceed the heavily risk-discounted gain attainable if entry is attracted via higher prices. The possible positions in which the established seller(s) in various industries may find equilibrium may be illustrated as follows. Suppose a single long-run marginal cost curve, for the initially established monopolist, or alternatively a uniquely determined aggregation of marginal cost curves for the initially established collusive oligopolists in any industry. This we label *MC.* Now first this marginal cost may in some industries lie at MC_1 (Figure 5.1), intersecting the relevant industry marginal revenue segment *am.*[12] Then the established seller(s) will almost certainly set price and output by this intersection, provided average costs are less than the resulting price. In this case, industry profit will be maximized at a price below the limit, entry will be forestalled, and the number of sellers in the industry will be in long-run equilibrium. Conventional monopoly maximization is possible without further entry being attracted. This case sublimes all those where entry is blockaded or where the limit price is so high as to be economically irrelevant.

Second, marginal cost may in other industries fall at MC_2, lying above industry marginal revenue but below price at the limit output OQ_a, with average costs less than Q_aA. In this case, provided the profit offered seems preferable to the gamble of inducing entry, the established seller(s) will produce OQ_a and sell at Q_aA. (They will then not choose the intersection of MC_2 and the marginal revenue *Da*, since this would give a price which would induce entry.) In this case entry is also forestalled and the number of sellers in the industry is in long-run equilibrium, but marginal cost exceeds industry marginal revenue and *industry* profits are not maximized.

Third, marginal cost may fall at MC_3, lying above price at the limit output OQ_a, but with the corresponding average cost lying below price at this output. The established sellers will still choose to produce OQ_a and sell at Q_aA, so long as the resulting profit is considered preferable to the gamble if entry is induced. Again the number of sellers will remain constant, but industry profits will not be maximized and *marginal cost will exceed price*—not a probable but nevertheless a quite possible and rational result.

The general argument developed for the last two cases may also be applied on the supposition that the limit price lies at some level Q_bB on the industry demand curve, where this demand is less elastic than unity and the relevant marginal revenue segment, *bm,* is entirely in the negative range. We may still have equilibrium with entry forestalled at the limit price Q_bB (not rationally below it) with marginal cost above industry marginal revenue and possibly above price, but with the difference that industry marginal revenue is negative.

These solutions involve the premises that potential entrants recognize a limit price below which they will not enter, and that the established seller(s) know this and do not overestimate the limit price. Should potential entrants fail to be influenced by price, a stable solution will not result if entry promises to be profitable; if they are so influenced but the established seller(s) set too high a price, there will be entry and a probably irreversible change in industry structure will result. One qualification may be added to the preceding argument. In

[12]In this and each of the succeeding cases we refer to distinct industry situations, each with a separate limit price, a separate initial marginal and average cost function, and a different relation of marginal and average cost to the limit price. We do not suggest different relations of cost to limit price in a single industry, but rather differences among industries in this respect.

deciding whether or not to go above the limit price, the established sellers should count in favor of the former course any transitional extra profit they may earn after going above the limit and before entry becomes effective.[13] This consideration has not been formally treated in the preceding model.

A fourth possibility is that average cost for the established seller(s) will lie above the limit price Q_aA at the output OQ_a, marginal cost lying above or below price. In this event price will presumably be set above the limit and entry attracted, provided there is some possibility of making profits at smaller outputs.[14] The number of sellers in the industry then could not be stable until further entry had occurred.

Considering the various possibilities, there is a very good a priori chance on the assumptions drawn for the threat of entry to force a significant departure from what have been viewed as the conventional long-run monopoly-equilibrium price and output in single-firm monopoly or collusive oligopoly industries. It has been conventionally supposed that the single-firm monopolist will set a price such as to maximize long-run *industry* profit, and that collusive oligopolists will do likewise. It has been further suggested that this may result, at least in collusive oligopoly, in the attraction of entry to the point where excess profits are small or absent and the industry contains an excessive number of firms.[15] But under the assumptions of anticipated entry and a response of entry to price, we see that, consistent with profit maximization *by firms,* the price in such industries may be lower and the output larger than would maximize long-run *industry profit.* A vigorous threat of entry which at an appropriate time is anticipated and forestalled, moreover, may serve to keep firms producing at outputs which give a fairly close approximation to optimum average costs. If the firms in an industry are so few that they would encounter serious diseconomies of scale in supplying the limit output, they may be unable profitably to forestall entry. But when the number of firms becomes such as to allow production of the limit output at near-optimum average costs, excessive entry may be profitably forestalled by limit-pricing policies and an economical adjustment of capacity to demand perpetuated.[16]

The preceding hypotheses are developed on the basis of certain crucial assumptions, of which the only really controversial one is that potential entrants to concentrated industries may be significantly influenced in their entry

[13]In a dynamic model, we might consider the possibility of a critical or maximum short period during which established sellers could temporarily go above limit price without attracting entry, returning price to the limit in time to discourage potential entrants.

[14]In this case, however, the potential entrants presumably being able to attain lower average costs than established firms, it is doubtful that any price stratagem would forestall entry.

[15]E. G. Chamberlin, *The Theory of Monopolistic Competition,* 1933, pp. 100-108.

[16]It is of course evident that if once an oligopolistic industry gets an excess number of firms–whether because the threat of entry is overlooked, or because the limit price fails to forestall entry, or because industry demand declines–then there is no evident force which will eliminate firms and give such a good adjustment. But it nevertheless holds that excessive entry *may* be deliberately forestalled in the manner described.

decisions by the prices set by established sellers. This assumption may or may not find extensive empirical support. But the observed price policies in a considerable number of oligopolistic industries with apparently effective collusion on price are consistent with hypotheses developed from the assumption, and we may have a thesis of real explanatory value.

The model discussed above also rests on the assumption that the established seller(s) are uncertain of the rivalry which will exist if new firms enter the industry. Its conclusions are not essentially modified, however, if we assume instead that the established seller or collusive sellers contemplate effective collusion with any new entrants. If this is assumed, together with the assumption of a determinate industry demand curve and an anticipated lump of entry above a given limit price, the analysis develops as follows. The long-run industry demand curve is DAD' (Figure 5.2) and the marginal revenue drawn thereto is *Dam,* as before. Similarly the limit price is Q_aA; above it the demand for the output of the established seller(s) is not *DA,* and the marginal revenue segment *Da* cannot be exploited by the established seller(s). If the established seller(s) go above the price Q_aA or below the output OQ_a, however, the resultant entry does not render the demand for their outputs indeterminate, since effective collusion with any entrant is contemplated. Presuming that the market share going to the entrant under such collusion is calculated, the established seller(s) anticipate a determinate loss of the total market volume to the entrant at each possible price. Then if they raise or attempt to raise long-run price above the limit, the anticipated long-run demand for their output becomes some determinate curve DD'', lying to the left of the industry demand curve by distances representing the share of the industry output an entrant would obtain at various prices. The corresponding marginal revenue is Dm'.

As an approximation we may say that the established sellers' demand function is discontinuous horizontally, made up of the segment AD' below the price Q_aA and the segment $A'D$ above that price. This is not precisely accurate, however, since the attempt by established sellers to charge more than Q_aA, involving attraction of new entry, might result in a collusive equilibrium price *after entry* which lay below Q_aA. The curve DD'' thus can have a meaningful price range which overlaps that of AD'. The diagram may therefore be read as follows: the established sellers can in the long run sell any of the price-output combinations on the line AD' (the quantities OQ_a or larger) without attracting entry. If they go above the price Q_aA, or attempt to, they thereafter in the long run can sell any of the combinations on the line DD'', with the remainder of the industry demand going to a new entrant or entrants. In effect, the established seller(s) are given the choice between the truncated industry demand curve AD' for exclusive exploitation and the non-truncated share of the industry demand curve, DD'', for exploitation via collusive agreement with the new entrant.[17] The AD' and DD'' curves adequately compare the revenue alternatives of the established

[17]The latter curve might also be truncated at a higher level due to an additional threat of entry, but we will focus attention here on a single increment of entry.

Figure 5.2

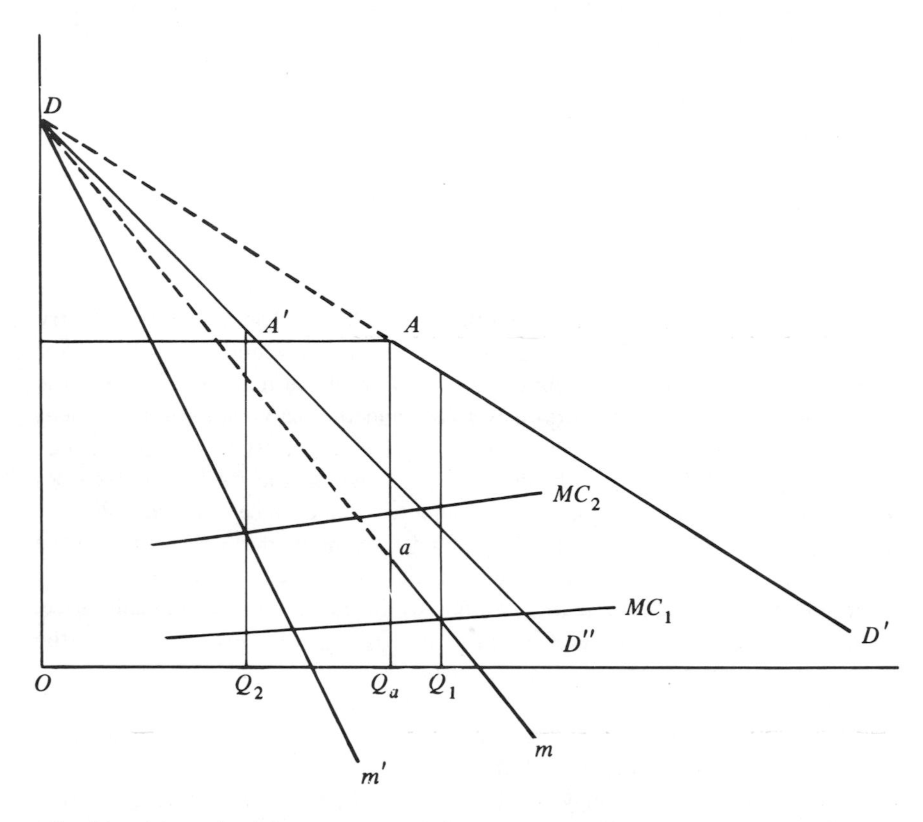

seller(s) with and without entry, so long as we neglect any transitional extra profit which the established seller(s) might enjoy while raising above Q_aA but before entry became effective. If such a transitional profit is significant, it must be considered as augmenting that long-run average profit which is obtainable by exploiting DD'' after entry.

If we place the long-run marginal cost of the established seller(s), as previously defined, against this demand complex, conclusions generally consistent with those already developed emerge. Suppose that the marginal cost of the established seller(s) lies at MC_1, so as to intersect industry marginal revenue in the range *am,* where price can be below Q_aA. Provided that total profit at the output OQ_1, determined by the intersection of MC_1 and *am,* is positive and exceeds profit at the intersection of MC_1 and Dm', the established seller(s) will produce OQ_1, charge a corresponding monopoly price below Q_aA, and maximize industry profits without attracting further entry.

Suppose instead that the marginal cost lies at MC_2, so as to lie above industry marginal revenue at the limit output and to intersect the marginal-revenue-after entry, Dm', at an output, OQ_2, which gives a price above Q_aA (average cost being less than Q_aA at OQ_a). The established firm(s) can supply the entire industry demand OQ_a at the price Q_aA, or part of the industry demand, OQ_2, at a higher price. They will choose between these discrete alternatives by comparing *the lump increment* to total revenue with *the lump increment to total cost* which are incurred in moving from OQ_2 to OQ_a.[18] If the revenue increment exceeds the cost increment (the area under MC_2 between Q_2 and Q_a), they will produce at OQ_a, sell at Q_aA, and exclude entry. The profits of the industry will not be maximized, but those of the established seller(s) will be. This holds for MC_2 in successively higher positions until the cost increment exceeds the revenue increment between Q_2 and Q_a; even production at OQ_a with marginal cost above price is possible. When the lump cost increment exceeds the lump revenue increment, price will be raised above Q_aA and entry will be attracted. (Average cost must of course always be covered at the best output or exit from the industry will occur in the long run.)[19]

On the supposition of collusion after entry, we thus arrive at conclusions regarding price similar to those developed when assuming uncertain rivalry after entry. It may be objected, of course, that if established sellers assume collusion after entry, and potential entrants assume it too, then these potential entrants should not be much influenced by the current prices of established sellers, and that a limit-price analysis is thus implausible. It becomes plausible evidently only if potential entrants are quite uncertain about industry demand and about how they will be welcomed by established sellers. But such an incongruity of attitudes is itself not implausible, and the model just developed may thus constitute a realistic variant of our first model.

In summary, a considerable elaboration of the theory of monopoly and collusive oligopoly price may be implied if we assume that potential entrants to an industry are influenced by the going prices therein, and that established sellers anticipate and, if it is profitable, forestall entry. Assuming correct appraisal of limit prices by established sellers, we get three major possibilities: (1) pricing to maximize industry profit with no entry resulting; (2) pricing to forestall entry with industry profit not maximized but the profit of established sellers maximized; and (3) pricing to maximize industry profit but with resulting attraction of additional entry. The first two cases find industries already in long-run equilibrium; the third finds industries in process of dynamic change in structure.

[18]This lump increment to revenue if the limit output is chosen (as aggregated over all future periods) must be considered as reduced by any transitional extra profit receivable after raising price above the limit but before entry becomes effective.

[19]The general conclusions also hold if the marginal cost lies so as to intersect Dm' where price would be below Q_aA, and to lie above industry marginal revenue to OQ_a. The limit output will be produced and entry excluded so long as the revenue increment exceeds the cost increment between the alternative outputs. In this case we have the situation that collusive price after entry would lie below the limit price which should presumably attract entry. If we remember that the limit price is not necessarily the minimum which entrants expect after entry, however, this situation is not necessarily anomalous.

EXTENSIONS AND APPLICATIONS OF THE "LIMIT-PRICE" ANALYSIS

The limit-price models just developed, tracing the effects of a sort of oligopolistic interdependence between firms already in a concentrated industry and potential entrant firms, are essentially variations on the general theory of oligopoly price. There is an apparent similarity of the construction to the familiar kinked demand curve analysis, but in the present case the average revenue as well as the marginal revenue is discontinuous, and it is a revenue function for all firms already in an industry rather than that for a single oligopolist which is so affected. The limit-price analysis applies to collusive oligopoly behavior, whereas the kinked demand curve model refers explicitly to the action of a firm in non-collusive oligopoly. And the essential conclusions of the two models are of course different.

Various extensions of "limit-price" reasoning suggest themselves. Thus some firms established within an oligopoly may hold price down for fear of "fattening" their smaller rivals sufficiently to encourage their expansion. Departing from the realm of pure oligopoly, established collusive firms might extend selling costs beyond the point of industry profit maximization in order to discourage entry, so that the threat of entry could cause increased costs rather than reduced prices. The model developed above could also be elaborated to take explicit account of dynamic changes, of varying time lags involved in the "gestation" of new entry, etc. Any extensions along these lines might contribute to a more realistic theory of oligopoly price.

The explanatory value of the limit-price hypotheses of course remains to be determined. On a priori grounds they appear to be fruitful, although alternative explanations of observed "low-price" policies may also be valid. Some systematic empirical check of the extent of "limit price" thinking within concentrated industries, and especially by price leaders, would seem desirable. Direct verification of the crucial hypotheses from ex post statistical results, however, would be difficult. The "limit price" in any industry, even if recognized, must change over time in response to variations in industry demand, in factor prices, in the availability of capital to potential entrants, in the age of the industry, and so forth. The single limit price of our static long-run analysis becomes in fact a dynamic variable, and would have to be treated as such. It would be difficult to establish in a strictly objective fashion, and knowledge of its recognition by sellers or of its magnitude might best be gained through interview techniques. It would be somewhat easier, on the other hand, to check observed price results for consistency with the hypothesis, without relying on the subjective impressions of sellers involved. That is, objective calculations of the probable limit price (or time series of limit prices) could be made for any industry, and the prices actually charged in a supposedly collusive oligopoly could then be compared both with such limit prices and with prices calculated to maximize industry profits. Wherever behavior consistent with the hypothesis was found, direct investigation of policies of price calculation might be indicated. The emphasis often placed on non-profit motives, uncertainty, irrationality, and oligopolistic rivalry as explanations of low-price policy in concentrated industries may be unduly heavy, and the effects of threatened entry seem certainly to deserve consideration.

Chapter Six

Conditions of Entry and the Emergence of Monopoly

INTRODUCTION

An economist's inquiry into the "forces making for and against monopoly" might reasonably involve a search for answers to the following questions with respect to enterprise economies: (1) What are the "forces," whether tendencies of human behaviour or environmental circumstances, which favour or discourage the establishment and stable maintenance of monopoly? (2) Why and in what way do these "forces" affect the prospect of monopoly, and is the character of any of them strategic to its emergence? (3) What is the relative importance of the various forces identified–both in a priori logic and in fact? (4) Are there strategic *controllable* forces affecting the emergence of monopoly, through the manipulation of which public authority can limit the extent of monopoly?

A potentially important set of forces affecting the emergence of monopoly in any industry is found in the variety of basic environmental circumstances which influence the ability and disposition of successive additional sellers to enter the industry. The character of these circumstances may very strongly affect the probability that monopoly will emerge and remain. These circumstances, moreover, need not be considered simply as a miscellany of separate forces for separate analysis. Their composite influence within a given industry will be reflected in a certain state of the ability and disposition of successive additional firms to enter the industry, or a *condition of entry* to the industry–and this condition of entry may be viewed as a single proximate force bearing directly on the probability that monopoly will emerge.

Our aim here is to evaluate the importance of the condition of entry and of the fundamental circumstances which determine it as influences on the emergence of monopoly. How and why is the condition of entry associated with

Reprinted from *Monopoly and Competition and Their Regulation*, edited by E. H. Chamberlin (Papers and Proceedings of a Conference Held by the International Economic Association, September 1951, in Talloires, France), courtesy of the International Economic Association and Macmillan, London and Basingstoke.

monopoly, and what is its relative importance among various other forces which favour or discourage monopoly? What fundamental circumstances determine the condition of entry, what is their usual character, how important is each, and what lines of public action are suggested by analysing them? Answers to these questions should be sought on both a priori and empirical levels. Because we lack essential data, however, we must proceed here mainly on the a priori level. The possible relation to monopoly of the circumstances affecting exit from an industry will not be analysed at length. A systematic relation of conditions of exit to monopoly is not obvious, and if it exists it is probably of secondary importance. We will thus deal mainly with the relation of entry to monopoly, including only brief comments on exit phenomena.

THE DEFINITION OF MONOPOLY

A first step is to identify the sort of "monopoly" the emergence of which we will analyze. From numerous alternative definitions of monopoly, differing in both the criteria of identification employed and the inclusiveness of the category established, two alternatives are chosen here. Monopoly will be found in an *industry*—defined strictly as a group of close-substitute products to buyers—where (1) a high proportion of the industry output is supplied by very few firms (or other effective control units), or where (2) there is a tendency, in the long run or on the average through time, toward a level of output at which price *substantially* exceeds the long-run marginal costs of the firms producing the bulk of industry output, and probably also substantially exceeds long-run average cost.

Some elaboration of these definitions may be required. First, an explicit meaning for "high concentration" among firms is not supplied by a priori theory. When monopoly is so identified, the presumed reference is to concentration at least high enough to make effective (express or tacit) collusion among sellers easy, and to lead to the sort of price results specified in the second definition. Upon the basis of findings on the relation of concentration to profits in American manufacturing from 1936 to 1940, we tentatively suggest that the lower limit of high seller concentration may be found about where 70 per cent of output is supplied by eight firms, given the typical dispersion of firm sizes with the first eight.

Second, although the alternative definition finds the necessary and sufficient condition for monopoly in a substantial excess of price over long-run marginal cost, and merely adds that price may similarly exceed long-run average cost, the latter condition is likely, in fact, to accompany the former. It is apparently common for firms to operate within a range where long-run average costs are approximately constant as output changes, and so far as this is true long-run average and marginal costs will, of course, stand in about the same relation to price. However, the existence either of a large long-run price-marginal cost disparity without substantial excess profits (still monopoly by this definition), or of substantial long-run excess profits while price is close to marginal cost (not monopoly by this definition), is possible. The meaning of a "substantial" discrepancy between price and cost is also an issue. Although any visible criterion for deciding this seems intrinsically arbitrary, the investigation of American manufacturing industry mentioned above suggests that a long-run average rate of return on owners' equity greater than 10 or 12 per cent would identify the "more monopolistic" American industries as a group.

The category of industries identified as monopolistic by the first definition need not be precisely co-extensive with that established by the second definition. Although ceteris paribus, there should be a strong tendency in this direction, it will be suggested below that the variations in the condition of entry may lead to substantial variation in price results with the same degree of concentration. We thus define monopoly in two genuinely alternative senses.

STRATEGIC TENDENCIES OF ENTERPRISE BEHAVIOR

The forces conditioning the emergence of monopoly may include both certain environmental circumstances within which enterprise activity takes place—whether these be technological, legal, institutional, geographical, or inherent in the nature of buyers' preferences—and certain tendencies of enterprise behavior. Whatever the importance of the environmental circumstances, their impact will necessarily be through their effects on enterprise behavior or on how its basic tendencies develop. An identification of such tendencies is thus fundamental to understanding the significance of these circumstances.

In brief, we will postulate that there are three tendencies in enterprise behavior especially relevant to the present issues. First, there is always a tendency for the established sellers occupying an industry at any time to strive for joint-profit maximization—for a concurrent adjustment of output such that their combined profit over whatever future time period may be relevant is at a maximum. This tendency may encourage concentration by merger, or cartels, or express or tacit agreements to facilitate concurrence in, and observance of, a joint-profit-maximizing policy by all producing units. All ownership groups established in an industry have a sort of mutual interest in a formal or informal federation or treaty for concerted exploitation of the market. Second, there is always among established sellers a counter-tendency which may forestall, disrupt, or impair the fulfillment of the first tendency. This is the composite tendency of diverse firms or ownership interests to disagree on the division of spoils from possible agreement, to be dissatisfied with the share gained, to question the extent to which the other members to any arrangement will fulfill it in all relevant ways, and to cheat on the arrangement when this is profitable and possible. Such a composite tendency reflects the fundamental antagonism of diverse ownership interests—their intrinsic rivalry for a single market—and the existence of a certain ethical level of behavior recognized by all. Thus, although some sort of treaty may be to the group's advantage, mutually satisfactory treaty terms need not be found, and each participant may be wary of yielding part of his sovereignty to group government.

These two opposed tendencies are continually at work in every market with more than one firm, and whether monopoly will emerge or not depends in part on their relative force. For industries as a whole, one cannot predict any certain outcome. But in specific environmental circumstances—which may affect the relative force of the opposed tendencies—a strong probability of some given outcome may be predictable.

A third strategic tendency in enterprise behavior is that of successive units of new enterprise, not currently established in an industry, to enter it (unless quite arbitrarily restrained) whenever the market after entry will allow them a perceptible excess profit. This tendency will influence the emergence of monopoly to the extent (1) that monopoly raises long-run price above the competitive level[1] (and probably allows excess profits to established firms) and (2) that such price increases lead potential entrants to anticipate excess profits for themselves after entry. With the extreme fulfillment of both possibilities, for example, all movements toward monopoly by established firms would be modified or reversed by induced entry. But though movements toward monopoly may generally bring higher prices, the extent to which these will cause potential entrants to anticipate excess profits may vary widely and correspondingly the margin by which established firms can raise their prices above the competitive level without inducing entry may differ substantially among industries. The actual or potential impact of the strategic entry tendency on attempted monopoly may thus be strong and immediate in some industries, modified in others, absent in still others. In analyzing the probability that monopoly will emerge, therefore, industries should be distinguished by the level, relative to the competitive, of the maximum price which established firms can charge without inducing entry.

THE CONDITION OF ENTRY

Three behavior tendencies affecting the emergence of monopoly have been outlined. The central issue is how the condition of entry—and the underlying circumstances determining it—will affect the interplay of these tendencies and its outcome. One is not at a loss for reasonably convincing, if slightly ambiguous, generalizations on this point. The condition of entry refers to the ability of new firms to enter and compete in an industry; it affects the emergence of monopoly by determining how far established firms can raise price without attracting entry, and by making entry probable if price is raised further; the circumstances determining the condition of entry have a corresponding importance. But in such typical assertions the precise meaning of the condition of entry, and its exact importance in determining whether and to what extent monopoly will emerge, are generally unspecified. We shall therefore explore below in some detail the relation of the condition of entry to monopoly, inquiring into: (1) the

[1] I.e., above the level identified by the price-cost relations attributed to long-run equilibrium with atomistic competition.

nature of an appropriate general definition of the condition of entry; (2) the identity of the various environmental circumstances which determine the condition of entry; (3) the relative importance of the condition of entry as a force favoring or discouraging monopoly, so far as this may be predicted through a priori theorizing; (4) the actual importance of the condition of entry—and of the several environmental circumstances determining it—as an influence on monopoly in modern industrial situations; and (5) possible public policy measures to modify entry conditions.

The term "condition of entry" as ordinarily used evidently refers to the ability and disposition of firms to enter an industry, given the potential inducement of various alternative price-cost relations within it. It thus also refers to the height of any barrier to their entry. Two things, however, are not clear about the ordinary usage. First, is the condition of entry an attribute with only two or three possible values, or is it a variable which may assume any of a continuous range of values and is potentially susceptible to quantitative measurement? Second, if the latter is true, is there an appropriate measure of the barrier to entry by which established firms are protected? Since the barrier which the condition of entry implicitly describes is presumably of continuously variable height and potentially measurable, any two- or three-fold classification of the condition—as, for example, into "easy," "blockaded," and "in-between"—seems unnecessarily crude if some meaningful system for measuring the barrier can be established. And a reasonably meaningful definition and measure of the condition of entry as a continuous variable is available. It may thus conveniently be treated in this fashion.

An appropriate definition of the condition of entry is suggested by a consideration of the properties of the "easy entry" often expressly or implicitly attached to models of atomistic competition. Among these properties are first that there are no arbitrary legal prohibitions on entry and second that there are never any differential advantages among established firms with regard to either demand or cost. Correlatively or in addition, *regardless of the going population of the industry or the number of potential entrant firms previously admitted,* the following must be true as between established firms and the most easily attracted (most favored) potential entrant firm or firms:

1. Established firms have no absolute cost advantage in the long run. That is, for an identical or equivalent product, the so-called "optimum-scale" average cost of one or more potential entrants after entry will not be perceptibly higher than the optimum-scale average costs of established firms before entry; thus a potential entrant can always attain average costs not perceptibly higher than those of established firms before entry. Fulfillment of this condition requires:
   a. No perceptible increase in hired factor prices because of an increment of entry, and absolutely no price or other advantage to established firms in access to any factors (including investible funds).
   b. Access by one or more entrants to all known techniques, and thus to optimal techniques, without disadvantage in cost.

2. The most favored potential entrant (or entrants) after entering will enjoy a relation of price to output not perceptibly less favorable than that then enjoyed by established firms. In homogeneous product markets, he will have the same demand curve for his output at the same market price; in differentiated-product markets, either he will have for an equivalent product a ceteris paribus demand curve for his output with the same position and shape as all others when incurring the same selling costs, or, more generally, he will have as favorable a relation of demand to production and selling cost as all others.[2] With identical scale curves and product differentiation, equal sales at equal prices with equal selling costs would be required. Fulfillment of this condition requires either:
   a. Product homogeneity in the industry, or
   b. Consumer preference patterns between established products and the entrant product which give the entrant an equal position.
3. The percentage increment to industry output resulting from the entry of an additional firm with competitive equality must always be so small that there will be no perceptible reduction of demand per firm (e.g., no smaller sales per firm at the going price), and no induced reactions by established firms. Fulfillment of this condition requires in effect that the smallest-scale firm permitting lowest attainable costs would supply a very small fraction of industry output. These conditions must apply to each of an indefinite succession of most easily attracted entrant firms, after successive increments of entry, over any potentially relevant range.

Under easy entry thus defined, monopolistic results would evidently be impossible in long-run equilibrium; with U-shaped scale curves, atomistic structure would similarly tend to be enforced in the absence of a cartel. However, a cartel could conceivably emerge and engineer a series of non-competitive disequilibria through time. The more general derived property of the easy-entry situation is the stricture on the ability of established firms in any stage of industry adjustment to raise prices concurrently above given levels of average cost without attracting entry. In homogeneous-product markets with easy entry, established firms can never concurrently raise price above their own (identical) optimum-scale average costs without attracting entry; as a corollary, therefore, long-run excess profits cannot be earned without attracting entry. In differentiated-product markets with easy entry, established firms can never raise their prices above the slightly higher-than-minimal average-cost levels at which their sloping ceteris paribus demand curves, as emergent with a large number of sellers and the given degree of product differentiation, would become tangent to their cost curves; as an added condition, excess profits cannot be earned without attracting entry. To a close approximation—since under conceivable circumstances the second level of average cost should diverge very little from optimum-scale average costs—the derived easy-entry property for all cases is that

[2] This condition and condition 1 above are in strict logic necessarily merged where there is product differentiation.

the general level of prices can never significantly exceed optimum-scale average costs without inducing entry (thus subsuming the excess-profit condition). This situation, where at any level of industry population there are no significant margins between minimal average costs and the concurrent prices which established firms can charge without inducing entry, is appropriately designated as one of easy entry. Let us designate the maximum-price to minimal-average-cost margin which can be attained with concurrent pricing[3] at any given point without attracting at least one further unit of entry as a measure of the *"immediate" condition of entry.* Then "easy entry" is found when this measure must always be zero or close to zero[4] for all sellers at every conceivable stage of industry adjustment.

This definition requires that there can never be perceptible differential advantages among established firms with respect to cost or demand; more generally, it might require simply that the immediate condition of entry always approximate zero (or less) when measured with respect to the most-favored established seller(s). Is extreme easy entry as ordinarily understood possible when the latter condition is *not* fulfilled and when there are differential advantages among established firms? It could exist in a possible alternative sense if at every stage of industry adjustment the stated price to minimal average cost relation held for the marginal firm but not for all. However, this condition will be fulfilled only under very special and improbable circumstances—such that at no point may the entry-excluding price significantly exceed the minimal average costs of all firms—and even then the possibility of a tendency toward substantial long-run price-marginal cost discrepancies for many firms is not excluded in strict generality. We will therefore, in general, identify easy entry with the existence, at every stage of industry adjustment, of an approximately zero (or lower) value of the immediate condition of entry as measured for every established firm. Correspondingly, the immediate condition of entry, in general, may be tentatively measured, small inter-firm differences being neglected, by the relation of the maximum entry-excluding price to the minimal average costs of the most-favored firm(s) in the industry.

The preceding analysis of the properties, definition, and measure of easy entry has suggested the properties of other conditions of entry, and a definition and measure of such conditions. In brief, barriers to further entry—or the departure of the immediate condition of entry in any given situation from approximately zero value—may result from:

1. Absolute production-cost advantages of some[5] or all established firms over the most-favored potential entrant firm, reflected in a higher position for an identical or equivalent product of the long-run average cost curve of the latter, with a higher optimum-scale cost (costs of investible funds being included).

[3]I.e., either with all prices identical, as in the case of homogeneous products, or with all prices moving together while in a given relationship which is determined by the character of buyer preferences among products and the character of inter-firm competition.

[4]Or where it is either zero or negative. All possible negative values may be lumped with the zero value. See below.

[5]I.e., one or more.

2. Product-differentiation advantages of some or all established firms over this entrant firm, because of favored positions in buyers' preferences, resulting for the potential entrant in a ceteris paribus demand schedule at a lower position than those of established firms with equivalent production and selling costs, or in higher costs to place its demand curve in the same position, or in smaller sales with equal prices and equal costs; or generally in a less favorable relation of cost to demand.

3. The fact that the percentage increment to industry output made by a firm of optimal (and possibly smaller) scale will be so great as significantly to reduce the market price or the sales per firm, and possibly to induce aggressive retaliation by established firms. (The size of this implicit advantage to established firms will necessarily depend on the shape of scale curve short of the optimal scale point or range as well as on the size of optimal output and the position and elasticity of industry demand.)

Two or more of these sources of advantage to established firms may co-exist to give rise to a given composite advantage over the most-favored potential entrant(s). The derived property of the existence of any or all of these barriers to entry is that established firms will be able to charge a price significantly above some or all of their own minimal average costs without attracting further entry, and may be able—in fact, probably will be able—at the same time to make an excess profit.[6] The immediate condition of entry in a given situation may then be measured as the excess above their optimum scale average costs of the maximum prices at which the most-favored established firms may exclude further entry (concurrent pricing by all firms being assumed), this excess being expressed as a percentage of the prices.

As soon as we depart from easy entry, we may not generally expect the immediate condition of entry to remain invariant at successive stages of industry adjustment or with the admission of successive entrant firms. A series of potential entrants may have different absolute cost disadvantages; buyer preferences may naturally solidify in favor of early-comer brands to the disadvantage of latecomers; where the barrier to entry rests on scale economies, successive entry may raise the price which can be charged without attracting more entry. Without discussing the matter in detail, it may be indicated (1) that at any point (with a given industry population) the immediate condition of entry is necessarily measured with reference to the price which will attract the most-favored entrant, and (2) that the general condition of entry to an industry must refer to a series of successive and potentially different values of the immediate condition of entry as they would emerge with the entrance of successive additional firms in the order of their advantage. Ordinarily, barriers to entry probably tend to rise as successive entry occurs. Strictly, entry to an industry is other than easy, or at least somewhat impaired, if at any attainable stage of industry adjustment the immediate condition of entry will depart significantly from a zero value. The general condition of entry to an industry is

[6]Excess profits while excluding entry will be possible except in extreme cases, such as where the industry demand curve is tangent to the monopolist's U-shaped cost curve.

essentially defined by the pattern of successive immediate values of the condition of entry (in the designated order) over any relevant range. It should be added that any immediate condition of entry, found at any given point in the progression of successive entry, may at least in some cases be affected by the internal structure of the industry—as determined by the relative size of established firms, extent of merger among them, etc.—and thus has a possible range of values. If this is so, the general condition of entry to an industry may thus potentially be described by alternative and somewhat divergent patterns of immediate entry conditions, depending on the evolution of internal industry structure with successive entry.

This measure of the condition of entry refers to margins by which price can exceed a certain level of cost in the long run without attracting added entry. As such, its meaning is reasonably unambiguous. Its relevance as a direct determinant of enterprise behavior is potentially reduced, however, by the facts that the measure recognizes no limits on the time period required for further entry to be accomplished if price exceeds the critical level, and that the length of this lag period may vary among industries. At least in some contexts a greater delay in the accomplishment of induced entry may have about the same significance as a lower barrier to ultimate entry, so that the condition of entry as defined does not provide a fully adequate comparison of the relative force of potential entry in different industries. The condition of entry to an industry might be more adequately described by two measures—one our condition of entry as defined, and the other measuring the lag period between entry undertaken and entry accomplished. We will not attempt here to combine these measures, but will interpret the significance of our condition of entry with various entry lags.

CIRCUMSTANCES CREATING BARRIERS TO ENTRY

The identity of the basic circumstances which may discourage entry is suggested by the foregoing description of the general properties of other-than-easy entry. They may be briefly listed as follows:

1. Circumstances giving an absolute cost advantage to some or all established firms.
    a. Control of production techniques by established firms, via patents or secrecy, which permits exclusion of entrants from optimal techniques or the levying of a royalty charge for their use.
    b. Imperfections in the markets for hired factors (including materials) which favor established firms, or ownership or control by agreement of strategic factor supplies by such firms.
    c. Requirement by the entering firm of enough factors to cause their market price to rise significantly (linked to the need for large scale to gain efficiency).

   d. Money-market conditions imposing higher interest rates or more severe rationing of investible funds on potential entrant firms.
2. Circumstances giving a product-differentiation advantage to some or all established firms.
   a. Patent control of superior product designs by established firms.
   b. The possible accumulative preference of buyers for established brand names and company reputations.
   c. Ownership or contractual control of favored distributive outlets by established firms.
3. Circumstances discouraging entry because of the size of an economical increment of entry.
   a. Real economies to the large-scale firm such that the optimal- and possibly smaller-scale firm will supply a significant share of the market.
   b. Strictly pecuniary economies of the same order. (The more steeply the scale curve falls toward the optimum level the greater the deterrent.)
4. Absolute legal prohibitions on entry.

Any number of these specific circumstances may affect the condition of entry to a particular industry. It is obvious that the existence of at least some circumstances which tend to discourage entry must be extremely common among modern industries. The crucial issues are how high the resultant barriers to entry are, and what effect the height of the barrier has on the probability that monopoly will emerge.

Before turning to these and related questions, two comments may be added. First, since the condition of entry to an industry is obviously a reflection of a congeries of underlying circumstances of the sort just outlined, it is clear that autonomous changes in these circumstances may alter the condition of entry to any industry over time. Second, established firms will presumably try to alter these circumstances so as to make entry more difficult. Since this effort may be countered in some degree, however, by that of potential entrants to break the barriers down, no net secular tendency of conditions of entry is necessarily predictable.

THE CONDITION OF ENTRY AND THE EMERGENCE OF MONOPOLY

To develop a complete theory of the relation of entry conditions to the emergence of monopoly would be a complex and prolonged task. At this point we will attempt only to develop certain general propositions to indicate the direction such a theory might take.

As a beginning, let us reconsider the prospect of monopoly under the extreme case of easy entry. Where the essential properties of easy entry are found—i.e., no absolute cost or product differentiation advantage to established firms, no significant economies of scale at any stage, and no significant inter-firm differences—certain conclusions follow. First, the pressure of entry in the long run will tend to induce the profitless tangency equilibrium of either pure or monopolistic competition; and, if there are significant diseconomies of large scale, also an atomistic structure. In general, however, significant concentration is not inconceivable. Second, any tendency of firms to raise price significantly above the designated competitive level will tend to induce entry and to drive price back, although entry may take place with a lag. Third, with entry lags it is possible that established firms may impose monopolistic pricing[7]—presumably with the aid of concentration via merger or cartel—sporadically and perhaps periodically, although induced entry will persistently tend to break down monopoly pricing tendencies. But even sporadic monopoly is unlikely—at least unless concentration by merger without diseconomies is possible—because of the attractiveness to any small firm of violating agreements and of the fear by all that others will do so. Easy entry—or close approximation thereto—thus makes monopoly price results improbable (in the absence of government regulation), though not impossible as a sporadic recurrent phenomenon. Fourth, the continued tendency toward zero long-run excess profits may create a situation of acute dissatisfaction among firms in the industry, and thus may especially favor the solicitation of political interference to establish monopolistic price-output results by regulation. Where industry demands decline and exit is difficult, such solicitation may be especially likely and, if undertaken, especially effective.

As we turn to the probability that monopoly will emerge under other entry conditions, one guiding generalization is self-evident. The immediate condition of entry to an industry at any stage of adjustment determines the extent to which price can exceed the minimal costs of the most-favored firms without attracting entry. If this price is exceeded, further entry will be attracted. Suppose now that each successive immediate condition of entry beyond a point is at the same value—as measured by the excess of the entry-inducing price over the minimal average costs of one or more most-favored firms; through any progression of successive further entry, the general condition of entry to the industry is, in effect, measured by a single value. Then this uniform condition of entry will determine the limit of stable monopoly price. Price cannot exceed the established limit without persistently setting in course adjustments which restore price at least to this limit. Only sporadic monopoly pricing above this level will be possible, though this may be more likely as entry lags are longer. If the limit is low, severe monopolistic pricing tendencies cannot persist regularly; if it is high, they may.

But this generalization is hardly adequate. First, even if the condition of entry should set the entry-inducing price at one or another uniform level regardless of the stage of industry adjustment, knowledge of this level alone does not permit

[7]The terms "monopolistic pricing," "monopolistic price raising," and "monopolistic restriction" will be used throughout to refer to price-output adjustments such that price significantly exceeds marginal cost for some or all of industry output.

us to predict the degree of concentration which is likely to develop or the share of the market which the most-favored firms will gain—since this will depend in addition on how many firms are so favored, on the extent to which diseconomies of large scale will be encountered if such firms attempt to supply the entire market, and on the length of entry lags. Nor can we be certain of whether or when established firms with the maximum possible or lower degree of concentration will reach, adhere to, or exceed an entry-excluding price, or of the price-marginal-cost discrepancy at any price. In short, the precise prospect for monopoly development will depend on several matters in addition to the general condition of entry as so far defined—so that sub-cases may be identified for any given general condition. Second, there is no particular reason to suppose that the immediate condition of entry remains invariant as successive entry occurs—there may be, for example, a pattern of rise of the entry-excluding price with successive entry. In this case the shape of the pattern must be specified, together with the determinants of the reactions of established firms to successive immediate entry conditions, in order to predict the net tendency toward monopoly. Given this complex of matters for analysis, we will attempt here only to describe the consequences of certain possibly typical entry-condition patterns, under certain assumed subsidiary conditions which also affect the emergence of monopoly.

Two factors which, along with the condition of entry as defined, will affect the emergence of monopoly are (1) the length of the entry lag, between the time when a firm is induced to begin entry into an industry and when it will set up production at its planned scale, and (2) whether or not and to what extent diseconomies of large scale will make production of the entire industry output by one or a few firms less efficient than production by many. In the succeeding discussion we will assume in all cases (1) that entry lags are of short or moderate length, so that any extra interim profits per annum to established firms, received only between the time when price is raised to an entry-inducing level and further entry is accomplished, will pass at a substantial discount relative to per annum profits receivable in the long run either without or after further entry, and (2) that there are no significant diseconomies of large scale to prevent one or a few firms from supplying a market as efficiently as more firms could. These circumstances are set forth as aspects of the typical environmental setting within which the condition of entry has its effects.

Given these circumstances, certain condition-of-entry patterns may be advanced as approximations to those which are typical in fact. These are distinguished primarily on the basis of the determinants of the condition of entry because the nature of these determinants is probably to a certain extent related to the pattern of entry conditions.

The following patterns, other than that of easy entry, will be considered here:

I. Conditions of entry which rest entirely or almost entirely on absolute-cost and product-differentiation advantages of established firms, with no significant economies of large scale.

A. Where either the only or the greatest advantage is held—approximately equally—by a few firms (entry being easy until they are in), and where
   1. The condition of entry, or excess of the entry-inducing price over minimal costs of these firms, remains the same through any progression of entry, and has
      a. A "low" value.
      b. A "medium" value.
      c. A "high" value.
   2. The condition of entry increases in value with a progression of entry because of differential advantages among potential entrants.

B. Where either the only or the greatest advantage is held—approximately equally—by at least a moderately large but limited number of firms (entry being easy until they are in), and where the sub-categories are as under A above.

II. Conditions of entry which rest almost entirely on economies of large scale, with no significant absolute-cost or product-differentiation advantages to established firms—and where any advantage thus tends to be shared by all firms in the industry at any stage. (A provisionally assumed behavior-pattern is that all entrant firms retain their identity and share the market with previously established firms—i.e., there are no rationalizing mergers to counteract the effects of entry.)

A. The condition of entry is approximately stable at relatively low levels through a progression of entry—a case found principally where the optimum scale is barely large enough to provide some deterrent to entry, or, if the optimum scale is large, where the scale curve slopes shallowly back to small scales, and moderate increases in price will bring in entry at negligible scales with no deterrent repercussions.

B. The condition of entry tends to increase in value with the progression of entry, as the average scale of established (and potential entrant) firms is reduced with substantially higher costs, thus providing successively less favorable prospect for entry at any given price—a case likely to be found where optimum scale output will supply a substantial fraction of the market and where the scale curve slopes rather steeply back from the optimum scale—and the condition of entry has, with one or a few firms:
   1. A "low" value.
   2. A "medium" value.
   3. A "high" value.

   Mixed cases will not be outlined in detail, but may be considered in conjunction with the simple cases.

What is the prospect of monopoly under any of this variety of alternative entry conditions? Space being limited, we will confine ourselves to the brief statement of evident corollaries of the various conditions, when found under the initially assumed general circumstances. Let us first consider the three cases under I-A-1, characterized in effect by absolute-cost or product-differentiation advantages of a few firms equally over all possible entrants, and effectively horizontal scale curves. In all these cases the few firms can, in effect, dominate the market if they will—thus securing stable "monopolistic concentration"—by not going above the maximum entry-excluding price. And in all cases the potentially small number of sellers makes effective collusion in some deliberate policy probable though not strictly necessary.

But the prospect both of monopoly pricing and of structural development will depend on the height of the entry-excluding price. Suppose first that this price is "low" relative to average costs, by which we will mean low enough so that, entry lags being taken into account, the few favored firms whenever occupying the market alone will find greater joint profits in the long run by raising price above the maximum entry-excluding level and reaping extra interim profits until entry is accomplished. Then price probably will sporadically exceed the low limit level, but will tend to be driven back to it by entry, and a recurrent "cleaning out" of unfavored entrants through price-cutting will probably occur, with a resulting unstable market structure. The degree of monopolistic price-raising which is persistently attainable is relatively slight, but sporadic price-raising to much higher levels is probable. And the latter is probable with higher levels of the maximum entry-excluding price as entry lags become longer.

Suppose second, that the entry-excluding price is in a "medium" range, by which we will mean that it is high enough to make an entry-excluding price policy offer larger long-run joint profits to the favored sellers than a policy of charging a higher price, but that it is lower—and perhaps substantially lower—than the price which would maximize *industry* profits. Then it is probable that a small to moderate degree of monopolistic price-raising will occur, but only to the limit level above which entry would be attracted. At this level stable monopoly pricing (in limited degree), together with a stable high concentration, can persist through time. Inter-firm rivalry which keeps price lower than the limit is, of course, possible. If the entry-excluding price is "high"—i.e., at least as high as that which will maximize industry profits—the preceding conclusion for a "medium" condition of entry applies, except that stable maintenance of extreme monopoly price results is probable. For these cases in general, concentration is likely to be high, and once the condition of entry is above "low," the degree of probable monopolistic price-raising increases with the height of the barrier to entry. A "low" barrier to entry, however, introduces added complications.

The cases under I-B-1—which are like those just discussed except that the strategic advantage is shared by a considerable number of firms—tend toward different price results so far as the larger number of favored sellers may be less likely to reach effective collusion for the exploitation of their position. Thus in each such case it will be less probable that the monopolistic pricing tendencies indicated will be consistently approached and maintained. In any event, monopolistic concentration will in all cases tend to be lower. However, all I-B-1 cases are convertible into I-A-1 cases by mergers among the favored firms, and these are likely to appear attractive. For these cases in general, the possible extent of persistent monopolistic price-raising again varies with the height of the barrier to entry, but attainment of this limit is significantly less probable, since (barring mergers) concentration will tend to be lower.

Cases of the I-A-2 or I-B-2 type, where entrants are at successively greater disadvantage to the most-favored firms, may follow a considerable variety of tendencies, depending on the potential number of firms at each level of advantage and the sizes of the gaps between the levels. Under collusive pricing successive entry may tend to be induced up to a point where a "medium" barrier to further entry is encountered, and where stability at the corresponding entry-excluding price can then probably be found, with a corresponding degree of monopolistic restriction. If so, the minimal height of the "medium" barrier will tend to be greater than in the I-A-1 case. But market instability and sporadic monopoly departing from a lower base level of price is equally possible. The probable degree of concentration which develops will similarly be influenced by the pattern of successive immediate entry conditions and the potential number of firms at each level. If concentration is low and collusion is not effective, perceptible monopolistic restriction may not be attained. The only general rule here is that a progression of successively more difficult immediate entry conditions linked to absolute advantages will tend to lead toward at least some degree of monopolistic output restriction unless, early in the process of approaching this point, numbers become such that collusion breaks down.

In the preceding cases it has been assumed that there are no significant diseconomies of large scale. Should these be encountered—as, for example, where the most-favored firms could not supply the market and cover average costs at the entry-excluding price—additional firms beyond the most favored may *necessarily* be induced to enter. If in this case there are no differential advantages among other firms, the situation should thereupon become one of easy entry in an alternative sense, as measured by the costs and prices of this second layer of marginal firms, but with extra profits to the first layer. Further possible cases need not be discussed in detail. In general, significant scale diseconomies—sufficient to limit the share of the market which firms at successive levels of advantage can profitably supply without inducing further entry—tend to make a progression of entry to a certain point inevitable and to cause some approach toward easy entry as measured with relation to the positions of the least-favored firms necessarily admitted. The closeness of the approach will depend on the gaps between the successive levels of advantage. Scale diseconomies also tend to favor atomistic structure, and whatever may follow from it. Where such diseconomies are present, a value of the condition of entry which departs substantially from zero (as measured by the discrepancy between the maximum entry-excluding price and the minimal average costs of the most-favored firms) will not systematically encourage significant price-marginal-cost discrepancies, but it will tend to give excess profits to some firms.

It is doubtful, however, that significant diseconomies of large scale are ordinarily encountered.

The preceding analysis of the emergence of monopoly under the entry conditions included under I (significant diseconomies of scale being assumed absent) has implicitly supposed that the structure and price behavior of the industry develops from the outset under a given condition of entry. It is possible, however, that a new and different condition of entry will emerge in any developed industry, and that the industry may then include some less-favored firms–now "unwanted and eliminable"–which the more-favored firms, had this new condition of entry been in effect earlier, would have excluded from entry by adhering to a limit price found at a point where a "medium" or higher barrier to entry was encountered. It then seems likely on balance that, with the new entry condition, the more-favored firms will be inclined to pursue a price policy which will force exit of any such now unwanted and eliminable firms, and that industries will thus approach the same levels of price and degrees of concentration previously predicted for the now-ruling conditions of entry. So far as this is true, our conclusions apply regardless of legacies from the past (or of temporary aberrations of adjustment due to irrational behavior.[8] It is, however, possible in these cases that prolonged exit lags and their potential consequences may forestall the tendency toward elimination of the unwanted and eliminable firms, and lead to the maintenance of a lower concentration, and possibly to a higher price than previously predicted. There is thus a potential modification of our previous predictions when applied under more general assumptions, and its practical importance is hard to evaluate.

Let us now consider cases in which the barrier to entry rests almost entirely on economies of large scale. Absolute-cost and product-differentiation advantages are unimportant, but one or a few firms can supply the industry at lower costs than more, and the size of an economical increment of entry will have repercussions which discourage entry to some extent. In case II-A, where small-scale entry involves average costs not very much higher than optimum-scale costs, the entry-inducing price can never go very far above the minimal cost level with any progression of entry, although it may increase slightly toward a limit as added firms come in. Here, there are two major possibilities. One or a few established firms, operating at efficient scales, may find it profitable to stay below the entry-inducing price–which is thus at least "medium" in height–or competition may conceivably keep price below this level, with stable high concentration and a small to moderate degree of monopolistic price-raising. Or, a few established firms may find it profitable to induce entry (the initial barrier is "low")–adding to short-run profits during entry lags. In the latter case stability with the same or a slightly higher degree of long-run monopolistic restriction may eventually result, with reduced concentration, or if there is periodic

[8] If the new entry condition places some established firms at a new disadvantage, but small enough so that there would now be a "low" barrier to their entry, they may tend to be periodically eliminated, but their presence on at least a temporary basis is consistent with previous conclusions.

rationalization of market structure by merger, there may be dynamic instability of market structure and severe sporadic monopoly tendencies. Barring periodic mergers, severe monopolistic restriction will not persist in either case, although in the first instance high concentration will.

In case II-B, a scale curve which rises rapidly behind the optimum scale may lead to progressively higher levels of entry-excluding price as successive entry occurs. At the same time, the average costs of established firms rise similarly as they operate at smaller scales. The strategic question is whether and where in the progression of entry an entry-excluding price is found at which established firms can make larger joint profits than at attainable higher prices, and how high it is. The answer seems to depend principally, given certain entry lags, on the size of optimal output (relative to industry demand), and on the curvature of the scale curve behind the optimum output.

The sub-cases listed above suggest the major possibilities. If with one or a few firms operating efficiently the value of the condition of entry is "low," price will probably be raised and progressive entry will be induced (unless competition keeps price down) to the point where further entry may be profitably excluded. This may easily lead to very substantial degrees of monopolistic restriction, so far as average costs pursue the entry-excluding price upward. Market structure may be dynamically unstable so far as mergers to restore efficiency (or price wars to drive out rivals) are an attractive possibility. Thus, so long as collusion remains effective, this case has clear monopolistic tendencies, although early price rivalry may forestall them. If the value of the condition of entry is "medium" or "high" with one or few firms, stability with high concentration and from a very moderate to a high degree of monopolistic price-raising is probable. But if the industry is "caught" (e.g., after a decline in demand or with the emergence of greater scale economies in a developed industry) with an excessive number of firms, a higher degree of monopolistic restriction is likely to persist, unless rationalization by merger occurs.

In brief, economies of scale may constitute a formidable barrier to entry and a basis for high concentration and monopolistic pricing. The size of optimum output and the shape of the scale curve is strategic, but it is impossible to say that the probable degree of monopolistic price-raising increases in simple relation to the size of optimum output and the steepness of the curve. Very shallow curves will not favor stable maintenance of strongly monopolistic results, and steep curves, especially with large optima, will favor severe monopolistic restriction. In some portion of the range between these extremes, however, we may find monopolistic tendencies first decreasing and then increasing as we move toward the second extreme.

The various possibilities with respect to "mixed" cases, where the barrier to entry rests simultaneously on scale economies and other advantages, should be obvious from the preceding and will not be developed in detail here. Certain generalizations comprehending all cases, however, may be offered. Any long-run monopoly pricing tendencies must rest on a departure from easy entry, although sporadic monopoly tendencies may emerge even with easy entry. As among industries without easy entry (and these are probably in the majority) there is a wide variety with respect to the condition of entry, either as a general value or as a pattern of values with successive entry. Generally, the value of the condition of entry, or the maximum immediate value it reaches with an achievable progression of entry, determines the maximum limit on the degree of stable long-run monopoly price-raising. If further circumstances favor high concentration, this limit may be approached, but where there is a distinct progression in the value of the condition of entry it is probable that neither the maximum attainable nor the industry-profit-maximizing price will be reached, and that further entry will be forestalled with a price which exceeds the competitive level by only a small or moderate amount. If a large number of firms must be admitted before the immediate condition of entry exceeds a low value, then monopoly results are improbable (though not impossible) even if the barrier to entry would rise with further entry. Some modification of the preceding conclusions would be required if significant scale diseconomies were present.

In general, relatively moderate immediate values of the condition of entry may encourage no more than a moderate degree of monopolistic price-raising, although they very possibly may engender high seller concentration. (High seller concentration can evidently be quite consistent with a variety of entry conditions and degrees of monopolistic restriction.) Low positive values of the condition of entry, however, may in several possible instances encourage sporadic monopoly tendencies and unstable market structures, and this possibility is enhanced by the lengthening of entry lags. The preceding is true regardless of the particular determinants of the value of the condition of entry. It will be relevant for policy purposes, of course, to inquire which are the more important determinants in fact. It may be noted that economies of scale as a source of barriers to entry are more likely than others to give rise to progressively higher barriers with successive entry, and thus to the possibility of extremes of monopolistic restriction. Also, these barriers are perhaps longer lived or less ephemeral, and present the severest potential difficulties in public policy.

THE ACTUAL IMPORTANCE OF THE CONDITION OF ENTRY AS A BASIS FOR MONOPOLY AND POLICY SUGGESTIONS

Except so far as we desire to test the validity of the conventional premises of economic theory, the principal factual question posed by the foregoing analysis is not whether the condition of entry is strategic to the emergence of monopoly. It is rather how high the existing barriers to entry are, and what are their sources. Currently available data unfortunately do not permit us to give a detailed and precise answer to this question. Systematic information on the sources of impeded entry is sufficiently lacking so that their character is not infrequently postulated ad hoc to justify a particular policy proposal. We are thus at best limited to a few general observations.

A primary issue concerns the relative importance as sources of impeded entry of scale economies, which may constitute wholly or largely ineradicable sources of impeded entry, and absolute-cost and product-differentiation advantages, which seem at least potentially eradicable. Although there are manifold evidences of the existence of the latter, data presently available on scale economies do not permit any safe judgment concerning their relative or residual importance. It is quite possible, for all we now know, that if all deterrents to entry other than scale economies were done away with, there would still be substantial barriers favoring monopoly in many or most of the industries where it now exists; it is also possible that scale economies would turn out to be quite unimportant. Much more investigation bearing on this issue is obviously called for. It seems safe to say, however, that whatever deterrents to entry do inhere in scale economies per se, they are in most cases substantially enhanced by absolute-cost or product-differentiation advantages of established firms; and further, that there is probably some range of cases where the only significant barriers to entry are of the latter sort.

Is it therefore true that the elimination of these further barriers would generally tend to make for less monopoly? As a general rule, perhaps yes, but there are conceivable exceptions. Where economies of scale alone impose a condition of entry which has a "low" value when firms are few and efficient, but which rises in value as further entry occurs, existence of this barrier by itself may favor a progression toward severe monopolistic restriction with an excessive number of excessively small firms. If it would, some added barrier might encourage stabilization with reasonable efficiency, small or moderate monopolistic restriction, and entry forestalled, whereas if this were eliminated less desirable results (though with lower concentration) would ensue. Or, in general, a moderately low barrier to entry may be preferable to a still lower one, as less likely to encourage the sporadic or persistent emergence of extreme monopoly tendencies, and more likely to encourage a stable but limited monopolistic restriction. Taking account of these exceptions, however, it would appear that monopoly tendencies might, in general, be considerably reduced by measures which would tend in part to erase the large absolute-cost and product-differentiation advantages of established firms.

How pervasive and how important are the barriers to entry resultant on the one hand from economies of scale, and on the other from absolute cost differences and product differentiation? Here we may venture a few hypotheses relative to the economy of the United States, based on casual observation. First, the effective barriers imposed by scale-economies, in those cases where they are evident, seem usually to be significant but not very high. This may, in part, account for the co-existence of rather high seller concentration and rather moderate or slight monopolistic restriction in many industries. But just how pervasive such barriers are is difficult to say. Second, absolute-cost advantages to established firms, resting on patent controls and on other foundations, appear to exist in a significant share of manufacturing industries, and product-differentiation advantages appear to be common in a substantial share of consumer-good manufacturing industries. The resultant barriers to entry appear to be quite variable in height, very often only moderately high, but in a number of extreme cases quite high. Where such advantages provide a deterrent to entry, they seem ordinarily to be shared by only a few firms, so that concentration is fostered. The variability of the height of such entry barriers is one plausible explanation of the widely varying degrees of monopolistic price-raising associated with high seller concentration.

With respect to absolute-cost advantages, as we have defined the category, there is a question as to the relative importance as a potential deterrent to entry of the condition of supply of investible funds to potential entrants. Certain writers have placed major weight on this factor, and financing difficulties certainly have some importance. It may be suggested, however, that this deterrent to entry may in some a priori theorizing have been charged as the chief culprit mainly because the existence of an army of alternative potential culprits was hardly recognized, and that the importance of capital-market considerations could very easily be overrated. Generalizations on this point applicable to all places and times are impossible, and detailed empirical analysis is called for.

In the preceding analysis, distinctions have been drawn between the probability of high concentration and the probability of prices substantially in excess of minimal average costs under various entry conditions. It perhaps deserves reiteration that although most barriers to entry (above a low minimal height) may generally tend to favor high concentration, the degree of monopolistic price-raising they engender may be quite variable. A severe monopoly pricing problem is not always—and perhaps not usually—associated with high seller concentration.

We may conclude with a few brief comments on public policy. First, barriers to entry inherent in real economies of scale are with a given technology ineradicable, at least without legislating for enforced inefficiency. Strictly pecuniary economies of scale might be attacked to advantage by a number of routes, but with the usual scatter-gun there is a genuine difficulty in shooting the hawk and missing the bird as they perch on the same limb. Where there are ineradicable economies of scale, some discretion should be observed in striking down other barriers, since some added low barriers may in some cases be to the social advantage. Second, reduction of other barriers to entry by the obvious variety of means—patent-law reform, capital-market policy, attacks on resource monopolization and unnecessary integration, consumer education, grade-labelling requirements, etc.—would, in general, tend to induce less monopolistic restriction and perhaps lower concentration. If low concentration per se is sought, genuine easy entry should be sought. But if reasonably low prices alone will do, reduction of existing barriers to moderately low levels would suffice. There is probably no especial danger that barriers will in effect be reduced below moderately low levels. But the erroneous belief that there must be a sort of one-to-one correlation between concentration and monopoly pricing tendencies could be a distinct potential handicap in policy formation. Third, any policy which may shorten entry lags should be a good one. Finally, genuinely easy entry has its political dangers, especially if slow exit is found in the same industries. A small margin of long-run excess profit coupled with "a little monopoly" may be a reasonable price to pay for diminishing the force and effectiveness of pressures for State-sponsored cartelization. But the limits of "a little monopoly" should be carefully drawn.

BIBLIOGRAPHICAL NOTE

The following recent works have been especially provocative of thought along the lines pursued above: William Fellner's *Competition Among the Few,* 1949, especially for its analysis of the counter-tendencies affecting the emergence of collusion, and Don Patinkin's "Multi-Plant Firms, Cartels, and Imperfect Competition" (*Quarterly Journal of Economics,* February 1947), for its analysis of entry phenomena under cartels. Much of the present analysis on the effects of the condition of entry on monopoly has grown out of this writer's analysis in "A Note on Pricing in Monopoly and Oligopoly" (*American Economic Review,* March 1949, and Ch. 5, this book) and "Workable Competition in Oligopoly" (ibid., May 1950, and Ch. 3, this book).

Chapter Seven

Theory Concerning the Condition of Entry

Economic theory concerning the condition of entry is fairly complex, and here we will present only a condensed and simplified version of it.[1] . . .

DEFINITION AND MEASUREMENT OF THE CONDITION OF ENTRY

A definition of the condition of entry rests on an initial distinction between (1) firms already established in an industry and supplying output to its market (hereafter *established firms*), and (2) firms not already established in the industry that might enter by building new plant capacity[2] and using it as sellers in the industry (hereafter *potential entrant firms*). In loose terms, the condition of entry is then defined as the "disadvantage" of potential entrant firms as compared to established firms—or, conversely, the "advantage" of established over potential entrant firms.

Somewhat more precisely, the condition of entry refers to the extent to which, in the long run, established firms can elevate their selling prices above the minimal average costs of production and distribution (those costs associated with operation at optimal scales) without inducing potential entrants to enter the industry. If the established sellers in an industry have some advantage over potential entrants, they will be able persistently to set selling prices at least

Reprinted from *Industrial Organization*, 2nd ed., edited by Joe S. Bain, pp. 252-269, courtesy of John Wiley & Sons, Inc.

[1]For a fuller exposition see Joe S. Bain, "Conditions of Entry and the Emergence of Monopoly," *Monopoly and Competition and Their Regulation* (E. H. Chamberlin, Ed.), 1954 (Ch. 6, this volume); and Bain, *Barriers to New Competition*, 1956, Ch. 1.

[2]New entry as defined is not accomplished if a firm previously not in an industry simply acquires the plant of an already established firm and operates it; that is, the mere change of ownership of existing plant capacity does not constitute new entry as that term is understood here. If an outside firm does acquire existing plant in an industry, therefore, it "enters" the industry only to the extent that it then adds to the plant capacity it has acquired.

somewhat above the level of minimal average costs (and supply smaller than competitive outputs) without making it attractive for other firms to enter. This is because potential entrants, with their disadvantages, could not make satisfactory profits either at such prices (if the prices are not expected to change because of entry), or at lower prices expected to prevail after their new outputs were added to market supply.

The highest selling price that established sellers in an industry can persistently charge without attracting new entry may be referred to as "the maximum entry-forestalling price." Then *the condition of entry is measured numerically as the percentage by which the maximum entry-forestalling price exceeds the minimum attainable average costs of established firms.*

Entry to an industry will not occur if selling prices do not exceed the maximum entry-forestalling level. Conversely, if established sellers set prices higher than this level, or at an "entry-inducing" level, potential entrants will be induced to enter the industry in spite of their disadvantages and will anticipate satisfactory profits after so doing. Somewhere in the progression of successively higher possible selling prices in any industry we will encounter the largest possible entry-forestalling price, followed immediately by the smallest possible entry-inducing price. For example, with minimal costs for product A at $1.00 per unit, any price charged up to $1.10 may be sufficiently low to forestall the entry of added sellers, so that $1.10 is the maximum entry-forestalling price. But prices above $1.10 per unit will induce entry, so that $1.11 is the minimum entry-inducing price. Then the numerical measure of condition of entry is 10 per cent.

A further word should be said about the meaning in this definition of the minimal average cost relative to which the maximum entry-forestalling price is measured. For production and distribution costs this refers to the lowest attainable average costs—those which the firm would have if operating at the optimal or most efficient scale of production and without any chronic excess capacity (It would tend to do this in the long run under conditions of theoretical atomistic competition.) So far as sales-promotion costs are incurred, it is difficult to set a similarly definite competitive standard, since even a competitive firm may spend more or less on promotion and correspondingly be able to charge higher or lower selling prices. This difficulty in definition may be dealt with by defining the condition of entry in terms of the percentage excess of (1) the maximum entry-forestalling selling price per unit of output *minus* the average promotional costs per unit accompanying it, over (2) minimum attainable average costs of production and distribution.

Greater precision can and should be introduced into the preceding rather rough definition of the condition of entry—and the need for it is occasioned by the facts that:

1. Different established firms in an industry frequently have differing degrees of advantage over potential entrants—reflected in some established firms having advantages over others—so that different firms already in an industry will

effectively have different maximum entry-forestalling prices (or the same entry-forestalling price but different minimal average costs). Therefore, we should distinguish the "most advantaged" established firms in an industry—those with the highest ratio of maximum entry-forestalling prices to minimal average costs—from other established firms.

2. Different potential entrant firms often have differing degrees of disadvantage as compared to the most advantaged established firms in an industry that they might enter. Consequently, we should distinguish the "least disadvantaged" potential entrants from other potential entrants, and if possible rank potential entrants according to the degrees of their disadvantage (from least through successively greater disadvantage).[3]

Given these circumstances, the "immediate" condition of entry to an industry should be defined in terms of the advantage of the most advantaged established firm or firms over the least disadvantaged potential entrant or entrants. It should be measured by the percentage excess over its minimal average costs of the highest selling price that the most advantaged established firm (or firms) can charge without inducing the least disadvantaged potential entrant (or entrants) to enter the industry. (As we will see later, the immediate condition of entry at any time will potentially exercise the strategic proximate influence on the pricing policies of established firms.)

The "general" condition of entry to an industry should correspondingly be measured as the series of values of the immediate condition of entry which would emerge if, successively, individual potential entrants entered the industry one by one in the order of increasing disadvantage (beginning with the least disadvantaged one, followed by the next least disadvantaged one, and so forth.) The general condition of entry to an industry will be measured by a series of constant or unchanging values only if all potential entrants are equally disadvantaged initially, and if also economies of the large-scale firm are unimportant. In the following abbreviated theoretical discussion, we will unless otherwise noted be referring either to immediate conditions of entry, or to general conditions wherein all potential entrants are equally disadvantaged.

The condition of entry, thus measuring the ability of established sellers to secure supercompetitive prices without attracting new competitors, is evidently an important characteristic of the structure of any industry. Although in practice it is frequently difficult to measure precisely from available data, it can be meaningfully estimated and comparisons of conditions of entry to different industries can be made. Let us next consider the typical determinants of the condition of entry.

[3]Potential entrant firms may have initially differing degrees of disadvantage which would remain unchanged after the least disadvantaged potential entrant had actually entered the industry. But also, where scale economies are a deterrent to entry (as discussed below), the disadvantages of remaining potential entrants, though not initially different from any others, would increase after one or more potential entrants had actually entered the industry. That is, entry to an industry by additional firms may become more difficult if economies of the large-scale firm are important.

SOURCES OF BARRIERS TO ENTRY

The existence of a condition of entry to an industry that permits established firms to elevate price at least somewhat above minimal average costs without inducing new firms to enter obviously reflects the existence of some barrier to entry—some source of disadvantage to potential entrants as compared with established firms. In general, these barriers to entry are of three types:

1. *Product differentiation advantages of established over potential entrant firms.*
2. *Absolute cost advantages of established over potential entrant firms.*
3. *Advantages of established over potential entrant firms due to economies of large-scale firms.*

Although two or more of these types of barrier to entry may combine to determine the condition of entry in a single industry, we will begin by discussing them separately, and also initially consider each one on the assumption that the other two are not present in the case at hand.

The established firms in an industry may enjoy a product-differentiation advantage over potential entrants because of the preference of buyers for the products of established firms over new ones. If so, any potential entrant may be unable to secure a selling price as high (relative to average costs) as established firms can when selling their products in competition with the entrant.

The resulting disadvantage to the entrant can be reflected in three alternative ways. First, it may be that established firms can charge prices above minimal average costs and the competing entrant would be able to charge only a lower price that does not cover his average costs. Second, it is possible that to secure a comparably favorable price, the entrant would have to incur sales-promotion costs per unit of output greater than those of established firms, again having average costs greater than his price. Finally, even if neither of these disadvantages is incurred so long as the entrant supplies a limited fraction of the market, he might be unable, at comparable prices and selling costs, to secure a sufficiently large market share to enable him to support an economically large production and distribution organization. Excluded from realizing available economies of large scale production and distribution, he might again find his average costs above his selling price, even though established firms were receiving prices in excess of minimal average costs.

In any of these circumstances, established firms have the power to elevate their prices by some amount above their minimal average costs without making it attractive for new firms to enter the industry. It is true of course that if a potential entrant did enter in the face of such disadvantages, these might tend to diminish and perhaps eventually vanish after a period of years during which his product gained acceptance and respect among buyers. Therefore, the duration of his product-differentiation disadvantage, as well as its initial and subsequent sizes, is to be reckoned in computing the net barrier to entry. The net deterrent effect on his entry might be calculated by averaging his declining disadvantages over all the years of his prospective operation (with appropriate discounting of more remote years), to arrive at that maximum excess of the prices of established firms over their minimal costs that would suffice to forestall his entry.

For example, an entrant firm might anticipate that for the average of the first ten years after his entry his selling prices would have to be 10 per cent below those of his rivals. But after ten years (and up to thirty years, which we will suppose is as far as he looks ahead) he would expect no disadvantage. This situation would probably not permit established firms to elevate prices above average costs by as much as 10 per cent without inducing entry. But they might well be able to make the early losses of entry unattractive, and deter entry, by setting their prices persistently only 4 to 5 per cent above average costs.

The preceding may be clarified by analyzing in a simple theoretical model the operation of a "pure" product-differentiation advantage of established firms in determining a maximum entry excluding price. (The advantage is "pure" in the sense that no economies of the large-scale firm are present and that established firms have no absolute-cost advantages over potential entrant firms, and also have no absolute-cost differences among themselves.) In this case, the long-run average cost or scale curves of all established firms and all potential entrants–showing the long-run relation of average costs of production and distribution to rates of output–are identical and also are horizontal (showing no change in average cost with variation in scale of firm). The scale curves of both the most advantaged established firm and the least disadvantaged potential entrant[4] are thus shown by the single line *ac* in Figure 7.1. Sales promotion costs are assumed to be absent.

Let us now suppose that the demand curve for the output of the most advantaged established firm, showing the long-run relationship of his sales volume to the price he charges, is D_sD_s' in Figure 7.1–this relationship being drawn on the assumption that all other established firms always match his price changes so as at all times either to charge the same price as his or to charge prices having the same ratios to or differentials from his. (All established firms, let us say, change prices concertedly and concurrently to maintain the same interfirm price relationships.) The question posed is how high a price the most advantaged firm can charge persistently without inducing the most advantaged potential entrant to enter the industry.

With no scale economies present, entry can be forestalled only if the established firm's price is such that there is no output (however small) that the potential entrant can sell at a price exceeding his average cost, *ac*. If the established firm has a pure product-differentiation advantage, he can set some price above his minimal average cost (also *ac*) and leave the potential entrant in a position where there is no output he can sell profitably. Let us suppose that the product-differentiation advantage is such that the maximum entry forestalling price is P_e in Figure 7.1. Then when this price is charged by the established firm,

[4]And, by assumption, of all established firms and all entrants.

Figure 7.1

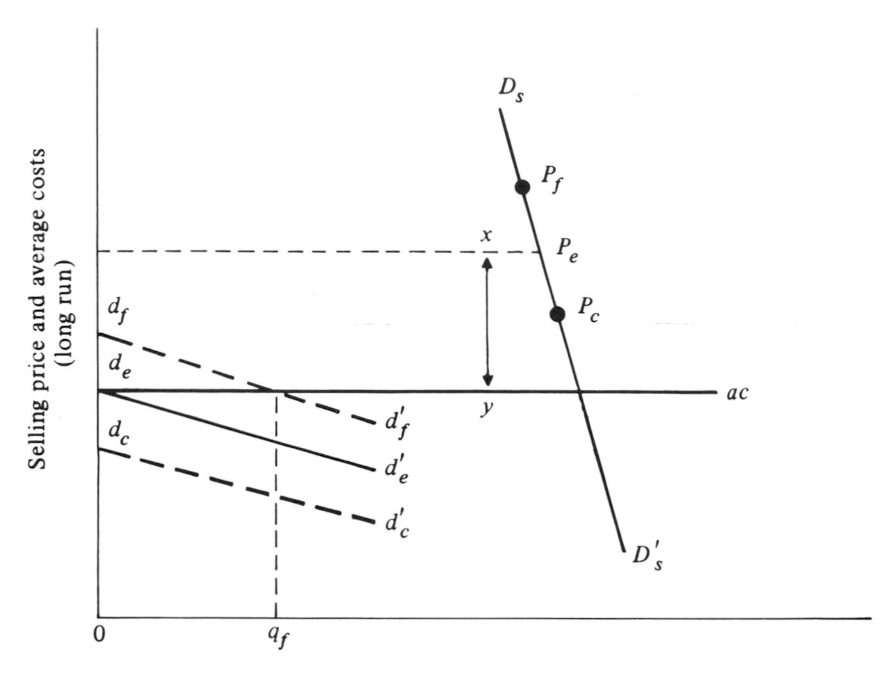

the demand curve for the potential entrant's output (drawn on the assumption of no reaction of established firms' prices to his entry[5] will lie at d_ed_e', showing that even at the smallest possible output the entrant could not gain a price above average cost.

The established seller's price P_e, however, is the highest price that will forestall all entry. If he charged a higher price P_f, the demand curve for the potential entrant's output would lie at d_fd_f'. He would then be attracted to enter and could make a profit by selling any output between zero and $0q_f$. (His profit-maximizing output would lie between zero and $0q_f$, and his corresponding price above *ac*.)[6] And if the established seller instead charged a lower price P_c, the demand curve for the potential entrant's output would lie at d_cd_c', whence he would not enter–but the price P_c would be lower than necessary to keep him from entering. The height of the immediate (and possibly general) product differentiation barrier to entry in Figure 7.1 is thus measured by the excess of P_e over *ac* (of the maximum entry forestalling price over minimal average cost), or the distance *xy*. (If there were no product-differentation barrier to entry, P_e would lie at the level of *ac*.)

[5]A valid assumption since the entrant would add so small a fraction to industry supply in this case that he would engender no price reactions from established firms.

[6]Precisely, he would choose the price and output at which his marginal revenue, derived from d_fd_f' (but not shown on Figure 7.1), was equal to *ac* (and thus to his marginal cost).

Figure 7.2

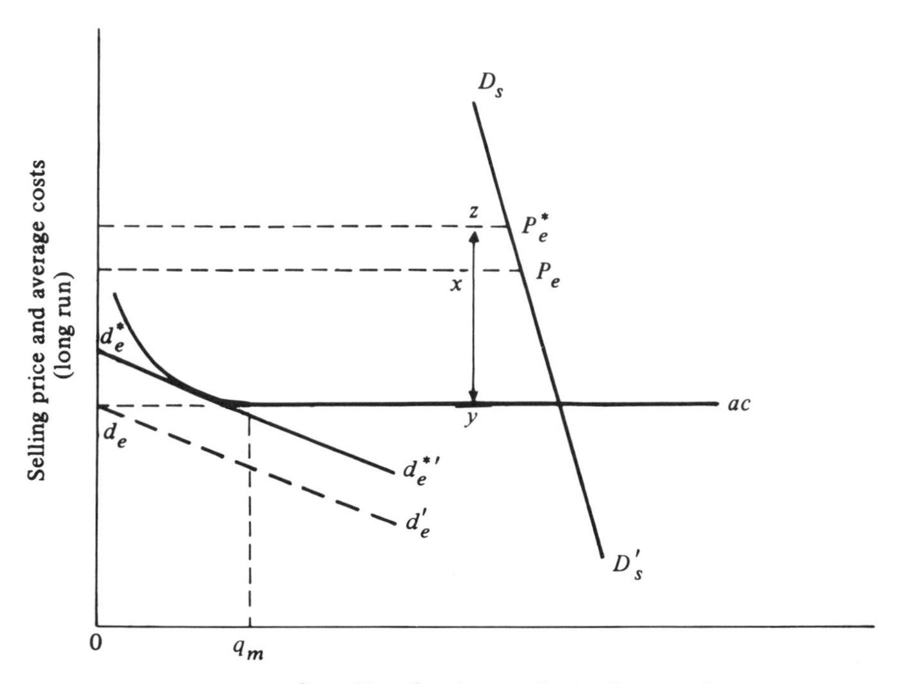

The model just presented becomes more realistic if we relax the assumption that there are no economies of the large-scale firm and suppose instead that there are some such scale economies, although the output of a firm of minimum optimal scale is nevertheless such a small fraction of industry output that entry at that scale would induce no price reactions from established sellers. (Consideration of the effect of important scale economies *per se* on the condition of entry is thus still excluded.) If some such relatively negligible scale economies are present, the barrier to entry resulting from a product differentiation advantage of established firms can be noticeably heightened even though the preference of buyers for their products is no stronger. This is because, if they suffer diseconomies of very small scale, potential entrant firms will require higher prices at small outputs in order to make production profitable. Therefore, established sellers can raise their own prices further and still forestall entry.

The argument is illustrated in Figure 7.2, which depicts the situation shown in Figure 7.1 exactly except that the common scale curve, *ac,* now shows some economies of the large scale firm up to a relatively small long-run output–Oq_m, the minimum optimal scale. When the most advantaged established firm now charges what the maximum entry excluding price would be in the absence of scale economies–that is, P_e . . . –resulting in the potential entrant's demand curve lying at $d_e d_e'$ as previously, it is clear that a still higher price set by the established seller will exclude entry, since $d_e d_e'$ is now not close to the backward-rising *ac*. In fact, the established seller can now set some higher price such as P_e*, which will result in the demand curve for the potential entrant's output lying higher at d_e*d_e*'–just enough higher that his selling price barely equals cost at his most profitable output. Only if the established seller's price exceeded P_e* would the potential entrant's demand curve shift upward from d_e*d_e*' to allow him (in view of diseconomies of very small scale) a profit at some output. Therefore, the maximum entry excluding price is higher because of diseconomies of very small-scale production even though the product preferences favoring established sellers are no greater. The effective barrier to entry–now measured in Figure 7.2 by the distance *yz* rather than by *xy*–is higher. When really important scale economies are encountered, as we will see later, they may interact with product-differentiation advantages of established firms to erect very high barriers to entry.

Further theoretical models and diagrams could be developed to illustrate the operation of higher sales-promotion costs (rather than lower selling prices) for the potential entrant in establishing comparable product differentiation barriers to entry, but the foregoing should suffice.

The possible sources of product-differentiation barriers to entry are fairly clear: (1) the accumulated preferences of buyers (often under the influence of long-sustained advertising) for established brand names and company reputations, either generally or except for small minorities of the buying population; (2) the exclusive control of superior product designs by established firms, through patent protection; (3) the ownership or control of favored systems of distributive outlets by established firms, in circumstances where alternative distributive systems can be established, if at all, only at a cost disadvantageous to the entrant. We will turn later to evidence on the importance of product-differentiation barriers to entry.

The second main type of barrier to entry reflects the "absolute" advantage, for one reason or another, of established firms in the matter of production and distribution costs. Their costs, at any comparable scale of operation, may be at a lower level than those of potential entrants. If this is so, they can obtain prices which are some amount above their own costs while potential entrants, competing with them, could not cover costs and so would not enter the market. (Again, the prospective duration of the entrant's disadvantage affects the calculation of the net resulting barrier to entry.)

The principal potential bases for such advantages to established firms seem to be the following: (1) control of superior production techniques by established firms, maintained either by patents or by secrecy; (2) exclusive ownership by established firms of superior deposits of resources required in production; (3) inability of entrant firms to acquire necessary factors of production (management services, labor equipment, materials) on terms as favorable as those enjoyed by established firms; and (4) less favored access of entrant firms to liquid funds for investment, reflected in higher effective interest costs or in

Figure 7.3

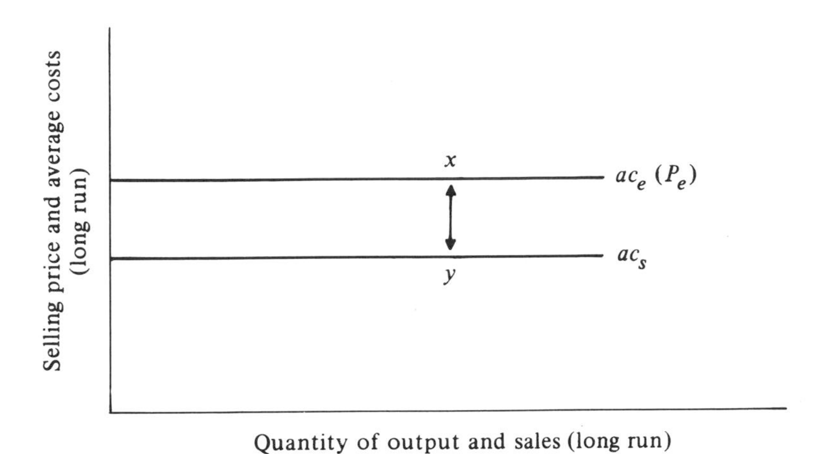

simple unavailability of funds in the required amounts. Any one or more of these circumstances can place the costs of potential entrant firms on a higher level and permit established firms to elevate selling prices somewhat above their own minimal average costs without making operations profitable for entrants and thus without inducing entry.

The case of "pure" absolute cost barriers to entry (unalloyed with economies of the large-scale firm or with product-differentiation advantages of established firms) is illustrated in Figure 7.3. The long-run average cost or scale curve of the most advantaged established firms is ac_s, and that of the least disadvantaged potential entrant is ac_e–the higher level of ac_e reflecting the absolute cost disadvantage of the potential entrant at any scale or rate of output. Clearly, the established firm may set his selling price as high as (but no higher than) ac_e without inducing entry, since the entrant would find production unprofitable at that price but profitable at higher prices. The maximum entry forestalling price is thus P_e (equal to ac_e), and the height of the barrier to entry is measured by the distance *xy*.

Absolute cost disadvantages of potential entrants, of course, may not always be unrelated to the scale of operations; they may increase as the scale of the potential entrant increases. This is especially likely, perhaps, if the disadvantage is reflected in the entrant's interest costs of securing funds for investment–a disadvantage which is likely to be greater as larger amounts of funds are sought.

Then the absolute cost disadvantage might be as illustrated in Figure 7.4, where again ac_s is the scale curve of the established firm and ac_e that of the potential entrant. (The existence of some economies of the large scale firm–not necessarily great enough that the added output of an entrant would induce reactions by established firms–is also depicted in Figure 7.4.) The potential entrant firm is depicted as having a scale curve which lies progressively farther above that of the established firm at progressively larger scales, because of

Figure 7.4

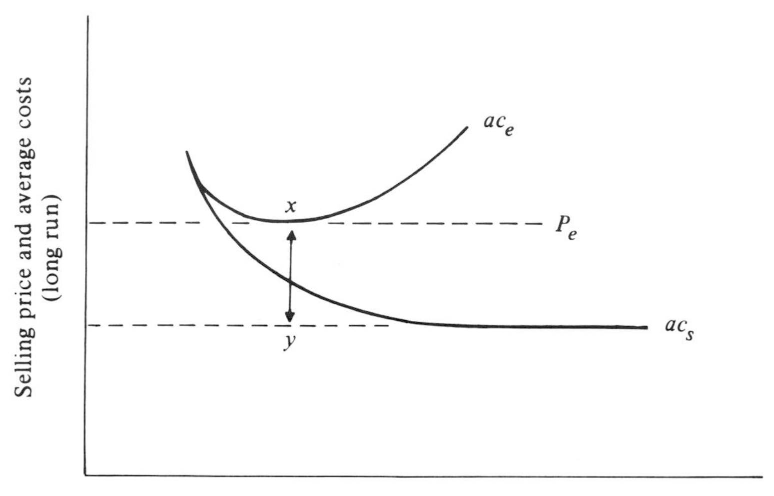

absolute cost disadvantages that increase with its scale (and that result in its experiencing diseconomies of increasing scale beyond a scale corresponding to x on Figure 7.4). In this case, the maximum entry-excluding price would correspond to the lowest level of average costs that the potential entrant could attain at any scale, and would thus be P_e. The height of the barrier to entry is the difference between P_e and the level of minimal average cost of the established firm, measured by the distance xy on Figure 7.4. It should be emphasized that P_e is unequivocally the maximum entry-excluding price only on the suppositions (1) that the entrant could secure a market share at least as large as that corresponding to output x and sell at the same price as established firms (he would have no effective product differentiation disadvantage) and (2) that his entry with an output as large as x would induce no reduction in market price by established firms (economies of the large-scale firm would not *per se* provide a deterrent to entry).

The third sort of barrier to entry may result from the fact that economies of the large-scale firm in the industry are such (*a*) that an entrant of minimum optimal scale (smallest scale at which lowest unit costs are attained) would supply a significant fraction of industry output, and (*b*) that at appreciably smaller scales, the entrant would have appreciably higher than the lowest attainable unit costs (would suffer significant diseconomies of small scale).

In the "pure" case of a barrier to entry due to scale economies (with no absolute-cost or product-differentiation barriers, and established and potential entrant firms supplying a homogeneous output), this situation would be reflected in the fact that the scale curve of every established and potential entrant firm was as illustrated by *ac* in Figure 7.5. Any firm's output

Figure 7.5

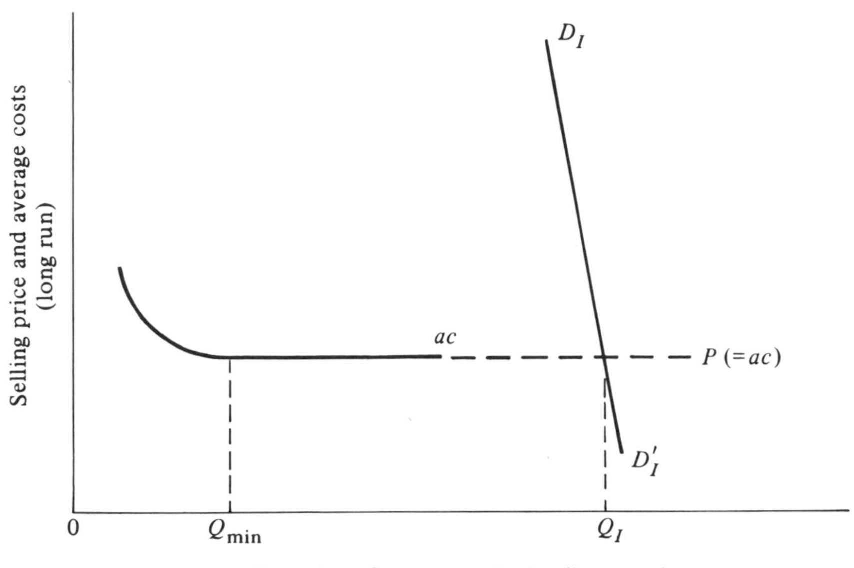

corresponding to minimum optimal scale (Q_{min}) would be a significant fraction of that total industry output (Q_I) which would be demanded at a price ($P = ac$) equal to minimal average cost (Q_I being codetermined by the demand curve for industry output, $D_I D_I'$). At progressively smaller scales than Q_{min}, any firm's average costs would increase progressively and by significant amounts. In Figure 7.5, Q_{min} is depicted as one-fourth of Q_I, so that four firms of minimum optimal scale could supply all industry output. But for scale economies to impede entry, it could be a larger fraction of Q_I, or a somewhat smaller one (so that the industry could accommodate fewer or more firms of minimum optimal scale), as long as Q_{min} was a large enough fraction of Q_I that its addition to total industry output would significantly reduce the market price of that output.

Now if economies of the large-scale firm are significant in the sense just described, established firms are likely to be able to set their selling price at least somewhat above the level of minimal average costs (P in Figure 7.5) without attracting entry, because one of the following situations is likely to be faced by any potential entrant firm:

1. It could enter at minimum optimal scale (or larger), secure a corresponding share of the market for industry output, and thus add enough to total industry output that selling price for that output would decline significantly. This price decline would occur, that is, unless established firms reduced their combined outputs by an amount about equal to the entrant's addition to output. In this case, however, it is probable that the potential entrant firm would not expect established firms to react to its entry by reducing their outputs sufficiently to

leave industry output unchanged. If they did not, its entry would cause the selling price for the enlarged industry output to fall. The post-entry selling price would therefore be lower than the pre-entry price.

Assume that the potential entrant firm conjectures that this price decline would occur because of its entry. Then established firms should be able to set a maximum entry-forestalling selling price that exceeded minimal average costs by the amount that the potential entrant firm expected this price to fall as a result of its entry. (If such a price were set, the potential entrant would expect that the price which would prevail after his entry would yield him no profit.)

2. It could enter at any of a number of scales somewhat smaller than the minimum optimal one but still large enough to add appreciably to industry output, secure corresponding shares of the market, and again conjecture that established firms would not reduce their pre-entry outputs by enough to keep the price for industry output from falling. The anticipated post-entry price would be below the pre-entry price, but probably below it by progressively less as the scale of entrant was progressively smaller. In addition, the potential entrant would incur average costs of production which were above minimal average costs—by increasing amounts as its scale was made smaller—because of diseconomies of small-scale production. In this case, established firms should be able to set a maximum entry-forestalling price that exceeded minimal average costs by an amount equal to (*a*) the expected reduction in this price resulting from entry, plus (*b*) the excess of the potential entrant's average costs over minimal average costs.

3. It could enter at some scale smaller than the minimum optimal one—either large enough to add appreciably to industry output or small enough not to do so—secure a corresponding market share, but conjecture that established firms would not reduce the pre-entry price perceptibly as a result of entry. It would expect, that is, that they would reduce their combined outputs by as much as the entrant's addition to output. (The likelihood of this conjecture by the entrant firm should increase as its proportionate market share was smaller.) Though not expecting industry price to fall as a result of his entry, the potential entrant would incur average costs of production above the level of minimal average costs. Established firms should therefore be able to set a maximum entry-forestalling price that exceeded minimal average costs by the same amount that the potential entrant's average costs would exceed them.

The first two situations are represented diagrammatically together in Figure 7.6. There *ac* is the scale curve of the potential entrant, already familiar to the reader. The curve pp'—not familiar—represents (by its varying distances from the horizontal axis) the excesses of the pre-entry over the post-entry prices that the potential entrant firm expects to be associated with its entry at various scales—or, in other words, the varying amounts by which the price for industry output are expected to fall as a result of its entry at varying scales. If we now add these expected differences between pre-entry and post-entry prices to the average costs of the entrant at each possible scale, we obtain the maximum

Figure 7.6

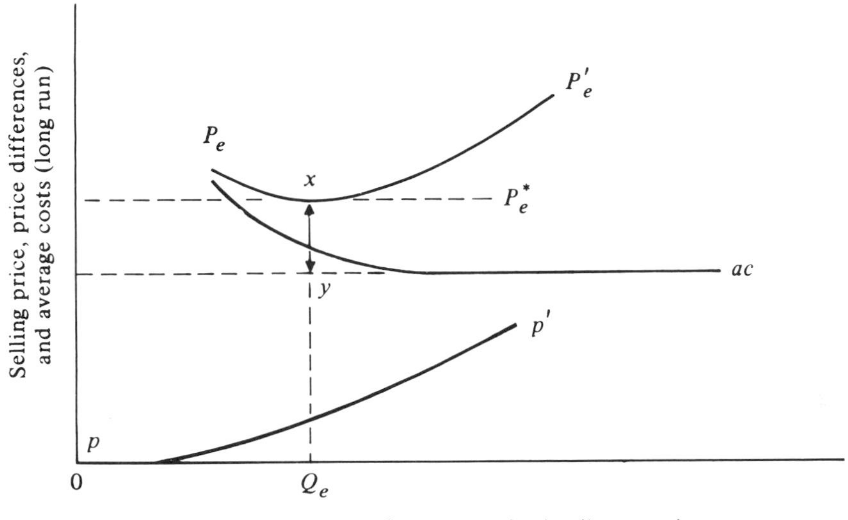

entry-forestalling price at every scale of entry. This is done diagrammatically by adding vertically to the values on *ac* the values on *pp'*, to obtain the curve P_eP_e', which shows the relationship of the maximum entry-forestalling price to the scale of the potential entrant. Assuming that the entrant firm is free to vary its scale, moreover, P_eP_e' shows by the lowest price on it, P_e*, the maximum entry forestalling price resulting from scale economies. No higher price could be entry-forestalling, because at any higher price the potential entrant firm could enter at the scale Q_e and expect a post-entry price in excess of its average costs. The height of the barrier to entry is *xy*.

In the general situation represented in Figure 7.6, the key to the determination of the maximum entry-forestalling price is found first in the potential entrant firm's general conjecture that after its entry established firms would not restrict their outputs by enough to maintain the pre-entry market price for industry output. It is found further in the entrant's specific conjectures concerning how much industry output would in the net increase, and the market price for it correspondingly fall, as a result of its entry at various scales. The general conjecture is comparatively pessimistic, and more so the less that the entrant firm expects established firms to reduce their outputs as a result of its adding a given amount to industry output.

But this is not the only conjecture the entrant firm may have. In the third situation just discussed, we indicated the possibility that it may entertain the more optimistic conecture that established firms would maintain the going industry price unchanged in the event of its entry, essentially by reducing their collective output by an amount equal to the entrant's output and market share.

Figure 7.7

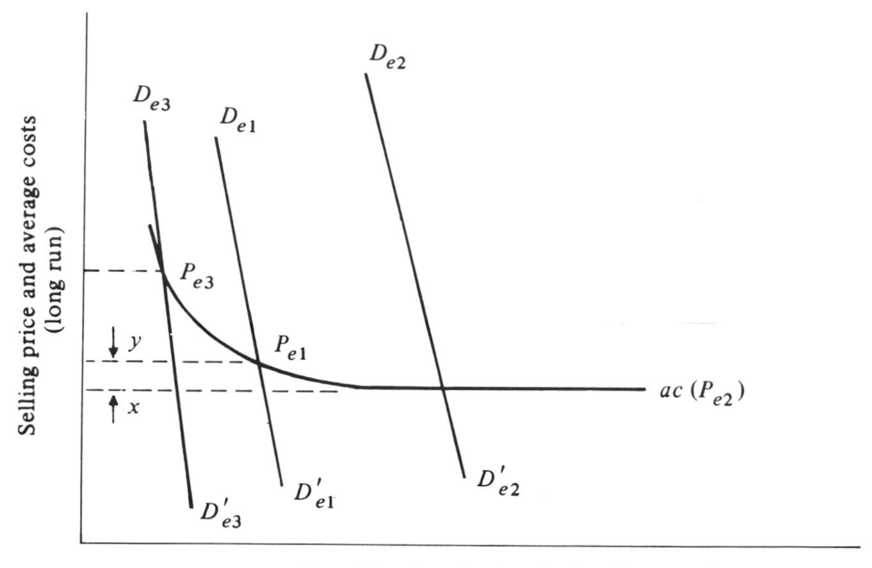

This third situation is represented in Figure 7.7. There *ac* is again the scale curve of the potential entrant firm. $D_{e1}D_{e1}'$ shows a possible demand curve for the potential entrant firm's output. It is drawn on the assumption (appropriate to a pure oligopoly) that the entrant and all established firms would always charge identical prices, and on the further assumption that the entrant's expected market share is insufficient to let it operate profitably at minimum optimal scale. $D_{e2}D_{e2}'$ shows the potential entrant firm's demand curve on the alternative assumption that its expected market share is great enough to allow profitable operations at a minimum optimal or large scale. (If the industry output is undifferentiated, the alternative *DD'* curves show the market shares of all firms after one more firm enters.)

Suppose that the expected market share of the potential entrant firm is as shown by $D_{e1}D_{e1}'$. Then, if the entrant firm expects pre-entry market price to be maintained after its entry (and if it cannot undercut it without drawing matching price cuts from the other firms), the established firms can set a maximum entry-forestalling price of P_{e1}, which is above minimal average costs. If the potential entrant firm expects a post-entry price of P_{e1} or lower, it cannot operate profitably with the market share shown by $D_{e1}D_{e1}'$, and will not enter. The height of the scale-economies barrier to entry is then measured by the distance *xy*.

Suppose alternatively that the entrant firm's expected market share is shown by $D_{e2}D_{e2}'$. Then it can operate profitably at or somewhat beyond minimum optimal scale and produce at minimal costs. The established firms therefore cannot elevate market price perceptibly above P_{e2} (equal to minimal average cost), and there is no scale-economies barrier to entry. (But there would be if the potential entrant expected a post-entry price lower than the pre-entry one, as supposed in Figure 7.6.) In industries where no product-differentiation or absolute-cost barriers to entry are also present, and where potential entrants optimistically expect pre-entry market price to be maintained, scale economies tend to impose a barrier to entry only after the industry has enough firms in it that the addition of one more firm would leave all firms with market shares too small for profitable operation at optimal scales.

The preceding analysis makes it plain that the height of the barrier to entry to an industry (if any) that results from significant scale economies alone is a function the conjectures of potential entrants concerning the reactions of established firms to their entry. The barrier may be higher or lower as these conjectures are more pessimistic or more optimistic. Since we are in no position to predict just what the conjectures of potential entrants will be, there is logically considerable uncertainty about how high a barrier to entry will result from the presence of scale economies of a given magnitude, though very important scale economies should probably provide some deterrent to entry.

It should also be noted that there may be some difference between (1) the "actual" barrier to entry due to scale economies, which depends on the actual conjectures of potential entrants concerning the reactions to entry of established firms, and (2) what established firms think that the barrier to entry is (how high they think the maximum entry-forestalling price is), this depending on their conjectures concerning the conjectures of potential entrants about their reactions to entry. This oligopolistic interdependence of crossed conjectures adds further uncertainty to the effects of significant scale economies on the price policies of established firms, as we will see later.

We have now considered product-differentiation, absolute-cost, and scale-economies barriers to entry. In any particular industry, one or more of the three types of barrier to entry may exist (sometimes in complex combination), and as a result some total or aggregate barrier to entry will determine the condition of entry, or the degree to which established firms can elevate their selling prices above minimal average cost while still forestalling entry. We will not go further with theory that analyzes the interaction of two or more entry barriers in the same industry except to note that the combination of important product-differentiation disadvantages of potential entrant firms with significant economies of large-scale production may result in exceptionally high barriers to entry.

Suppose that, because of product-differentiation disadvantages, the least disadvantaged potential entrant firm can secure only a rather small share of the market, though it can secure it (and because of oligopolistic interdependence perhaps must secure it) at the same selling price as established firms. (This is unlike the case of "pure" product differentiation disadvantage illustrated in Figures 7.1 and 7.2, where the entrant has a price disadvantage as well.) And suppose further that economies of large scale (conversely diseconomies of small scale) are such that with the market share the entrant firm can secure it, it will have average costs far above the minimal level. Then established firms may be able to set maximum entry-forestalling prices that are very high relative to minimal average costs. This possibility is illustrated in Figure 7.7 by the relationship of $D_{e3}D_{e3}'$—showing the putative minor market share of a potential entrant with product differentiation disadvantages—to his scale curve, *ac*. Even if the potential entrant entertains the optimistic conjecture that the pre-entry market price will not react to his entry, established firms could forestall entry while charging the high price P_{e3}. The aggregate barrier to entry is far higher than the mere sum of component barriers individually attributable to product differentiation and to scale economies.

There will presumably be a wide range of different conditions of entry among different industries, varying from those in which barriers are so high that entry is effectively blockaded almost regardless of the price policies followed by established firms, to those in which there are practically no barriers to entry at all.

The extreme at this latter end of the range is completely "easy" entry, with no barriers and with new entry being attracted if established firms persistently raise their selling prices at all above their minimal average costs. With such "easy" entry, it will of course be true that established firms enjoy no product-differentiation advantage over potential entrants, and no absolute-cost advantage, and that economics of scale are sufficiently unimportant that an optimal-scale firm will supply an insignificant percentage of total market output. As we depart from these polar easy-entry conditions in one or more of the three dimensions, the condition of entry becomes progressively more difficult.

Chapter Eight

Economies of Scale, Concentration, and the Condition of Entry in Twenty Manufacturing Industries

Ever since the merger movement of the late nineteenth century, American economists have been recurrently interested in the extent to which large size is necessary for business efficiency. Was the merger movement necessary; was the rule of reason economically justifiable; can this or that concentrated industry be atomized without loss of efficiency? These continue to be important questions to students of recent industrial history and contemporary antitrust policy. In the last three decades, with the notion that plant or firm size is related to efficiency formalized in long-run average-cost or scale curves, there has been much speculation and some inquiry concerning the shapes and positions of those scale curves in various industries and the placement of existing plants and firms on them.

To the economist qua economist, a knowledge for its own sake of the scale curves in particular industries is obviously unimportant. Only idle curiosity could justify his learning without further purpose how many barrels of cement a plant should produce to attain the lowest unit production cost, or how many passenger cars an automobile firm should make to minimize its production costs. But inferences which can be drawn from such knowledge may be important in several ways.

First, the proportion of the total output of its industry which a plant or a firm must supply in order to be reasonably efficient will determine the extent to which concentration in that industry is favored by the pursuit of minimized production costs. In any industry, the minimal scales of plant and of firm which are required for lowest production costs—*when these scales are expressed as percentages of the total scale or capacity of the industry* and are taken together with the shapes of the scale curves at smaller capacities—determine the degree of

Reprinted from *American Economic Review,* 44, March 1954, pp. 15-39, courtesy of the American Economic Association.

concentration by plants and firms needed for reasonable efficiency in the industry.

Second, the same relation of productive efficiency to the proportion of the market supplied by a plant or firm in any industry will have a profound effect on *potential competition,* or on the disposition of new firms to enter the industry. If a plant or firm needs to supply only a negligible fraction of industry output to be reasonably efficient, economies of scale provide no deterrent to entry other than those of absolute capital requirements. If, however, a plant or firm must add significantly to industry output in order to be efficient, and will be relatively inefficient if it adds little, entry at efficient scale would lower industry selling prices or induce unfavorable reactions by established firms, whereas entry at much smaller scales would give the entrant a significant cost disadvantage. In this situation established firms can probably raise prices some amount above the competitive level without attracting entry. In general, the "condition of entry"–measured by the extent to which established firms can raise price above a competitive level without inducing further entry–becomes "more difficult" as the ratio of the output of the optimal firm to industry output increases.[1]

Third, the amount of money required for investment in an efficient plant or firm–as determined by size–will affect the availability of the capital necessary for new entry. When the supplies of both equity and loan capital in the range needed for a unit investment are either absolutely limited or positively related to the interest rate, the number of dollars required to establish an efficient plant or firm will clearly affect the condition of entry to an industry.[2]

Finally, a comparison of the scales of existing plants and firms in any industry with the most efficient scales will indicate whether plants and firms are of efficient size, or whether or not the existing pattern of concentration is consistent with reasonable efficiency. Have plant and firm concentration proceeded too far, farther than necessary, just far enough or not far enough–from the standpoint of productive efficiency? A knowledge of scale curves is prerequisite to an answer.

Although information on the relation of efficiency to scale thus has some importance, relatively little has been done to develop this knowledge through empirical research; economists have relied mainly upon a priori speculations and qualitative generalizations of the broadest sort. A popular American view is that economies of large-scale plant do exist–and that the efficiency of plants as large as are built may be conceded–but that further economies of large multiplant firms do not exist, or if they do, are strictly pecuniary in character and hence not to be sought or justified as a matter of social policy.[3] At the extreme it is

[1]See J. S. Bain, "Conditions of Entry and the Emergence of Monopoly," *Monopoly and Competition and Their Regulation,* E. H. Chamberlin, ed., London, 1954, for a development of this theory (Ch. 6, this book).

[2]But the absolute capital requirement for efficiency need not, as we move from one industry to another, be systematically related to the proportion of industry output needed for efficiency.

[3]See, e.g., TNEC Monograph No. 13, *Relative Efficiency of Large, Medium-sized, and Small Business,* Washington, 1941, pp. 95-139. It may be noted that the income-

argued that increasing the size of the firm beyond that of an efficient plant does not normally lower costs at all, so that the scale curve is approximately horizontal for some distance beyond this point. The dominant British view, expressed by such writers as Steindl, Florence, and E. A. G. Robinson, gives more credence to the alleged economies of large-scale firms. Both schools rely upon qualitative and substantially untested generalizations about productive and commercial techniques which supposedly determine the response of production costs to variations in the scale of plant or firm. Yet in spite of the extremely sketchy nature of this sort of knowledge, it is common to presume, for instance, that there are numerous examples of each of two sorts of oligopolistic industries—those where scale economies encourage a high concentration, and those where such economies do not but something else does.[4]

Direct empirical investigation has not added much to our knowledge of scale curves. The principal studies employing accounting cost data are found in TNEC Monograph No. 13, and in later work by J. M. Blair,[5] of the Federal Trade Commission. Unfortunately the industries studied have been so few, the periods of time reviewed so remote and brief, and the use and interpretation of the statistical data in most instances so open to question that no reliable generalization regarding scale curves can be drawn from this body of material. There is more available in the way of profit-rate data for firms of various sizes, but here the unsupported assumptions which are normally necessary to argue from higher profits to lower costs are so numerous as to vitiate any attempt to infer scale curves from profit rates. Somewhat more satisfactory information has been developed, for a very few industries only, through "engineering" estimates of the scale curve for plant or firm. But in general our information is such that we are ill-prepared to say much about actual scale curves and their implications.

SCOPE OF THE PRESENT STUDY

In the course of a recent general study of condition of entry to American manufacturing industries,[6] it has been possible to develop some further data on economies of scale therein. The portion of this information presented here concerns, for each of twenty selected manufacturing industries: (1) the relationship of the output capacity of a plant of lowest-cost size to the output capacity of the industry, together with the shape of the plant scale curve at

---

distribution effects of strictly pecuniary economies may not be inconsequential in many settings.

[4]See, e.g., William Fellner's "Case 1-a," "Case 1-b," and "Case 2" oligopolies, in his *Competition Among the Few,* New York, 1949, pp. 44ff.

[5]See, e.g., "Technology and Size," *American Economic Review,* Proceedings, XXXVIII, May 1948, pp. 121-152, and "Relation between Size and Efficiency in Business," *Review of Economics and Statistics,* XXIV, August 1942, pp. 125-135.

[6]I wish to acknowledge the generous assistance provided for this study since 1951 by the Merrill Foundation for the Advancement of Financial Knowledge, through a grant made to the Research Group on the Monopoly Problem at Harvard University, directed by Dean E. S. Mason. Acknowledgment is also due for the assistance in preceding years of the Bureau of Business and Economic Research, University of California, Berkeley, where essential initial background studies were undertaken.

smaller sizes; (2) the relationship of the capacity of a firm of lowest-cost size to industry capacity, and the firm scale curve at smaller capacities; and (3) the absolute amount of money capital required to establish an optimal plant and an optimal firm as of the current decade.

These data have been developed almost entirely from managerial or "engineering" estimates supplied by certain firms in the industries involved; precisely, they reflect estimates of scale economies and capital requirements which were prepared, in response to detailed prearranged questioning, either by or at the direction of high-level executives in these firms. The general procedure for securing such data included: (1) a lengthy preliminary survey of each of the twenty industries, based on available monographs, documents, and other published and unpublished secondary materials; (2) the subsequent preparation for each industry of a separate, special, and rather lengthy series of questions designed to elicit certain information having bearing on the condition of entry; (3) securing, after explaining the project involved and assuring confidentiality of replies, an advance offer of cooperation in answering these questions from executives in a large number of firms; (4) actual submission of the questions, followed (except in those cases where cooperation was subsequently withdrawn) by obtaining answers, in writing or orally or both. The method used thus involved neither shot-gun dissemination of an all-purpose questionnaire nor postprandial armchair quizzes, but rather a more or less hand-tooled questionnaire procedure in the case of each of twenty industries.

The questions submitted relative to scale economies in each industry were designed in general to elicit information concerning the minimal plant size requisite for lowest unit costs and the shape of the plant scale curve at smaller sizes, the same information for the firm, and the capital required to establish a plant and a firm of most efficient size. Direct and (with exceptions to be noted below) explicit answers to these questions were normally secured. In many cases, there was abundant evidence in the length and documentation of replies of a careful estimating procedure; in some, figures submitted were frankly characterized as unsubstantiated armchair guesses, though in most of these the respondents were very well qualified to guess. By and large, the writer is inclined to feel, on the basis of checks against other sources and of comparisons of different and independent replies to the same questions, that this is generally a fairly reliable body of data, in which the bulk of individual industry estimates are likely to be fairly accurate. The data have the advantage, so far as they are reliable, of reflecting "engineering" estimates in the sense that they represent expert ex ante predictions of the net relations of cost to scale, rather than an ex post comparison of gross cost results at different achieved outputs. Thus they refer in general directly to scale curves as understood in economic theory.[7]

[7]The general time reference of all estimates is the period 1950 to 1952. From two to five such estimates were received in each of the twenty industries in question. Other sources of data which were available for some industries—such as comparisons of accounting costs or the personal estimates of authors of industry studies—have been deliberately neglected here in order to give a more uniform consistency to the data presented. The only other data presented here, and these largely for expository purposes, are plant and firm concentration

The twenty manufacturing industries studied may be designated as those producing cigarettes, soap, distilled liquor, shoes, canned fruits and vegetables, meat products, passenger automobiles, fountain pens, typewriters, flour, rubber tires and tubes, refined petroleum products, farm machinery, tractors,[8] steel, copper, cement, gypsum products, rayon, and metal containers. The sample was obviously not drawn at random. It was selected to obtain a maximum possible diversity of industry types consistent with the availability of data, but the fact that data have been more frequently developed for large and for highly concentrated industries than for others has resulted in some systematic differences between the sample and the whole population of manufacturing industries.

The following characteristics of the sample deserve brief note: First, it features large industries, with fifteen of the twenty having value products above a half billion in 1947. Whereas it includes only a little over 4 per cent of the total number (452) of manufacturing industries in 1947, it accounts for about 20 per cent of the value product of all manufacture in 1947.[9] Second, it contains a substantially larger proportion of moderately and highly concentrated manufacturing industries than the total population. Nine industries of the sample had 75 per cent or more of value product controlled by four firms, three had 50 to 75 per cent so controlled, eight had from 25 to 50 per cent, and none less than 25 per cent controlled by four firms.[10] In the total population of manufacturing industries, the corresponding numbers in the four concentration classes were 47, 103, 164, and 138. This bias must be recognized in interpreting findings.

Otherwise, the sample is fairly representative. Eight industries are classed as making consumer goods, eight producer goods, and four goods bought by both producer and consumers. The outputs of eight are nondurable in use, whereas twelve are durable or semidurable. As to type of technique or process, five industries may be classified as engaged in processing farm products and four minerals, three as chemical industries, five as manufacturing or assembling mechanical devices, and three as in miscellaneous fabrication.[11]

---

data prepared from the 1947 Census of Manufactures. Since the engineering estimates which supply the bulk of our data were generally secured under guarantees of secrecy as to source, no acknowledgments or references to source can be supplied.

[8]For present purposes only we follow the Census in the dubious experiment of segregating tractors from other farm machinery.

[9]The total population of industries described, as well as all data on value products and on concentration by firms, is derived (except as otherwise noted) from the 1947 Census of Manufactures, and in particular from a special analysis of concentration prepared from this Census and published as an appendix in *Hearings, Subcommittee on Study of Monopoly Power, Committee on Judiciary, H. R., 81st Cong., Serial 14, Part 2-B.*

[10]In three of the twenty cases, value added rather than value product figures were used by the Census in calculating concentration. For automobiles, registration rather than Census figures are followed in describing concentration, in both the sample and the total population, because of deficiencies in Census data.

[11]One further characteristic of the sample may be noted–Census industries have been selected which correspond fairly well to "theoretical" industries, or for which industry concentration as computed tends to reflect closely the relevant theoretical concentration of corresponding or component theoretical industries. This matter is discussed at length in J. S. Bain, "Relation of Profit Rate to Industry Concentration," *Quarterly Journal of Economics,* LXV, Aug. 1951, 297-304 (Ch. 4, this book).

OPTIMAL PLANT SIZE AND PLANT CONCENTRATION

Our first question concerns the shape and position of the plant scale curve (relating unit costs of production to the size of the individual factory or plant) in each of the twenty industries, and the apparent consequences of economies of large plants for entry and for seller concentration. We are interested initially in the scale curve reflecting the relation of production cost to the output or capacity of the plant *when the latter are expressed as percentages of the total output or rated capacity supplying the market to be supplied by the plant.* When output or capacity is expressed in these percentage terms, what is the lowest-cost or "optimal" size of plant and what is the shape of the plant scale curve at smaller sizes?

An initial clue to the potential importance of economies of large plants is supplied by certain data on plant size assembled in the 1947 Census of Manufactures. This Census shows for each of many industries the number of plants in each of several size-classes (size being measured by number of employees), and also the proportion of Census industry employment and of total industry "value added" accounted for by each size-class of plants. From these data[12] certain inferences can be drawn about the sizes of existing plants. For exploratory purposes here I have tried to develop from them some upper-limit estimates of the plant sizes requisite for greatest efficiency in the sample industries, by computing first the average size of plants in the largest size-class in each industry (expressed here as the percentage supplied per plant of the total value added of the Census industry), and second the maximum possible average size (similarly expressed) of the largest four plants in the industry.[13] If we neglect such obvious limitations as those of using value-added data, these estimates may be considered maximum percentages of the national industry outputs requisite for efficiency, on the grounds that in nearly every case we refer to the average size of a few of the largest plants actually built, and that the firms operating them were not restricted from building them to optimal scale. That is, they are generally multiplant firms which could bring a single plant to optimal scale before adding another, if indeed they did not in some cases duplicate optimal technical units on a single location.

The results of these estimating procedures are as follows: Eighteen industries were examined (automobiles and copper being eliminated because of gross deficiencies in Census data); for the eighteen the number of plants in the largest

[12]The data were previously used by the Federal Trade Commission for its study *The Divergence between Plant and Company Concentration, 1947.* The staff of the commission has kindly made available its tabulated calculations on plant concentration as based on the Census data.

[13]The latter figure is derived in general by attributing to all but the first four plants in the largest size class the minimum possible market share (i.e., for each the mean share of plants in the second size class) and by dividing the remainder of the total market share in the largest size class among the first four plants.

size-class lay between 3 and 15 in all but three cases; in those three it was large enough to make our estimates quite hazardous. The average share of Census industry value added supplied by plants in the largest size-class ranged from 20.1 per cent (typewriters) to 0.7 per cent (shoes), with a median at 3.8 per cent. The maximum possible average share of the largest four plants ranged from 19.1 per cent (cigarettes) to 1.7 per cent (shoes), with a median at 7.9 per cent.

The character of the data is more fully revealed in the frequency distributions in Table 8.1. The first frequency column therein (f_1) classifies industries according to the market-share interval within which the average size of plants in the largest size-class of plants falls, market share being measured by the percentage of the Census industry value-added supplied by a plant. The second frequency column (f_2) shows the same information when the plant size referred to in each industry is the maximum possible average market share of the largest four plants.

Table 8.1 Classification of Eighteen Census Industries According to Percentages of Industry Values-Added Supplied by the Largest Plants, 1947[a]

	Number of industries with the largest plant size in the specified percentage interval	
Percentage of census industry value added supplied by the average of the largest plants	*When "largest plant size" refers to average size of plants in largest size class of plants* (f_1)	*When "largest plant size" refers to maximum possible average size of the largest 4 plants in industry* (f_2)
0 - 2.4	6	2
2.5- 4.9	5	4
5.0- 7.4	2	3
7.5- 9.9	3	2
10.0-14.9	1	3
15.0-24.9[b]	1	4
Total	18	18

[a]From 1947 Census of Manufactures. The composition of sample is described in the text above.

[b]The highest value in this class was 20.1 per cent.

These findings, showing that in from seven to twelve of the 18 Census industries (depending on the method of estimate) the value added of the largest plants amounted to over 5 per cent apiece of total industry value added and that in from two to seven cases the figure was over 10 per cent apiece, suggest an importance for economies of large-scale plant which is substantial in some of these industries and small in others. But a detailed interpretation of the findings is not justified for several reasons. First, value added in a single year is a rather unsatisfactory measure of "scale" as that term is ordinarily understood. Second, the largest plants as identified by the Census may have resulted from building multiples of optimal technical units on single locations, and if so, the figures presented may overestimate optimal scales. Third, the data in question express the output of the plant as a percentage of the total national value added within the Census industry, whereas in fact the theoretical industry or separate market which a plant supplies may be somewhat smaller.[14] In these cases—where a Census industry is in fact made up of several theoretical industries corresponding to distinct regional markets or product lines—the "percentage-of-industry-output" derived from Census data for large plants is very likely to be below the theoretically relevant figure,[15] and revisions are in order. We thus turn at once to direct engineering estimates of optimal plant sizes.

Table 8.2 reviews the engineering estimates of the optimal scales of plants for twenty industry groups. In each case, the plant size referred to is the minimal physical production capacity of plant required for lowest production costs, this capacity being expressed as a percentage of total national capacity within the Census industry. In each case also the costs referred to are total production costs, including costs of out-shipment where the latter are strategic to the determination of optimal plant scale.

Table 8.3 summarizes the data of Table 8.2 by classifying industries according to the market-share interval in which the mean estimated size of an optimal plant falls, when size is measured as a percentage of the national industry capacity. These "engineering" data seem generally more satisfactory than those previously developed from Census figures. They reflect rational calculations rather than historical happenstance, and designed plant capacities rather than transient additions to value of output, although they still reflect percentages of the national capacities of Census industries.

It appears from them that in nine of the twenty industries an optimal plant would account for a quite small fraction of national capacity (under 2½ per cent), whereas in five others the fraction would run above 7½ per cent. In general, the industries with slight economies of scale of plant are engaged in processing of agricultural or mineral materials, whereas greater plant economies are frequently encountered in industries making mechanical devices. The engineering estimates of the importance of economies of large plant present an over-all picture for these industries not greatly different from that derived by calculating average plant sizes in the largest plant-size intervals (column f_1 of Table 8.1), but they clearly ascribe less importance to such economies than the estimates of the maximum possible average sizes of the largest four plants in each of these industries (column f_2 of Table 8.1).

Before we interpret these findings, however, two further matters must be discussed: the shapes of the plant scale curves at capacities short of the estimated optima, and the revisions in the estimates of optima which are needed if the division of Census industries into separate regions or product lines is recognized.

As to the shapes of plant cost curves at capacities short of the estimated optima, relatively fragmentary information has been received. In four industries

[14]It may also conceivably be larger, as in the case where imports are omitted from Census data or where the Census industry is too narrowly defined, but these contingencies are not realized in any important degree in this sample.

[15]It will be if the plant specializes as to area or product line.

Table 8.2 Proportions of National Industry Capacity Contained in Single Plants of Most Efficient Scale, for 20 Industries, per Engineering Estimates circa 1951

Industry	*Percentage of national industry capacity contained in one plant of minimal efficient scale*	*Industry*	*Percentage of national industry capacity contained in one plant of minimal efficient scale*
Flour milling	1/10 to 1/2	Rubber tires and tubes[g]	3
Shoes[a]	1/7 to 1/2	Rayon[h]	4 to 6
Canned fruits and vegetables	1/4 to 1/2	Soap[i]	4 to 6
Cement	4/5 to 1		
	4/5 to 1	Farm machines, ex tractors[j]	4 to 6
Distilled liquors[b]	1 1/4 to 1 3/4	Cigarettes	5 to 6
Petroleum refining[c]	1 3/4	Automobiles[k]	5 to 10
Steel[d]	1 to 2 1/2	Fountain pens[l]	5 to 10
Metal containers	1/2 to 3	Copper[m]	10
Meat packing:[e]		Tractors	10 to 15
fresh	1/50 to 1/5		
diversified	2 to 2 1/2		
Gypsum products[f]	2 1/2 to 3	Typewriters	10 to 30

[a]Refers to shoes other than rubber.
[b]Capacity refers to total excluding brandy. Costs refer explicitly to 4-year whiskey, packaged but ex tax.
[c]Optimal balanced integration of successive processes assumed. Outshipment largely by water assumed; optimal scale may be smaller with scattered market and land shipment.
[d]Refers to fully integrated operation producing flat rolled products.
[e]Percentages are of total nonfarm slaughter; diversified operation includes curing, processing, etc.
[f]Combined plasterboard and plaster production assumed.
[g]Purchase of materials at a constant price assumed; production of a wide variety of sizes assumed.
[h]Refers to plant producing both yarn and fibre.
[i]Includes household detergents.
[j]Refers primarily to complex farm machines.
[k]Plant includes integrated facilities for production of components as economical. Final assembly alone—1 to 3 per cent.
[l]Includes conventional pens and ballpoints.
[m]Assumes electrolytic refining.

the plant scale curve appears to be horizontal back to the smallest size considered, or ¼ per cent of national industry output; these are flour, shoes, canned fruits and vegetables, and "fresh" meat packing. In ten cases—steel, metal containers, diversified meat packing, gypsum products, farm machinery, automobiles, fountain pens, copper, tractors, and typewriters—quantitative estimates of the shapes of the plant cost curves are not available, although in some cases (e.g., diversified meat packing and metal containers) it is suggested that substantially smaller than optimal plants would entail only slightly higher costs, whereas in some others (e.g., typewriters, automobiles, and tractors) a distinct rise in costs is suggested at half the optimal plant scale. For the seven remaining industries, the estimated relation of production cost to plant scale is shown in Table 8.4, where costs of 100 represent the lowest attainable costs.

Table 8.3 Classification of Twenty Industries According to Percentages of National Industry Capacities Contained in Single Plants of Most Efficient Scale (from Table 8.2)

Percentage of national industry capacity contained in a plant of optimal scale	*Number of industries with optimal scale plant (per mean estimate) in the specified percentage interval* (f_3)
0- 2.4	9
2.5- 4.9	2
5.0- 7.4	4
7.5- 9.9	2
10.0-14.9	2
15.0-24.9	1
Total	20

A mixed picture again emerges. In some cases (liquor and cigarettes, for example) the rise of production costs at suboptimal scales is evidently quite small; in others (soap, petroleum refining, tires and tubes) it is moderate but by no means negligible; in some—e.g., rayon and cement—the rise is great.[16] One might hazard the guess that in from a half to two-thirds of all the industries sampled the upturn of the plant scale curve at suboptimal scales is such as to discourage very much smaller operations unless there are forces counterbalancing production cost disadvantages. In the other one-third to a half of cases, a wide variety of plant sizes might prosper indefinitely in only slightly imperfect markets.

Table 8.4 Relation of Production Cost to Plant Scale in Seven Industries

	Percentages of national industry capacity in one plant					
	5%	*2½%*	*1%*	*½%*	*¼%*	
Cement	100	100	100	115	130	Relative costs of production
Distilled liquor	100	100	100.5	101	102	
Petroleum refining	100	100	102	104	107	
Tires and tubes	100	100.3	103	104	105.5	
Rayon	100	107	125	Very high		
Soap	100	103	105	Above 105		
Cigarettes	100	101	102	Above 102		

The findings of Tables 8.2 and 8.3 however—reflecting as they do the percentages of national Census industry capacities supplied by single plants—can hardly be taken at face value so long as the suspicion remains that many Census industries may be broken into several separate and largely noncompeting

[16]It will be noted that the industries with the highest degree of plant concentration are generally those on which it has been most difficult to secure quantitative estimates of the shape of the scale curve. In general, our information on plant scales seems sketchier and perhaps less reliable at this end of the sample.

regional or product submarkets and that a plant may specialize in only one such submarket. In these cases the relevant measure of plant size must be the proportion of the capacity supplying a submarket which is provided by an otpimal plant, and this proportion will be larger than the proportion of national capacity provided by the same plant.

In eleven of the twenty cases listed in Table 8.2, a revision of plant-size figures is in order because of the apparent division of the national market into distinct submarkets, coupled with plant specialization among them. In seven of these cases—flour, cement, petroleum refining, steel, metal containers, meat packing, and gypsum products—the important segmentation of markets is geographical in character; national markets are broken into regions, and a single plant will mainly supply only one region. In the other four cases—shoes, canned fruits and vegetables, automobiles, and fountain pens—markets are divided to a significant extent among distinct product lines. In all cases, the relevant measure of plant size is the percentage it may account for of the total capacity supplying any submarket it may supply.

The industries in which market segmentation is important are predominantly those for which the percentages of national industry capacities represented by single plants are quite small. The data for nine of the first ten industries in Table 8.2 require revision because of market segmentation, and only two for which revision is required lie in the range of high plant concentration nationally. Where technology does not give some importance to plant economies in industries of our sample, geography and product specialization (by plants) apparently do. Correspondingly, revised plant-size data showing percentages of individual submarket capacities will differ markedly from those in Tables 8.2 and 8.3.

To make the revision mentioned, the optimal plant capacity for each of the eleven industries involved has been restated first as a percentage of the capacity supplying the largest submarket identified, and second as a percentage of capacity supplying the smallest of the major submarkets identified. For example, four major regional markets were identified in the petroleum refining industry. The proportion of national capacity supplied by a single optimal refinery had been estimated at 1¾ per cent (Table 8.2); the corresponding percentages for the largest and smallest of the four major regional markets were 3 1/3 per cent and 11½ per cent. In the fountain pen industry the proportion of aggregate national capacity supplied by an optimal plant was estimated at from 5 to 10 per cent. Dividing the market into high-price or gift pens and low-price pens including ballpoints (and recognizing differences in techniques for producing the two lines) the corresponding percentages become 25 to 33 1/3 per cent and 10 to 12½ per cent.

When these revisions have been made for the eleven industries, and the results combined with the unrevised data for the remaining nine, we are prepared to present two frequency distributions parallel to that in Table 8.3 above. They classify industries according to the percentage of market capacity provided by an optimal plant, in the first case (column f_4 of Table 8.5) when the capacities of optimal plants in the eleven revised industries are expressed as percentages of the

Table 8.5 Classification of Twenty Industries[a] by Percentages of Individual Market Capacities Contained in a Single Plant of Most Efficient Scale

Percentage of individual market capacity contained in a plant of optimal scale	*Number of Industries with optimal plant scale in the specified percentage interval*		
	Where percentage is that of the total capacity supplying the largest recognized submarket (f_4)	*Where percentage is that of the total capacity supplying the largest recognized submarket* (f_5)	*Where percentage is that of the total capacity supplying the national market* (f_2 *from Table 8.3*)
0- 2.4	4	2	9
2.5- 4.9	5	2	2
5.0- 7.4	5	4	4
7.5- 9.9	0	1	2
10.0-14.9	5	3	2
15.0-19.9	0	2	0
20.0-24.9	1	2	1
25.0-29.9	0	2	0
30.0-34.9	0	1	0
35.0-40.0	0	1	0
Total	20	20	20

[a]The meat packing industry is considered for purposes of this table as only involving so-called *fresh* meat packing.

total capacities supplying the largest submarkets in their industries, and in the second (column f_5) when optimal capacities in the eleven industries are expressed as percentages of the total capacities supplying the smallest major submarkets identified. The last column in Table 8.5 repeats column f_3 from Table 8.3 for purposes of comparison.

Subjective judgments have inescapably influenced the content of columns f_4 and f_5, particularly in the identification of regions, the decision as to what is a "major" region or product line, and the decision as to whether market segmentation is significant, but we have tried to follow available information and industry practice systematically. If there is a bias, it is in the direction of defining areas and product lines quite broadly, of considering only a few dominant areas for analysis, and of recognizing segmentation only if there is strong evidence supporting the recognition.

Interpreting Table 8.5 with appropriate reference to the earlier discussion of the shapes of plant scale curves, we may emphasize the following conclusions about the importance of economies of large-scale plants within the industries of our sample. First, if the reference is to the largest submarkets of industries with segmented markets (plus the national markets of those with unsegmented markets), then in nine of the twenty cases an optimal plant would supply less than 5 per cent of its market, and in five additional cases less than 7½ per cent. If this is true and if, further, the plant-scale curve is usually fairly flat for a moderate range of suboptimal scales, then in many of these fourteen cases the scale requirements for an optimal plant should not provide a serious deterrent to entry. A firm constructing one reasonably efficient plant should not ordinarily induce serious repercussions from established firms in its market.

On the other hand in six cases'–gypsum products, automobiles, typewriters, fountain pens, tractors, and copper–the proportion of the total capacity supplying either the national market or the largest submarket which is provided by a single optimal plant runs from 10 to 25 per cent. Precise data are largely lacking on the shapes of scale curves in these industries, but if they are much inclined upward at suboptimal scales (as is suggested qualitatively in several cases) then the economies of large plant should provide a very significant deterrent to entry to the markets in question. Further, a substantial degree of oligopolistic concentration by firms might easily be justified by the pursuit of plant economies alone. The substantial diversity of situations among industries of moderate to high concentration deserves considerable emphasis.

The picture changes markedly if our attention shifts in the case of the eleven segmented industries from the largest to the smallest major submarkets. Now we find that in eleven of the twenty cases (rather than six) the proportion of the relevant market capacity supplied by an optimal plant exceeds 10 per cent, and in six cases it exceeds 20 per cent. Plant economies sufficient to impede entry very seriously are potentially present in half or more of the cases, and high plant and firm concentration is encouraged by technology. The importance of plant economies thus potentially bulks large indeed in the smaller regional submarkets and the smaller product lines, whereas it is evidently less in the major submarkets and frequently so in the industries with relatively unsegmented national markets.

OPTIMAL FIRM SIZE AND FIRM CONCENTRATION

The extent to which further economies of large scale are realized if firms grow beyond the size of a single optimal plant has been a subject of controversy among economists. If a distinction is drawn between "production cost" and other advantages of scale–so that sales promotion, price-raising, and similar advantages of big firms are properly distinguished from cost-savings in production and distribution–there is no general agreement among economists as to whether or to what extent the multiplant firm is more economical.[17] It thus may come as no surprise that business executives questioned on the same matter with regard to our samples of industries evidenced a similar diversity of mind. Very distinct differences of opinion relative to the existence or importance of economies of multiplant firms were frequently encountered in the same industry, and in a pattern not satisfactorily explicable in general by the hypothesis that the individual would claim maximum economies for his own size of firm. Any findings presented here on estimates of economies of large-scale firm should thus be viewed as extremely tentative.

[17]This disagreement is, as noted above, complicated further by difference of opinion as to whether the disputed economies are real or strictly pecuniary in character.

Whatever the ostensible importance of economies of the multiplant firm, exploitation of them will not *necessarily* require the multiplant firm to control a larger proportion of any submarket than is needed for one optimal plant. In those instances where national markets are segmented regionally or by product lines, the multiplant firm *may* realize its economies while operating only one plant in each submarket. Then concentration by firms in individual submarkets is not further encouraged and entry is not further impeded[18] by economies of the multiplant firm. An optimal cement plant may supply about 1 per cent of national capacity, or percentages of regional capacity ranging very roughly from 5 to 30 per cent in eleven regional submarkets. The fact that a multiplant cement firm could secure lower costs than a single-plant firm by operating one optimal plant in each of the eleven regions—thus accounting for 11 per cent of national capacity—would not imply that it need have a higher proportion of capacity in any one region than a single-plant firm of optimal size. Except for an increase in absolute capital requirements, the assumed economies of the multi-plant firm would not encourage regional market concentration or impede entry.

Suppose on the other hand that there are economies of multiplant firms which are to be realized through operating two or more optimal-size plants either in a single submarket or in a single unsegmented national market. This will evidently encourage a concentration by firms in the relevant submarket or national market greater than that encouraged by plant economies alone, and will further impede entry. If a single plant of most efficient size would supply 5 per cent of the relatively unsegmented national cigarette market, whereas a single firm operating three such plants could lower costs of production and distribution perceptibly, economies of the multiplant firm would favor greater effective concentration and provide further deterrents to entry to the cigarette industry.

Findings relative to the economies of multiplant firms, together with certain related data, are presented in Table 8.6. The second column therein repeats the estimates of percentages of national Census industry capacities required for optimal plants, from Table 8.2. The third column indicates the estimated extent of economies of multiplant firms (i.e., firms of sizes beyond those of single optimal plants), costs of distribution but not of sales promotion being included. The fourth column indicates the percentages of national industry capacities required for firms with lowest production plus distribution costs, while the final column shows the average percentage per firm of the national market supplied by the first four firms in 1947. The last provides a measure of actual concentration by firms. The estimates in question are entirely those of executives queried in connection with the investigation underlying this study.

The data presented in Table 8.6 shed light on two questions: (1) to what extent do the economies of the multiplant firm tend to enhance concentration and impede entry, and (2) to what extent is the existing concentration by firms greater than required for exploitation of economies of large plants and of large firms?

[18]Except for the increase of absolute capital requirements.

Table 8.6 The Extent of Estimated Economies of Multiplant Firms in 20 Manufacturing Industries

Industry	Percentage of national industry capacity contained in one optimal plant	Estimated extent of multiplant economies (as a percentage of total cost)	Percentage of national industry capacity contained in one optimal firm	Average percentage share of the national market of first 4 firms in 1947[a]
Group 1:				
Canned fruits and vegetables	1/4 to 1/2	None	–	6.6
Petroleum refining	1 3/4	None	–	9.3
Meat packing:[b]				
Fresh	1/50 to 1/5	None	–	–
Diversified	2 to 2 1/2	None	–	10.3[c]
Fountain pens	5 to 10	None	–	14.4
Copper	10	None	–	23.1[d]
Typewriters	10 to 30	None	–	19.9
Group 2:				
Flour	1/10 to 1/2	No estimate	–	7.3
Distilled liquor	1 1/4 to 1 3/4	No estimate	–	18.7
Metal containers	1/2 to 3	No estimate	–	19.5
Tires and tubes	3	No estimate	–	19.2
Rayon	4 to 6	No estimate	–	19.6
Farm machines, ex tractors	4 to 6	No estimate	–	9.0
Automobiles	5 to 10	No estimate	–	22.5[e]
Tractors	10 to 15	No estimate	–	16.8
Group 3:				
Shoes	1/7 to 1/2	Small, or 2 to 4	1/2 to 2 1/2	7.0
Cement	4/5 to 1	Small, or 2 to 3	2 to 10	7.4
Steel	1 to 2 1/2	2 to 5	2 to 20	11.2[c]
Gypsum products	2 1/2 to 3	Small	27 to 33	21.2
Soap	4 to 6	1/2 to 1	8 to 15	19.8
Cigarettes	5 to 6	Slight	15 to 20	22.6

[a]Market shares are average percentages of 1947 national values of shipments unless otherwise indicated.

[b]Plant percentages refer to total of nonfarm slaughter, firm percentages to wholesale fresh meat packing only.

[c]Expresses average percentage of total value added rather than value of shipments.

[d]Expresses average percentage of electrolytic plus other national copper refining capacity, 1947.

[e]Expresses approximate average percentage of total 1951 passenger car registrations.

Concerning the first question a varied picture appears. In eight industries (Group 2 in Table 8.6) no definite estimate could be obtained of the extent, if any, of economies of the multiplant firm. This is in spite of the fact that in most of these industries the degree of concentration by firms substantially exceeds that requisite for exploitation of estimated economies of the large plant. In six industries (Group 1 in Table 8.6) it was the consensus that economies of the scale of firm beyond the size of a single optimal plant were either negligible or totally absent. In these cases estimated cost savings of the multiplant firm cannot justify concentration beyond that required by plant economies alone (either in submarkets or in unsegmented national markets) nor can they make entry any more difficult than it is already made by plant economies. With respect to the first four industries in the group, a multiplant firm with plants in several regions or product lines would, according to the estimates received, realize no net cost savings by virtue of this aspect of its organization. In the second three industries in this group, however, economies of the large plant alone are sufficient to support a high degree of concentration by firms and to impede entry.

In the remaining six industries (Group 3 in Table 8.6) perceptible economies were attributed to the multiplant firm. The extent of these economies is in no case huge, being characterized as slight or small in three cases and as in the two to five per cent range in the remaining three. Nevertheless, two or three percentage points on total cost can be significant in any industry if the ratio of operating profits to sales is not beyond five or ten per cent and if product differentiation and other market imperfections are not dominant. What further tendency toward concentration and what further impediment to entry would the existence of these economies imply?

The optimal multiplant firm as estimated in Group 3 of Table 8.6 includes two or three optimal plants in the soap industry, three or four in the cigarette industry, four or five in the shoe industry, and about ten in the gypsum products industry. Estimates for the steel and cement industries run all the way from one or two to ten plants per optimal firm, and the range of disagreement among authorities is wide. Applying these estimates, the proportion of national industry capacity needed for best efficiency in a multiplant firm is raised; but is the proportion of the capacity supplying any particular regional or product submarket also raised? It will not be if the efficient multiplant firm includes only one optimal plant per submarket, and it will be if it includes two or more per submarket or if the national market is unsegmented.

In Group 3 in Table 8.6 no more than one optimal plant per region is attributed to the optimal firm in cement or in steel, and the proportion of any regional market which need be supplied for efficiency is thus not increased by the incidence of economies of the multiplant firms. In the remaining four cases the conclusion is different. Soap and cigarettes have relatively unsegmented national markets, and the proportion of the market required for best efficiency is doubled, trebled, or quadrupled by the emergence of economies of the multiplant firm. In shoes the assumed specialization to a single product line of the four or five plants needed for efficiency raises the requisite firm concentration by product lines by corresponding multiples. In the gypsum industry it was evidently assumed that an optimal firm would operate several plants in each of one or more major regions. In all of the last four cases, therefore, economies of the multiplant firm encourage greater effective concentration by firms and impede entry. But in these cases (possibly excepting shoes) the economies of the large firm were characterized as slight, so that the effects just listed may be weak.

With respect to the effect of the economies of multiplant firms on concentration and on entry, these conclusions appear. In eight of twenty industries in our sample, no estimate was obtained of the extent of these economies. In two-thirds of the remaining cases, economies of the multiplant firm were held either to be absent, or to take such a form that exploitation of them would not require higher proportions of market control by the firm in any submarket. In one-third of the remaining cases, some encouragement to higher concentration by firms in submarkets was provided, but it was a small encouragement in view of the generally slight economies attributed to the large firm. Economies of the large-scale firm apparently do not represent a major force encouraging concentration or deterring entry in this sample of industries. The data on which this guess rests, however, are far from adequate.

Our second question concerns the extent to which the existing degree of concentration by firms within industries is justified by the estimated economies of large plants and firms. This is a rather complicated question, and may be broken down into three subquestions: (1) Is the existing concentration by firms for national Census industries justified by the economies of single large-scale plants? (2) If not, is the existing concentration by firms nevertheless consistent with no higher concentration within individual submarkets than is required by a single efficient plant–i.e., need there be more than one optimal plant per large firm in any one submarket? (3) In any case, to what extent is the multiplant character of large firms apparently justified by the economies of such firms?

A first approximation to answers to these questions may be made by taking the concentration figure in Column 5 of Table 8.6 as a simple and crude measure of national industry concentration by firms.[19] On the basis of this measure, the answer to the first subquestion is simple and unsurprising–concentration by firms is in every case but one greater than required by single-plant economies, and in more than half of the cases very substantially greater. Generally it is only within some of the industries with very important economies of large plant–e.g., fountain pens, copper, typewriters, autos, tractors, farm machines–that concentration by firms has not been much greater than required by single-plant economies. Even in these cases it may be two or three times as great as thus required. In the other cases concentration by firms tends to be a substantial or large multiple of that required by single-plant economies. Remembering that we are dealing in general in this sample with the more concentrated industries, it might be said in summary that nearly all of the industries tended to become moderately or highly concentrated (by firms) whether economies of the single plant were important or not.

The second subquestion is whether the existing degree of concentration by firms is consistent or inconsistent with the existence of a single optimal plant per firm in each recognized submarket. In seven of the nine cases where the national market has been considered substantially unsegmented–copper, typewriters, liquor, tires and tubes, rayon, farm machines, tractors, soap, and cigarettes–the degree of concentration by firms within a single market is greater than required by such plant economies, although in all but two of the seven cases (liquor and

[19]The average share of national industry output per firm for the first four firms obviously is smaller than the market share for the first firm, larger than that for the fourth firm, etc.

tires and tubes) it is greater by at most a multiple of three or four. This last is found probably in part because economies of the large plant seem very important in most of these industries.

In eight of the remaining eleven cases—canned goods, petroleum refining, meat packing, fountain pens, metal containers, cement, steel, and gypsum products—the degree of national concentration by firms is not grossly inconsistent with the larger firms on the average having but a single optimal plant per submarket in each of several submarkets. *(This is certainly not to deny that the largest single firms may have more than this and probably do; we refer only to the average of the largest four firms.)*

In the last three cases—flour, automobiles, and shoes—the degree of concentration by firms exceeds by a multiple of two or three that required for each of the four largest firms on the average to have an optimal plant in each submarket. In general, our showing is that in ten of twenty industries the existing degree of concentration by firms, as measured by the average size of the largest four firms, is significantly greater than required for these firms to have only one optimal plant per submarket; in the other ten cases concentration is at least roughly consistent with such a condition.

The third subquestion concerns the extent to which the existing degree of concentration by firms is justified by the exploitation of economies of multiplant firms. We will go no further with this question here than a comparison of the fourth and fifth columns of Table 8.6 will take us. In Group 1 in that table, the alleged absence of any economies of multiplant firm implies that there is no justification in terms of costs for the excess of concentration by firms over that required for single efficient plants, although in one case (typewriters) the existence of an excess is uncertain, and in four others (all but copper) it is not necessarily accompanied by accentuated concentration in individual submarkets. Here, therefore, the lack of an evident cost justification for multiplant firms raises not so much the issue of concentration in separate markets as the issue of the other advantages and disadvantages of a diversified firm operating in each of several related submarkets.

In Group 2 no estimates of multiplant economies are available; we need say no more than that in five of eight cases (excluding metal containers, farm machines, and tractors) there is a concentration by firms much greater than that required for efficient plants in each submarket, and that this requires evaluation from a cost standpoint. In only one of the industries in Group 3 (shoes) does the degree of concentration by firms seem to have clearly exceeded that required for economies of production and distribution by the large firm.

In the sample as a whole the existing degree of concentration by multiplant firms lacks a clear cost justification in perhaps thirteen of twenty cases, although in seven of these we have a simple lack of any definite estimates. In two more cases the multiplant phenomenon is not very important. Further information is needed on this matter, particularly with reference to cases in which multiplant firm organization has increased effective concentration in individual submarkets or in unsegmented national markets.

ABSOLUTE CAPITAL REQUIREMENTS AND ENTRY

The effect of scale economies on the condition of entry so far emphasized is transmitted through their influence on the share of market output which an efficient plant or firm will supply. This impact is important, but it is not proportional to the importance of scale economies measured in such terms as the absolute number of employees or the absolute size of investment required for an optimal plant or firm. This is because the proportion of a market supplied by an optimal plant or firm (which determines the degree of oligopolistic interdependence between the potential entrant and established firms) depends not only on the absolute size of the plant or firm but also on the size of the market. Thus an investment of over $200 million dollars might add only one per cent to national steel capacity, whereas an investment of $6 million might add five or ten per cent to the capacity for producing fountain pens. In addition to the effect of scale economies on entry via the proportion of the market an efficient entrant will supply, there is a distinct and not closely correlated effect via the absolute size of the efficient plant or firm, or, to choose a popular measure, via the total money investment needed to establish such a plant or firm.

To determine the importance of scale economies in establishing sufficient capital requirements to impede entry seriously, we have queried the same sources on the investment requisite for the most efficient plant or firm in the twenty industries sampled. The findings relative to capital requirements for the large plant are fairly comprehensive, and are summarized in Table 8.7. Column 2 of this table shows the estimated percentage of national industry capacity provided by one efficient plant, and Column 3 the total investment required to establish such a plant (ordinarily including working capital) as of about 1951. The industries are grouped according to the importance of scale economies from the previously emphasized percentage standpoint. The first category of industries are those in which a single efficient plant will supply no more than 5 per cent of the largest submarket or unsegmented national market; the second includes those where the corresponding percentage is 5 to 10 per cent; the third includes those where the percentage is above 10 per cent. We may thus observe the extent to which the "percentage effect" of scale economies is of the same order as their "absolute capital requirement effect."

The findings in Table 8.7 speak fairly clearly for themselves, but a few comments may be in order. First, there is no evident correlation of the absolute capital requirements for an efficient plant with the percentage of market output supplied by it. The size of the market is an erratic variable forestalling such a correlation. Second, absolute capital requirements for an efficient plant in all the manufacturing industries examined are large enough to restrict seriously the ranks of potential entrants; even 500,000 dollars, the smallest amount listed, will not be forthcoming from savings out of salary or from the winnings in a poker game.

Third, the absolute capital requirements in some cases reinforce but in other cases weaken the "percentage effect" on entry of economies of scale of plant.

Table 8.7 Estimated Absolute Capital Requirements for Plants of Estimated Most Efficient Scale, circa 1951, for 20 Industries

Industry	*Percentage of national industry capacity provided by one efficient plant (from Table 8.2)*	*Total capital required for one efficient plant*[a]
Category 1:		
Flour milling	1/10 to 1/2	$700,000 to $3,500,000
Shoes	1/7 to 1/2	$500,000 to $2,000,000
Canned fruits and vegetables	1/4 to 1/2	$2,500,000 to $3,000,000
Cement	4/5 to 1	$20,000,000 to $25,000,000
Distilled liquor	1 1/4 to 1 3/4	$30,000,000 to $42,000,000
Petroleum refining	1 3/4	$193,000,000 ex transport facilities
		$225,000,000 to $250,000,000 with transport facilities
Meat packing[b]	1/50 to 1/5	Very small
	2 to 2 1/2	$10,000,000 to $20,000,000
Tires and tubes	3	$25,000,000 to $30,000,000
Category 2:		
Steel[c]	1 to 2 1/2	$265,000,000 to $665,000,000[d]
Metal containers[c]	1/2 to 3	$5,000,000 to $20,000,000
Rayon	4 to 6	$50,000,000 to $75,000,000[e]
		$90,000,000 to $135,000,000[f]
Soap	4 to 6	$13,000,000 to $20,000,000[g]
Farm machines ex tractors	4 to 6	No estimate
Cigarettes	5 to 6	$125,000,000 to $150,000,000
Category 3:		
Gypsum products[h]	2 1/2 to 3	$5,000,000 to $6,000,000
Automobiles	5 to 10	$250,000,000 to $500,000,000
Fountain pens	5 to 10	Around $6,000,000
Copper	10	No estimate
Tractors	10 to 15	Around $125,000,000
Typewriters	10 to 30	No estimate

[a] These estimates generally exclude anticipated "shakedown losses" of new entrants, which in some cases may be large and prolonged.
[b] The two rows of estimates refer alternatively to fresh and diversified meat packing.
[c] Percentage of an efficient plant in the largest regional market may exceed 5 per cent.
[d] Excludes any investment in ore or coal.
[e] Acetate rayon.
[f] Viscose rayon.
[g] Excludes working capital.
[h] Percentage of an efficient plant in the largest regional market may exceed 10 per cent.

For each of the eight industries in Category 1 in Table 8.7, for example, the percentage of market output supplied by a single plant seems small enough to provide no serious-deterrent to entry. In three of these cases—flour milling, shoes, and canned goods[20]—the absolute capital requirements are also so small that entry may not be seriously restrained thereby. But in four others, capital requirements ranging from 10 to 42 million dollars per plant provide a greater

[20]As well as in fresh meat packing.

deterrent, and in one (petroleum refining) they impose a truly formidable barrier.

In the six industries of Category 2, where the "percentage effect" on entry of economies of scale of plant is moderate, it is strongly reinforced in four cases (possibly excepting metal containers, and farm machines, for which there is no estimate) by absolute capital requirements. The effect is very much increased in both the steel and cigarette industries. In the six industries of Category 3, where the "percentage effect" appears quite important, it is strongly reinforced in the cases of automobiles and tractors by absolute capital requirements, but in the fountain pen and gypsum industries capital requirements are relatively small. Thus a generally mixed picture regarding the dual effects of economies of large plant emerges.

The extent to which economies of multiplant firms as already noted increase the capital requirements for efficiency may be readily ascertained by comparing the findings of Table 8.6 with those of Table 8.7. Since the existence of such economies was denied in six industries, not estimated in eight others, and held to be slight in at least half the remaining six, detailed comment on this matter does not seem justified.

CONCLUSIONS

When the answer provided by empirical investigation to an initial inquiry concerning the values of certain economic data is that the values are highly irregular and variegated, and when the answer is therefore found only in a great array of numbers, any brief summarization of the findings may be difficult to make and misleading if attempted. Since this situation is encountered with respect to each of the major questions posed at the beginning of this paper, no comprehensive summary of findings will be attempted here. Certain salient conclusions may be restated briefly, however, in each case with the proviso that they may have general validity only so far as the sample of industries selected is generally representative of moderately to highly concentrated manufacturing industries in the United States.

Regarding the importance of economies of large plants, the percentage of a market supplied by one efficient plant in some cases is and in some cases is not sufficent to account for high firm concentration or to impede entry. Where it is, these economies might easily propagate high concentration and serious impediments to entry; the number of cases where it is sufficient increases as we refer to the smaller regional or product submarkets in various industries. A significant corollary of these findings is that the following popular horseback observations are apparently *not true:* that economies of scale of plant are never or almost never important in encouraging oligopoly or impeding entry, and that such economies always or almost always are important in these ways. The picture is not extreme in either direction and not simple.

The economies of large plants frequently erect formidable barriers to entry in the shape of absolute capital requirements. Moderately to very high barriers of this sort were found in all but four or five of the industries studied. The height of such barriers is not clearly correlated with percentage of the market supplied by a single plant, so that a relatively independent influence on entry is discovered.

The economies of large multiplant firms are left in doubt by this investigation. In half the cases in which definite estimates were received, such economies were felt to be negligibile or absent, whereas in most of the remainder of cases they seemed slight or small. Perhaps the frequently expressed suspicion that such economies generally are unimportant after all is supported, and perhaps we are justified in saying that we have had difficulty in accumulating convincing support for the proposition that in many industries production or distribution economies of large firms seriously encourage concentration or discourage entry.

Our reference here has of course been strictly to the effect of the size of the plant or firm on the cost of production and distribution, and thereby on entry and on concentration. Needless to say, parallel studies of other factors bearing on entry, including the effects of scale on price and on sales promotion, are required for a full evaluation of the entry problem.

Chapter Nine

Advantages of the Large Firm: Production, Distribution, and Sales Promotion

QUESTIONS AT ISSUE

Policy Issues

In recent decades, an important aspect of American industrial organization has been the existence in many industries of high seller concentration—of concentrated oligopolies wherein a very few dominant firms supply most of the output—and, concomitantly, of firms of very large absolute size. This situation has posted a number of problems for public policy, one group of which is considered here. They concern the character and extent of the advantages which large firms have over smaller ones and, derivatively, the social desirability and feasibility of measures which would require a decrease in seller concentration in industries of concentrated oligopolistic structure. To what extent in these industries do economies of large firms justify the existing degree of concentration, and to what extent could deconcentration be imposed without raising the costs of supplying goods? In view of the character of the advantages of large firms, what sorts of public policy measure, if any, would suffice to secure deconcentration efficiently and more or less permanently?

Economic Questions

In the vocabulary of economic theory, we ascertain several implied questions:

1. What are the character and extent of economies of large-scale production in various concentrated industries via large plants or multiplant firms, and how large are existing firms as compared to the minimum size required for maximum efficiency?

Reprinted from *Journal of Marketing,* 20, April 1956, pp. 336-346, courtesy of the publisher, the American Marketing Association.

2. What are the character and extent of economies of large-scale distribution of goods and services in various concentrated industries, and, again, what about the actual sizes of existing firms?

3. What are the character and extent of advantages of large-scale sales promotion, and what are their implications with reference to the policy questions posed?

Other questions are also implied, such as that regarding the relationship of scale of firm to effectiveness in propagating progress in product and technique, but the analysis is restricted here to the three just enumerated.

Development of Findings

These questions have been treated at length in a priori economic theory but on the whole inconclusively. The highly qualitative indications of the theory have done little more than to pose the essentially empirical questions involved. And economists have been slow in developing satisfactory factual answers. This paucity of essential information encouraged the author several years ago to undertake a systematic study of twenty manufacturing industries—seventeen of them either moderately or highly concentrated—emphasizing among other things the economies and other advantages of large-scale firms. The industries sampled—omitting those of rather low concentration—include those producing cigarettes, soap, distilled liquor, meat, automobiles, fountain pens, typewriters, rubber tires, petroleum products, farm machines, tractors, steel, copper, cement, gypsum products, rayon, and "tin cans." Some tentative suggestions concerning possible or probable answers to the three questions stated—restricted to concentrated manufacturing industries alone—are offered here. They consist in part of a summary report on empirical findings and in part of some ad hoc theorizing based on these findings.

ECONOMIES OF LARGE-SCALE PRODUCTION

Basic Questions

The first question concerns economies of scale in production and refers to the extent to which unit costs of production (to but not beyond the factory gate) decline as the scale of the plant or firm increases. Here, the two strategic issues in any industry are (a) what is the minimum optimal scale of the plant or firm—that is, the smallest size at which lowest cost can be attained—and (b) how rapidly do unit production costs rise as scale is made successively smaller than the minimum optimal? These questions may be asked, in turn, with respect to the scales of individual plants and of multiplant firms.

Findings

Production economies of plant scale in the seventeen moderately or highly concentrated manufacturing industries do not follow any single pattern. A first indicator of the extent of such economies is the percentage of market output which will be supplied by one plant of minimum optimal scale. Referring either to the unsegmented national market or the largest separate regional or product submarket in cases where the national market is segmented, this minimum optimal scale is estimated to run above 10 per cent of market output in six of the seventeen industries, between 5 and 7½ per cent in another six, and below 5 per cent in the remaining five. Many of the plant-scale curves, however, are apparently fairly flat so that plant scales may be reduced to one half or even one fourth of the minimum optimal while elevating unit production cost by only 2 or 3 per cent. When the shape of plant-scale curves is taken into account, the seventeen industries fall into groups as follows:

In *two,* plant-scale economies are very important, in the sense that the output of a plant of minimum optimal scale exceeds 10 per cent of the designated market output, and unit costs would be up at least moderately at one-half optimal scale.

In *five,* plant economies are moderately important in that the output of a plant of minimum optimal scale is around 4 or 5 per cent of the designated market output, and unit costs would be up moderately at one-half optimal scale.

In *six,* plant economies are unimportant, either because a plant of minimum optimal scale would supply a small percentage of market output or because plant-scale curves are almost flat back to very small scales.

In *four,* information does not permit definite classification, but in two of these important scale economies may well be present.

The extent of the advantage of large firms via large plants for production is variable among concentrated industries; there is no central tendency.

In any event, economies of plant scale are not generally sufficient to explain the existing sizes of larger firms in these industries, as they ordinarily have grown to scales much larger than those of minimum optimal plants. Some indication of this is given by expressing the average size of the first four firms in each industry as a multiple of the estimated size of one minimum optimal plant, overlooking the shape of the plant-scale curve. The number of minimum optimal plants which a firm of the average size of the first four firms could contain is:

one to two in four industries;
three to five in six industries;
seven to nine in five industries; and
twelve to seventeen in two industries.

Of course, the size of the single largest firm in an industry will, in general, be a larger multiple of the size of an optimal plant and of the fourth firm, a smaller multiple.

Deconcentration and Plant-Scale Economies

A related question is how much *deconcentration* could be imposed, or obtained without sacrificing economies of large plants. Pursuing a purely arithmetical operation with the statistics available (and overlooking many essential details, including the shape of plant-scale curves), the following appears. In thirteen of the seventeen industries, concentration is quite high—from 65 to 90 per cent of the national market is controlled by the first four firms, and the modal percentage about 80 per cent by four. For such industries on the average, deconcentration of the top four firms down to optimal one-plant firms would on the average result:

in no significant change in top-four concentration in *two* cases;
in halving the concentration (roughly to 40 per cent of the market controlled by four firms) in *two* more;
in reducing it to one third or one fourth (roughly to 20 to 25 per cent by four) in *five* more; and
in reducing it to one eighth or less (roughly to from 5 to 10 per cent by four) in another *four*.

Actually, practical deconcentration could not go quite this far without breaking up plants, since, for example, a few plants of the large firms in most industries are built to superoptimal scale. On the other hand, flat plant-scale curves in some cases would permit greater deconcentration without much loss. In general, the numbers calculated indicate—possibly with some overstatement—the general possibility of deconcentration consistent with maintaining efficient plants. If plant economies were the only consideration, very significant decreases in concentration as measured for national markets could be obtained without sacrifice of efficiency. It is worthy of note, however, that in about one third of these thirteen cases, the present multiplant development of the large firms involves specialization of plants to separate regional or product markets and that in these cases deconcentration down to one-plant firms would have a much smaller (and sometimes negligible) impact on the effective seller concentration within distinct regional or product submarkets included within national industries. In the other two thirds of cases, a stronger impact on market structure as it affects competition might be expected.

In the remaining industries where concentration runs lower, with around 30 to 50 per cent of the market being controlled by four firms, national concentration could be reduced to around 5- to 10-per cent control by the four largest firms without encountering inefficiencies of small plant, but in each case there is regional or product segmentation of the market so that the impact on concentration in individual markets would be less, though generally significant.

Deconcentration and Multiplant Economies

The question now arises whether, given the apparent insufficiency of production economies of large plants to explain existing concentration, there are nevertheless economies of large and ordinarily multiplant firms which do justify or explain this concentration. Here, economies in *production* are distinguished from those in *physical distribution* of goods; reference is made to the former now, economies in distribution being reserved for later discussion.

According to estimates developed, multiplant economies of production are probably absent or negligible in most of the seventeen industries examined and are present, though relatively small, in a minority of them. Small multiplant production economies (around 2 or 3 per cent of cost) were indicated in three of the seventeen industries examined. The economies were held to result from greater efficiency in some or all of the following: central management, accounting and financial departments, legal departments, production control, labor relations, procurement, engineering, and research and development, and financing costs. In these three cases in general, the scale held necessary for exploitation of such economies was roughly such as to justify a firm of the average size of the first four in the industry, though ordinarily not of the size of the largest firm. In these cases, according to estimates, not much deconcentration could be had without at least some sacrifices in productive efficiency. In seven of the seventeen industries, the existence of perceptible production economies to multiplant firms was more or less denied, and these included six industries in which there is actually a significant degree of multiplant development. Here, we have an as yet unexplained or unjustified degree of concentration, which could be significantly reduced without imposing inefficiencies in production. In the remaining seven cases, no definite estimates on multiplant production economies were developed, and we can only speculate as to how these seven industries (most of them with distinct multiplant developments in their larger firms) may ultimately be classified.

Our findings on multiplant production economies alter slightly our previous conclusions on the possibilities of deconcentration without production diseconomies. The list of industries in which much deconcentration would raise production costs is increased from two to five industries out of seventeen; for seven of the remaining industries, there is an undemonstrated possibility of multiplant economies in production.

ADVANTAGES OF LARGE-SCALE SALES PROMOTION

For reasons developed below, the advantages of large-scale sales promotion are considered next, saving for the last economies of scale in physical distribution.

Definition and Scope of Scale Economies in Promotion

Sales promotion here refers to activities designed to increase or maintain demand, and costs of sales promotion to the costs of these activities. Emphasis centers on sales-promotion costs borne by the manufacturing firms, directly or indirectly, whether or not the activities are carried out by personnel of the firms proper. Sales promotion and its costs tend to become important in cases where the product of the industry is readily *differentiable*—and hence in practice differentiated—in an important degree. It appears that this is the case in about ten of the seventeen concentrated industries examined. In such industries, amounts ranging from 2 or 3 up to 6 or 8 per cent of sales revenue may regularly be spent on sales promotion, mainly either for advertising or for the maintenance of exclusive distributing outlets which play a role in sales promotion.

In these industries, are there systematic advantages of large-scale sales promotion such that, by increasing the scale of its promotional activities and the cost thereof, the firm will obtain a lower promotional cost per unit of sales at a given price, a higher price relative to unit promotional cost, or both? Further, to what extent does the existence of such promotional economies explain or justify the existing scales of dominant firms?

Some relevant empirical observations with respect to the ten industries are as follows: (1) in each, there are a few large firms which hold much larger individual market shares than the other firms; (2) apparently, they maintain these market shares while obtaining either the same or higher prices with a sales-promotion expenditure per unit of sales which gives them either no disadvantage or a net advantage in per-unit revenue net of sales-promotion cost as compared to other firms; (3) thus, they have advantages (accompanying and perhaps consequent upon large-scale sales promotion) over smaller firms—reflected either in larger profitable volume with no net price disadvantage or, more frequently, in this accompanied by a net price advantage. Frequently, these advantages are those of the multiplant over the single-plant firm, although in some cases they involve comparisons between firms with optimal and suboptimal scales of plant.

Bases for Scale Economies in Promotion

There are some general institutional considerations, moreover, which suggest the distinct possibility that in some sense large-scale sales promotion will tend to be more effective than smaller-scale promotion. First, it may be that advertising is most effectively conducted through national media and that an increasing degree of saturation of these media will, up to a point, yield better results per advertising dollar. Second, sales promotion is frequently facilitated by the establishment and (if necessary) subsidy of retail distributive and product-servicing outlets, and an increasing spatial density of these outlets over some appropriate market area may confer net sales-promotion advantages. One or both of these considerations appears to operate in each of the ten industries in question.

But whether or not, and in what sense, there are systematic functional relationships of sales-promotion outlay to sales volume or to price is a complicated question on both the theoretical and the empirical level. For example, there is no reason to suppose in theory that, if on certain assumptions there are such systematic relationships, all firms in the same industry—old and new, large and small—face the same one. Sales-promotion expenses, as they are made historically, probably alter consumer preferences in such a way that subsequent expenses by other firms will not be comparably effective. Thus, though encountering advantages of large-scale promotion, small or late-comer firms may operate on inferior functional relations such, for example, that at every commonly attained sales volume their unit costs of sales promotion are higher than those of the larger, established firms. Further, the net relation for a firm of sales-promotion outlay to volume or price is not an easy thing to define in oligopolistic industries, since some sort of assumption about the reactions of rivals to increased promotional cost and volume must underlie the definition. The only evident net relation would be of a ceteris paribus variety, assuming no retaliatory reaction by rivals. (The validity of this assumption in practice might go a long way to explaining why small or new-entrant firms may be deterred from exploiting economies of large-scale promotion, with other economies of scale, by reaching for larger market shares.) Finally, there is the possibility that, although the large firms in a sense enjoy favored promotional-cost positions because they are already big—or perhaps more fundamentally because they have historically secured absolutely preferred positions in consumer preference patterns—smaller or new-entrant firms may encounter either no economies or even diseconomies of large-scale promotion in attempting to attain comparable size.

How far does the evidence carry us in selecting among theoretical alternatives beyond indicating that large, established firms can typically maintain their dominant positions on either equal or favored terms as compared to small firms concerned with maintaining or extending their positions? Not very far. But the weight of assorted evidence tentatively favors the notion that small firms would be more likely to encounter economies rather than diseconomies of extended sales promotion if only they would not thereby induce competitive reactions from their large rivals—and this perhaps especially where development of large, exclusive distribution networks is a strategic phase of sales-promotion strategy. But reactions would probably be induced, and even if they were not, the smaller firms would probably exploit inferior functional relationships of promotional costs to the results thereof. As to how much the scales of large, established firms could be reduced without raising the costs of maintaining their reduced market shares—either with unchanged outlays by rivals or because nonprice rivalry was stepped up with lowered concentration—we have no pertinent information.

Concentration, Promotion, and Production Economies

Without theorizing further, let us pose two policy-oriented questions and attempt to answer them to the extent that our very tentative findings permit:

1. Does the existing degree of concentration in these ten product-differentiated industries permit and is it essential to a lowering of sales-promotional costs?

Given the history of product differentiation and given the continuation of restricted efforts by sellers to differentiate their products, large firms in these industries have and probably will continue to have a going promotional advantage. This advantage is sometimes reflected in lower unit monetary and real costs of conducting promotional efforts; it is more frequently reflected either in price premia with the same or higher promotional costs or in larger market shares with equivalent promotional costs. Some sort of virtual social advantage is apparent in the former cases, but it is not generally apparent in the latter.

The really relevant question in either event, however, is what sort of change in unit promotional costs a deconcentration involving splitting up of larger firms would entail. If we assume the continuation of unrestricted sales-promotional efforts after deconcentration, the answer is that we don't know, though increased promotional costs due to diseconomies of smaller-scale promotion and to increased nonprice rivalry are a distinct possibility and thus a hazard.

If we were to assume a fundamental and effective attack on the bases of existing product-preference patterns—large-scale national advertising and distributive integration or quasi-integration—then lower promotional costs might be had either with or without deconcentration, but deconcentration probably would not raise promotional costs much. Further, market forces alone might then induce deconcentration. With unrestricted promotional effort, as at present, the pattern of promotional advantages of large firms supports and perpetuates high concentration even in the face of substantial growth of markets; this probably would not be so in an important degree if the bases of product differentiation were altered. In general, in these product-differentiated oligopolies, an effective and economical deconcentration policy would probably require some fundamental attack on the bases of contemporary product differentiation and sales promotion.

2. Is the current exploitation of apparent advantages of large-scale sales promotion essential to the realization of economies of large-scale production? That is, would lower concentration—perhaps induced by competition in the absence of these advantages—give us firms of inefficiently small scale from the standpoint of production?

This is an old chestnut, somewhat bruised by careless handling. Among the handlers are those who have concluded that, because in abstract theory very large-scales sales promotion up to some point *could be* essential to exploiting large-scale production economies, therefore in fact it was—even to the point of justifying existing degrees of concentration in highly concentrated, product-differentiated industries.

For one answer to this question, it is sufficient to refer to findings on the extent of production economies. In eight of the ten industries in question, the average size of the first four firms (all involving multiplant scales) is substantially greater than would be required to exploit all evident production economies of large plant or of multiplant firms. Therefore, deconcentration consequent upon an inability to exploit so effectively advantages of large-scale sales promotion could proceed a significant distance without making production less efficient than it is. Advantages of large-scale sales promotion and related phenomena have enabled the dominant firms in these industries to become on the average a good deal bigger than productive efficiency probably requires. Whether or not a particular revision in the opportunities for product promotion would tend to lead to *too much* deconcentration cannot be answered in simple terms; it would depend on the nature of the revision and on effects of it which are not realistically predictable.

In two of the ten industries–both with large optimal plant scales from the standpoint of production–any substantial deconcentration would probably impose diseconomies in production, and it is quite possible that the exploitation of existing promotional economies facilitates the maintenance of an efficient degree of concentration in production. In these cases, any partial tampering with the bases of sales promotion could have adverse results. In general, it is not consistent with the facts to paint all industry with one brush.

For another answer, it is reasonably clear that, with the substantial elimination of product differentiation and sales promotion, there would be no exceptional intrinsic barriers within competitive processes to the attainment of an efficient degree of concentration in production. This can be demonstrated in theory; that it works out in fact is suggested by the finding that in the seven industries of our sample in which product differentiation is of slight or negligible importance, the incidence of inefficient plant and firm scales is on the average proportionally about the same as in the industries with strong product differentiation. It is conceivable, of course, that we might discover or impose some peculiar pattern of restricted product differentiation which conduced to productive inefficiency.

ADVANTAGES OF LARGE-SCALE DISTRIBUTION

Have advantages of the large firm been fully covered? One possibility has been reserved–advantages of the large firm in physical distribution, including outshipment freight costs, handling, order taking and filling, storage, administration of distribution functions, etc. Do large firms have such advantages? And do such advantages extend so that a firm can realize them more fully by growing to a size greater than that of one plant of minimum optimal size from the standpoint of production?

Types of Physical Distribution Economies

In general, it appears that there are three main sorts of physical distribution economies. One might be referred to as *central distribution economies,* reflecting primarily economies realized in conducting a larger distribution operation from a single plant. These will reflect economies of mass or bulk in transactions–handling, shipping, and so forth, from the plant–offset in some degree by diseconomies of rising average costs of outshipment freight as volume expands and more distant customers are reached. They will result in some distributional optimum scale for the plant. It is conceivable, though not necessary, that these central distribution economies of the plant will be reinforced by further central economies of the multiplant firm, resulting in the main from more efficient administration of central distribution functions of plants.

A second might be referred to as *nodal distribution economies,* realized in the performance of distribution functions at and through particular geographical nodes—such as recognized wholesaling and retailing centers—throughout the country. These economies are roughly those of mass or bulk in the volume passing through any node.

The third sort of economy is potentially encountered only if two or more distribution nodes *must* for some reason be reached by the single firm and if the shipping cost of the product is significant. It is an economy *to the scale of firm,* reflecting a reduction in outshipment freight costs to individual nodes which must be reached, through a multiplant development involving regional dispersion of plants.

Importance of Distribution Economies

How important is each of these economies in practice? As we attempt to answer this question, we find that the industries of our sample fall into two groups. In the first group of about eight industries, it is generally true (1) either that product differentiation is unimportant or that sales promotion effort is effectively conducted on a local or regional basis, so that national sales promotion does not confer significant advantages; and (2) that the firm is able without sales-promotion disadvantage to concentrate its distribution in a single region. In these cases, neither nodal economies nor multiplant freight economies are likely to be critical. The firms need to use no greater a number of nodes than are required for a volume to exploit the central distribution economies of one plant (plus possible multiplant central distribution economies); nodal economies will increase scale requirements only if they require at single relevant nodes larger scales than central plant economies of distribution do.

In the eight industries in question, the evidence roughly and generally is (1) that relevant single-node economies do not require larger scales than central plant economies do; (2) that multiplant central economies of distribution are not significant; (3) that the central distribution economies of plants are thus critical or strategic, the optimal scales for distribution not exceeding those determined by central plant economies; and (4) that the distribution optima for plants are not greater than the production optima, so that scale and concentration requirements are not increased by the incidence of distribution. In these industries, that is, one-plant firms would tend to be efficient in both production and distribution except so far as multiplant economies of production were encountered.

This is not to deny that many of the firms in these industries do have multiplant organization and do make multinode and even nationwide distribution economical by being so organized. The point is that this multinode distribution is pretty much optional from the standpoint either of evident distribution economies or of evident sales-promotional advantages so that production-economy requirements rather fully specify what scales are needed for efficiency in any sense.

Differentiation and Nationwide Promotion

There is a second group of about eight industries, however, to which the preceding observations do not generally apply. In these industries, product differentiation and sales promotion are important, and in addition promotional effectiveness generally appears to require *nationwide promotion*—generally, through advertising via national media and also in some cases through nationwide distributive and servicing outlets. The firm is at a substantial and often overwhelming disadvantage if it attempts to promote sales locally or regionally; thus, it generally operates on a sales-promotion function presupposing nationwide promotional effort. If this is so, the firm must in general match its nationwide promotional effort with multinode distribution over a wide area, dispersing its output among many nodes. And if that is so, both nodal economies and multiplant freight economies in reaching many nodes definitely affect the determination of the most efficient scale and organization of the firm. For maximum efficiency (presupposing multinodal or nationwide distribution), the firm requires something like a total scale for production at least equal to the aggregate of the minimum optimal scales for distribution at all nodes to be reached. In addition, it requires such a geographical dispersion of plants as will minimize total outshipment freight plus production costs when distances, unit freight costs per unit of distance, and production economies of the plant are taken into account. Total scale requirements may exceed the sum of nodal optima if freight costs are important and production economies of individual plants require large scales. Given these requirements, it is conceivable that the optimal scale of the firm, from the standpoint of production plus distribution economies, could be quite large and could substantially exceed the optimal scale for production alone. A great deal depends, of course, on the extent of nodal economies in distribution and on the importance of freight costs.

The evidence on the importance of such scale economies of conducting nationwide distribution is far from complete. Briefly, existing multiplant scales of large firms are expressly justified on the basis of distribution economies in estimates for two of the eight industries involved, and in four others the accumulated evidence suggests that such economies are probably present in a degree such as to justify at least a considerable excess of firm scale over that of single plant which is optimal for purposes of production. But in none of these cases can we state definitely whether larger scales than attained would be still more efficient, or whether somewhat smaller scales would be just as efficient. Both possibilities are open. In the remaining two industries involved, multinodal distribution economies enter, but the apparent optimal scales for distribution do not much exceed the rather large optimal plant scales for production.

Over all, it appears possible that there is an important category of concentrated industries—those selling highly differentiated consumer goods in situations where nationwide sales promotion is the superior alternative to the firms—in which distributional economies of increased firms scale *in a sense* justify much larger scales of firm and higher degrees of concentration than production economies alone would. They may—in that sense—justify somewhat less, as much, or even more concentration than we have at present.

It is, however, a very special sense in which they do this—that is, subject to the condition that there will be unrestricted sales-promotion activity and that firms in these industries will generally find it advantageous to pursue nationwide sales-promotion policies. If we concede this, then distributional economies probably tend to justify much larger scales than production economies do. Moreover, intensive exploitation of advantages of large-scale sales promotion may then be held to be conducive to the realization of physical distributive efficiency. If we do not concede it, and suppose the alternative either of no sales promotion or of its restriction to regions or localities, then the order of distributional economies just discussed dwindles in importance toward a vanishing point, and our earlier conclusions about the concentration requirements for efficiency would probably not be seriously altered.

DECONCENTRATION AND OVER-ALL ECONOMY

Let us now return to our main policy question. All things considered, could substantial deconcentration of concentrated industries be consistent with over-all economy in production, distribution, and sales promotion? Considering production economies alone, we concluded that very much deconcentration might interfere with production economies (plant or multiplant) in five of seventeen industries, but that in the others significant deconcentration without inducing productive inefficiency was either possibly or probably feasible. Of these other twelve industries, it would appear that in six more industries selling nationally distributed consumer goods, distributive economies of very large firms may well justify existing concentration and existing multiplant scales so long as unrestricted nationwide sales promotion is presupposed. In these industries, moreover, the large firms have superior efficiency in promotion. In five of the remaining six industries (omitting one for lack of certain data), deconcentration might proceed a considerable distance without impairing either productive or distributive efficiency and, in nearly all cases, without much impairing effectiveness in sales promotion.

There is thus a sphere within concentrated industries—in our sample, a little less than one third of the industries examined—in which considerable deconcentration could probably be imposed with impunity if efficiency is the concern. There is another sphere—again, a little less than one third of industries in our sample—where production economies would probably be at least somewhat impaired by any significant degree of deconcentration and, in some cases, distributional and sales-promotional economies also. There is yet a third sphere—in our sample, over one third of the industries examined—in which the interaction of the exploitation of nationwide sales-promotion opportunities and of economies of scale in nationwide distribution confer lower promotion-plus-distribution costs on very large firms, and in which deconcentration might well be an uneconomical operation *unless* the institutional bases of sales promotion were seriously and directly altered. Deconcentration per se in this area would be a questionable operation; deconcentration together with alterations of the bases of product differentiation and sales promotion would, if feasible and desired, probably be economical.

Various policy suggestions have been implied or stated as the issues involved have been discussed. In the interest of brevity, only one summary statement and one policy conclusion are offered. The character and incidence of advantages of scale are complicated and are variegated as among concentrated industries. Pending a development of regulatory law not yet attained, deconcentration measures ought to be highly selective and perhaps hand-tailored.

Chapter Ten

Price Leaders, Barometers, and Kinks

In the economic literature of the last ten or fifteen years, a variety of hypotheses have been advanced concerning the character and consequences of "price leadership" in American industries. The reference is generally to a mode of making selling prices through which a principal firm within an industry typically takes the lead in announcing or posting an official price or price schedule, or change therein, and through which most or all of the rival firms in the same industry, selling identical or closely similar products, always or usually follow the leader and announce or post the same official prices or price changes. Some of these hypotheses hold that price leadership is essentially monopolistic in effect as well as purpose, or that a tacit collusion of sellers with such intent and consequences is revealed by the existence of price leadership. Others hold that much or most price leadership is essentially competitive in effect, since the price leader is really led by strong market forces of supply and demand and is a "barometer" reflecting them. On the level of broad and sweeping generalization, either one or both of the differing schools of thought must be wrong.

Connected with the discussion of price leadership has been the issue of whether, as some sort of alternative to price leadership, all principal sellers in concentrated or oligopolistic industries act as if the demand curves for their individual outputs are significantly "kinked," so that each principal seller would feel that his rivals would not ordinarily follow his individual price increases but would indeed match his price reductions—a type of reasoning or conjecture by sellers which would favor relatively rigid prices and would make price leadership generally not feasible.

The immediate purpose of this essay is to examine the validity and usefulness both a priori and as applied, of these popular hypotheses concerning price leadership and possible "kinky" alternatives to it. This inquiry should be regarded, however, as a stage in a more general appraisal of the ability of

Reprinted from *Journal of Business,* 33, July 1960, pp. 193-203, courtesy of the University of Chicago Press.

economists to develop valid and rigorous theories which classify and project the consequences of the *market conduct* of sellers in concentrated industries and to apply such theories meaningfully in interpreting available empirical evidence of such conduct.

An analytical system concerning oligopolistic market phenomena which recognizes a distinction among the market structure, market conduct, and market performance of sellers is useful in this connection. *Market structure* refers to the basic, long-term, and rather slowly changing organizational characteristics of a market—to the market "situation," in legal terms—which determine the general character of interseller, interbuyer, and buyer-seller relationships. The structural characteristics of a market usually emphasized include the degree of seller concentration (number and size distribution of sellers), the degree of buyer concentration, the degree of differentiation of the products of rival sellers, and the height of barriers to the entry to the market of additional sellers. *Market performance* refers to the end results which the market engenders in the dimensions of efficiency, profit rates, relation of price to marginal costs, progressiveness in technique and product, and so forth.

Market conduct, which is in some sense a link between the structural situation in which sellers find themselves and the end results or performance they produce, refers generally to the patterns of behavior which sellers follow in adapting or adjusting to the markets in which they deal. As such, market conduct—at least in its dimensions which affect the determination of prices and outputs in an industry—has two crucial aspects. The first involves the nature of the means or mechanism which sellers employ to obtain a coordination or compatibility of their price and output policies with those of their rivals. Such mechanisms may include, for example, complete cartels, incomplete collusive agreements (affecting price only, for example, but not market shares), price leadership, systematic exchange of cost and price information, or simple and unadorned oligopolistic interdependence. The second involves the principle of price-output calculation which is effectively employed by the firms involved, whatever the means or mechanism of coordination may be. Such a principle might be one of joint profit maximization by the member firms of the industry (pricing together to get the largest possible collective profit). It might be one of independent profit maximization (pricing independently to enhance individual profits without regard to rivals' reactions). It might very possibly be one of "hybrid" profit maximization, in which some expedient compromise is struck between acting together for maximum collective profits and pricing individually for maximum individual profits. It could also be a more or less arbitrary principle, such as that of always adding a "fair" margin to normal costs in order to arrive at a price.

In terms of the preceding analysis of market conduct, we should note that price leadership is ostensibly and only a pattern for interseller coordination. and is not rigidly or necessarily linked to any particular principle of price-output calculation. What principle is implemented by price leadership will depend on many things—among them the structure of the industry—and may vary widely from case to case. "Kinked demand-curve" reasoning by rival sellers, on the other hand, reflects the application of a sort of independent profit-maximizing principle subject to the constraint of considerable oligopolistic interdependence among sellers. In the net, in this latter case, we find a coordinative mechanism reflecting interdependence without express or tacit agreement, plus the application of some sort of hybrid profit-maximizing rationale.

Let us center for the moment, however, on price leadership as a prominent variety of mechanisms for interseller coordination, or, more generally, on such coordinative mechanisms as a group. With respect to the genus, a safe generalization is that the classification of market conduct patterns simply according to the means of interseller coordination is in large part otiose description, having doubtful meaning in theory or in theoretically oriented applications. It is only when specific patterns of interseller coordination can be systematically linked with specific principles of price-output calculation, and thus with specific tendencies of predicted market performance, that the identification and classification of patterns of interseller coordination become meaningful in theory. Even if meaningful theoretical links could be established, moreover, the classification would be useful in application only so far as available data would permit a defensible empirical distinction among different theoretical types of coordinative mechanism.

Faced with these constraints, prominent taxonomists of oligopolistic market conduct have first attempted to imbue various a priori classifications of patterns of interseller coordination with some meaning by claiming that specific principles of price-output determination, and resultant patterns of market performance, are uniquely linked to specific patterns of interseller coordination. Second, they have attempted to apply (and justify) their a priori classifications by identifying a few empirical industry cases which assertedly fit one or another category of a taxonomy. The numerous relevant writings have a certain superficial plausibility and persuasive power. But it cannot be said that, in general, they have established theoretically valid associations of patterns of interseller coordination (in oligopoly) with the principles (and performance results) of price-output determination or that they have usually succeeded in drawing meaningful distinctions among "total" market-conduct patterns (which embrace coordinative mechanisms and pricing principles together) in various limited assortments of empirical cases.

Their difficulty on the theoretical level inheres in the fact that no general association of patterns of interseller coordination to principles of price-output determination can, in the oligopoly context, really be deduced. Briefly, each of the more common devices for interseller coordination in oligopoly–including simple price agreements, price leadership, tacit collusion based on exchanges of cost and price information, formula pricing for a "fair" margin, and apparently unadorned oligopolistic interdependence–can hypothetically be associated with practically the full possible range of effective price-calculating principles from joint profit maximization to independent maximization and, on the level of performance, with a corresponding range of attained price-cost relationships from truly monopolistic to atomistically competitive. In a context wherein the mutual antagonism of rival oligopolists goes hand in hand with their desire for a maximum joint profit, many outcomes from a given coordinating mechanism are possible. The pricing principle followed and the price result obtained will vary according to whether or not there are competitive clandestine reductions of nominal posted prices, whether or not all members of the industry are parties to any express or tacit agreement, whether or not the price terms of such express or tacit understandings are initially lowered so as to discourage or avert open or secret defections from an agreed-upon price, whether or not there is a serious threat of new entry if prices exceed a certain level—and according to a number of related considerations. Basically, the most probable outcome may depend on the structure of the market in question. But if we lump together all cases in which a given sort of coordinative mechanism, such as price leadership, is observed—cases which will present a wide variety of structural situations—little of an a priori character can be said of them in general, other than that a more or less maximum range of pricing principles and price results is possible and that no one outcome has a dominant probability. (An exception might be made for the full cartel as a coordinative mechanism—*rara avis* in American industry—but even here it is difficult to predict that a certain pricing principle will always be applied).

In general, then, no valid a priori generalizations concerning fixed relationships of patterns of interseller coordination to pricing principles or market performance can be advanced. As a substitute we may receive ad hoc inductive generalizations from one or a few empirical instances, in which the fact that an apparent pattern of interseller coordination was once or twice associated with a certain apparent performance (and implied price-determining principle) is evoked as the basis for asserting that such an association holds in general. Or we may receive open-end deductive generalizations, such as the one above, to the effect that each of several patterns of interseller coordination among oligopolists may be associated with any of a full variety of price-determining principles and performance outcomes, with the "facts" about actual associations to be determined by empirical application of the model. This approach, which has no especial content on the a priori level, usually throws the emphasis back on casual induction from a few empirical cases. In general, the authors of the received literature have been unsuccessful in developing more than ad hoc theorems concerning the association of patterns of interseller coordination to pricing principle and market performance.

One difficulty encountered in testing a priori hypotheses concerning the association of patterns of interseller coordination with price-determining principle and with market performance is thus that there is frequently not much of a hypothesis to begin with. The association is really read backward from observed performance to the implied price-determining principle coupled with the observed coordinating mechanism (in one or a few specific cases) and usually emerges in a form not amenable to generalization. But even if a sophisticated general hypothesis is developed, which draws adequate a priori distinctions among different total-conduct patterns and associates performance with them, it is typically very difficult to apply it to received data.

This is mostly because the relatively fine distinctions among total patterns of market conduct which such a theory requires cannot practically be drawn from available empirical data concerning conduct in different instances. Although the means or devices of interseller coordination can be ascertained with relative ease, the crucial added element of each total-conduct pattern—involving the effective principle of price-output calculation employed by the industry—cannot in the usual case be independently determined from available data; it can at best be inferred from evidence of the market performance which emerged from whatever conduct sellers engaged in. The investigator is therefore ordinarily unable to test either the association of independently established total-conduct patterns with similarly established patterns of performance or the association of patterns of interseller coordination with price-determining principles.

It should be emphasized that I do not view the preceding as an indictment of price theory for its poverty as a source of useful explanations and predictions of market performance in various industries. It is rather a criticism of certain varieties of ad hoc pseudotheorizing about the consequences of observable patterns of market conduct, which has traditionally rested on rather shaky foundations.

The deficiencies of various attempts to say something meaningful and convincing about oligopolistic market conduct are aptly illustrated by some notable recent discussions of price leadership and alternatives to it, to which we will now turn.

NOTIONS ABOUT PRICE LEADERSHIP, BAROMETRIC AND OTHERWISE

It has long been recognized that there are at least two general kinds of price leadership. The first, dominant-firm or partial-monopoly leadership, requires one firm supplying a large fraction of an industry market and a number of much smaller firms competing. It involves the large firm setting a market price, at which the smaller firms supply all the output they wish to supply or can sell, and the large firm supplying the remainder of the industry demand at the price set. Necessary conditions for the long-run stable operation of this model are that no smaller firm shall be large enough to have significant circular interdependence with the dominant firm (that is, there is no duopoly or oligopoly element present) and that either the cost conditions or individual demand conditions of the smaller firms induce them to limit their combined outputs to a minor fraction of the market at any market price the partial monopolist is likely to establish. The second, common-garden-variety or oligopolistic price leadership, requires an ologopoly of several large firms (at least two) in a market, with circular interdependence inter se, these firms being surrounded or not, as the case may be, by a competitive fringe of small sellers. It involves some one large firm persistently or typically taking the lead in changing announced selling prices for the industry, with its rivals generally following its lead with reasonable promptness by matching its prices or price changes and ordinarily not altering their announced prices independently. Conspicuous parallelism of price changes (and usually conspicuous identity of rival announced prices) is secured through the mutual observance by the sellers involved of a leader-follower convention.

Since the first variety of leadership model has scant theoretical interest or practical application, I will consider here only the second variety—oligopolistic price leadership. The latter clearly constitutes an empirically identifiable device, of a rather general sort, for interseller coordination of price policies within an oligopolistic industry. Employment of the device could ostensibly reflect or implement an express (but not necessarily discoverable) collusive agreement among leader and followers to eliminate price rivalry, or a tacit agreement or understanding of the same sort or no agreement at all. What, if anything, can be said of the general implications of the use of such leadership for the price-calculation principle which is implemented or for the market performance which emerges?

A good general answer to this question might be "very little," or "anything can happen." Unfortunately for the cause of pure logic, a number of economists have reacted to the distressing ambivalence of the implications of oligopolistic price leadership by advancing special assertions (usually based on the casual observation of a scattering of data) as to what it really implies. An early version of such assertions was to the effect that oligopolistic price leadership is in general inherently monopolistic, in the sense, presumably, that it implements joint profit maximization by the sellers involved and that it is conducive to price and output results similar to those a single-firm monopolist would impose. This assertion is not supportable as a generalization in economic logic (any respectable theory of oligopoly behavior would indicate at least the equal probability of each of a wide range of alternative outcomes), and it is not confirmed by numerous empirical observations. But, partly in reaction to this implausible assertion, counterassertions of no greater general plausibility or validity have been made. I refer in particular to those which identify, characterize, and predict the results of something designated as "barometric" price leadership.

The trouble begins, in my reading, with George Stigler's noted article on oligopoly kinks and rigid prices.[1] In the course of proving that most oligopolists do not act as if they had kinks in their demand curves, Stigler casually designated all price leadership which is not of the dominant-firm type as being "barometric" price leadership. This latter form of (or new name for) plain oligopolistic price leadership is not defined precisely by Stigler, since he relies mainly for a definition on the lengthy quotation of an oil-company executive's apologium for price leadership in his industry. The main point of the quotation is that in the instant situation, typically beset by all sorts of secret price cuts or

[1]George J. Stigler, "The Kinky Oligopoly Demand Curve and Rigid Prices," *Journal of Political Economy,* LV, October 1947, 432-49.

concessions from quoted price, all that the recognized price leader does is to bear the burden of formally recognizing current market conditions and to announce prices accordingly—and also that the leader cannot set prices for a maximum joint profit and force others to conform. Stigler himself describes the generic (and barometric) situation only as one in which there is "a firm that conventionally first announces price changes that are usually followed by the remainder of the industry" and in which "the barometric firm commands adherence of rivals to his price only because, and to the extent that, his price reflects market conditions with tolerable promptness."

This is a fairly vague definition, in the degree that recognizing market conditions is a pretty elastic notion; therefore, the content and consequences of barometric leadership are not precisely defined. Whatever they may be, however, Stigler seems to designate all price-leadership cases (other than those of dominant-firm leadership) as belonging to a single barometric category and to attribute to the mechanism of interseller coordination in question (oligopolistic price leadership in general) whatever degree of competitiveness in price-calculating principle and market performance is implied by a leader's policy of "reflecting market conditions." Perhaps so pliable a characterization of the implications of price leadership requires no defense in the form of deductive argument or evidence; in any event, none was supplied.

The trouble deepens with Jesse Markham's essay on price leadership, four years later.[2] In pursuit of the commendable end of arguing that price leadership or conspicuous parallelism is not the most appropriate citadel for anti-trust attack, Markham adopts Stigler's barometric concept, refines it, and extends it. He refines it by arguing that there are really two sorts of barometric (oligopolistic) price leadership, one competitive and innocuous and the other monopolistic and dangerous. Competitive barometric price leadership is hard to identify without a thorough case-by-case investigation, but its presence is suggested by one or more of the following: occasional changes in the identity of the price followers to the leader's lead; and frequent fluctuations of individual sellers' market shares, especially in periods of changing price. Monopolistic barometric price leadership, on the other hand, is a rarer bird and emerges only when most or all of these conditions are fulfilled: a small absolute number of firms, all relatively large; severely restricted to the industry; no extreme product differentiation within the industry; a market demand not much more elastic than unity; sufficient similarity of the cost curves of rival firms to allow of mutually compatible collusive determination of price. (This is hardly a complete principle of classification, since we can envisage and identify cases which fulfil both sets of criteria as well as cases which fulfil neither set, but it has the anemometric virtue of suggesting how the winds of thought are blowing. It may also be noted, for future reference, that competitive barometric price leadership is identified primarily in terms of certain observable details of market conduct,

[2]Jesse W. Markham, "The Nature and Significance of Price Leadership," *American Economic Review,* XLI, December 1951, 891-905.

or of the working of the coordinative mechanism, whereas monopolistic barometric price leadership is identified wholly in terms of market structure.)

Given this refinement, Markham extends the implications of competitive barometric price leadership quite drastically:

> Barometric price leadership which follows the above lines probably does not greatly circumvent the public interest . . . . The barometric firm . . . simply passes along information to the "Big Three" or the "Big Four" on what the rest of the industry is doing in a declining market, and proceeds with initiating price increases in a market revival only so rapidly as supply and demand conditions dictate.

And further: "The barometric price leader, as defined by Professor Stigler and as visualized for purposes of this paper, appears to do little more than set prices that would eventually be set by forces of competition." All this is apparently attributed to oligopolistic price-leadership patterns in which leaders and followers sometimes change places, lag in followership responses, and/or have somewhat unstable market shares, the only exception being for cases where "more overt arrangements" (however discovered) that support monopolistic tendencies supplement the working of the otherwise innocuous price leadership. The monopolistic barometric form of price leadership, however, is dire, and it may serve "all the ends of a strong trade association of or a closely knit domestic cartel."

Markham thus goes much further than Stigler in associating principles of price determination and patterns of market performance with loosely designated mechanisms of interseller coordination involving price leadership. There are still some ambiguities (for example, the meaning of the "forces of competition" which would otherwise eventually arrive at a price), and there are some escape hatches (the possible existence of "more overt arrangement" to rationalize monopolistic pricing in a context of otherwise competitive barometic price leadership). But, in general, fairly definite implications of observable patterns of interseller coordination have been postulated, and it is time to ask questions. Do the postulated associations have any validity in theory, or can they be verified by the analysis of empirical data?

SOME CRITICISMS OF PREVAILING DOCTRINE

If we explore any theoretical model which represents with reasonable generality the conditions ascribed to barometric price leadership by Stigler or to competitive barometric price leadership by Markham, it does not appear that a competitive outcome, on the level of price-calculation principle or of price-output performance, can be deduced either as uniquely necessary or as dominantly probable.

An appropriate model, following the lead of the writers in question, might refer to an industry in which structurally there were a few large firms, none "dominant" and each with a significant share of industry output, which together supplied a large share of industry output (from two-thirds to four-fifths for example), and a number of smaller firms (from relatively few to many) which had individually insignificant market shares and together supplied the remainder of industry output. In other words, we envisage an industry of a type commonly found, with an oligopolistic core and some competitive fringe. In addition, on the structural level there are probably some moderate barriers to the entry of new firms and to the expansion of existing small ones but no severe barriers. As to visible manifestations of conduct, one of the oligopolists is a generally recognized price leader for the industry as regards quoted prices. But the identity of the leader has occasionally shifted; his lead has at least occasionally been followed in a lagging fashion; and market shares both within the oligopoly core and as between it and the competitive fringe have fluctuated somewhat. Finally, there is either persistent or periodic shading of the leader's quoted price through "secret" price concessions; the leader has at least occasionally been "led" by the increase in such concessions to reduce his quoted price; and his price increases have frequently followed intervals in which the balance of supply and demand has been such that secret price concessions were minimal.

Assuming all this (which grants a good deal more than the apparent minimum conditions for competitive barometric price leadership), can we deduce a competitive outcome for the market? If by a competitive outcome we mean, first, pricing according to independent (as distinct from joint or hybrid) profit-maximizing calculations and, second, a performance closely approximate to that ascribed to atomistic competition (output such that price equals average and marginal costs, at least on a long-run average), the answer is definitely negative. As a matter of fact, we cannot deduce much of anything of a definite sort. But, looking for general theorical indications, we must note that oligopolistic interdependence is clearly present as among the principal firms, that the adoption and perpetuation of the price-leadership convention strongly suggests the existence of some tacit understanding among such firms at least not to set announced prices independently, that the member firms of the competitive fringe which undercut the leader's price are subject to some probable disadvantages which limit their competitive power and ability to expand, and that the larger firms' "secret" price concessions are limited by recognized interdependence. Therefore, the process of various sellers making concessions from the leader's price by no means inevitably proceeds to the point where all or most sellers are acting as independent profit-maximizers or to where a competitive adjustment of price to cost is reached.

The leadership-plus-price concession pattern may thus reflect a generally hybrid principle of profit maximization, somewhere between independent and joint maximization, involving qualified jointness and restrained independence. In this event, oligopolistic interdependence, as implemented in the leadership system, may very well succeed in the net in keeping price somewhat above and output somewhat below the competitive level. Such an outcome seems, on a priori grounds, at least as probable as a competitive outcome.

The preceding, of course, does not argue that a fully monopolistic outcome, with maximized industry joint profits, is especially likely in theory. The structural and conduct indications are, generally, that the price-leader's price is more likely than not to be held below a full monopolistic level because of actual or threatened defections from his leadership and that actual prices will, because of secret concessions, tend to run somewhat below the leader's quoted prices. But this is not to say that the price-output solution is therefore necessarily "competitive" in the usual sense of the term; significant monopolistic output restriction and perceptible monopolistic excess profits may, quite possibly, still persist, just as strictly monopolistic and strictly competitive outcomes are at least possible. Note also that, if the structural conditions of the model were altered in the direction of substantially higher seller concentration and more difficult entry, an approximately monopolistic outcome would become more probable; conversely, if we had a less concentrated or more dilute oligopoly, it might be more likely to come close to a competitive outcome. Markham distinguishes the first of these alternatives, but not the second.

The foregoing raises the question of what writers like Stigler and Markham intended to mean by terms such as "reflecting market conditions" and "set by the forces of competition," when characterizing the market outcome ascribed to barometric price leadership. If they meant competitive price calculation and performance in the accepted rigorous sense used above, theory does not adequately support their predictions. If they only meant less-than-fully-monopolistic calculation principles and performance or, alternatively, the sort of oligopolistic solution which would be arrived at in the absence of price leadership (both tentatively acceptable), their assertions have been seriously ambiguous, and the suggestion that barometric price leadership generally leads to "competitive" results is misleading.

Markham's predictions concerning monopolistic barometric price leadership seem to rest on firmer theoretical ground, fundamentally because the basis for identifying the category is predominantly structural. If all the structural conditions established for this category are simultaneously fulfilled, there would seem to be a predominant theoretical probability that significant departures from competitive price calculation and performance should take place, although attainment of a full monopoly would be less certain. It might only be commented in passing that Markham has specified more conditions than are necessary for such a probability and that he has therefore defined the limits of this category in an unduly restrictive fashion.

To return to competitive barometric price leadership: the appraisal of empirical evidence has supplied no more support than has a priori theory for the assertion that industries with the attributes of structure and conduct specified by Markham in general actually behave competitively. To subject the Markham assertion to a meaningful empirical test, it would be necessary to select at random a considerable number of industries with the specified attributes (such as those suggested in the model described above) and to determine in what proportion of them either (1) price calculation effectively followed the principles of independent profit maximization or (2) market performance, as measured by price-cost relations, efficiency, and so forth conformed to the competitive norm. Actually, only the second sort of association could be directly tested from obtainable data, since there is no feasible means of determining independently what principles of price calculation are being employed in a market—this must, in practice, at best be inferred from the evidence of market performance. Thus, the central tendency and variance of market performance in a substantial group of industries having the attributes specified by Markham would have to be determined. His assertion might be confirmed if the distribution of performance measures were unimodal, if the central tendency of performance were at or very close to a competitive level, and if the variance were not such as to place an important proportion of cases significantly up the scale toward monopolistic performance.

Such a systematic test has not been described by Markham or by anyone else, to my knowledge, and I have not made such a test; we may thus regard the assertion in question as neither confirmed nor disconfirmed by convincing empirical evidence. My own casual observations, however, lead me to suspect strongly that the results of such a test would reveal a bimodal tendency in (or perhaps even a more or less rectangular distribution of) the market performance of industries with so-called competitive barometric price leadership and that variances would overwhelm central tendencies.

In this connection it may be noted that empirical evidence may be adduced in support of the Markham assertion in at least two ways which really prove nothing. One is to identify industries which have the specified attributes of structure and conduct, to discuss these attributes, and then to assert that they perform competitively (without scrutinizing their performance very critically). Another is to select some industries with apparently competitive performance plus the attributes in question and to cite them as supporting the basic assertion. This process is facilitated if the requirements of competitive performance are rather loosely or liberally construed. Most of the empirical support presented to date for the barometric price-leadership hypothesis is of the sort just described.

Even if we are concerned only with identifying industries which evidence aspects of conduct conforming to the competitive barometric model, there are some further practical difficulties in interpreting data, of which I will mention two. The first is that of the occasionally erratic barometer, which once in a while rises when it should fall. This phenomenon was brought to my mind once in tracing, in a series of classified industry price data, the response of the leader's quoted price over ten years to movements in average actual prices for the industry, as calculated after all concessions and discounts. In general, the leader's price followed actual prices down and was raised only as actual prices started pushing up. But twice in ten years the leader's price responded to severe declines in actual prices by being raised sharply, after which actual prices followed it up. Was this a case of competitive barometric price leadership? Should one suspect the periodic emergence of a more overt form of collusion? Avoiding pure rationalization, I am uncertain. The second difficulty concerns how we should interpret the contemporary price leadership and followership behavior of a group of firms whose attorneys have read the new "Tobacco decision," have become sensitive to the possible legal dangers of conspicuous parallelism, and have advised their clients accordingly. It would not be too difficult for a group of firms deliberately to rotate leadership, lag in their following responses, and allow market shares to fluctuate a bit—and still to secure all of the results of a tight leadership system which had none of these marks of barometry. (Antitrust-oriented "dramatic conduct" may become important in the contemporary economy.) This difficulty goes back to the essential unreliability, as indicators of competition, of the superficial hallmarks of competitive barometric price leadership.

ON KINKS, AND ON PUBLIC POLICY

It might be emphasized in conclusion that, although I have been generally critical of the Stigler and Markham concepts of barometric price leadership, I am not in disagreement with the conclusions of the main arguments in the course of which they made use of these concepts. That is, first, I would agree with Stigler that most oligopolistic industries do not act as if their sellers were usually in a position where they had very sharp kinks in their individual demand curves—or very long discontinuities in their marginal-revenue functions. This is empirically apparent and is consistent with a variety of theoretical explanations. One qualifying remark is that it is quite conceivable that the price leader may frequently face a sort of ceiling price at which he encounters some kind of a kink, in the sense that his followers would not really follow him higher (if they did so nominally, they would seriously undercut the price through secret concessions) and that they would follow him downward (but might also precede him downward, via clandestine concessions). Considering the fact that the leader may or may not be at this ceiling at various times, the existence of such a kinky phenomenon seems quite consistent with any of the empirical evidence so far presented.

Second, I would agree with Markham that attacks on price leadership or similar conspicuous parallelism are likely to be relatively fruitless devices of antitrust policy. The basis of my agreement, however, would be that the proper focus of attack is found in the structural situations of which various phenomena of conduct are only reflections and not that the bulk of industries with apparently barometric price leadership provide us with satisfactory competitive performance. Conversely, the Justice Department would be ill advised to accept signs of barometric price leadership, as defined, as evidence that an acceptably competitive structure and performance exist.

Chapter Eleven

Survival-Ability as a Test of Efficiency

At least since the days of the Temporary National Economic Committee before the second World War, economists have shown recurrent interest in determining empirically, in each of many industries, the comparative efficiency of firms of different sizes. As we progress from the smallest toward the largest firm in any industry, do unit costs of production, distribution, and perhaps also sales promotion tend to vary systemically with firm size?

One type of study has attacked this question directly by attempting to measure the long-run average cost or scale curve of "the firm" in each of a number of industries. Two things may be noted about such measurements. First, they generally attempt to abstract from interfirm cost differences due to differences in productive technique, in money prices paid for productive factors, and in rate of utilization of plant. Second, they generally admit sales promotion costs into a scale curve only provisionally and with qualms, because of a priori and empirical indications that unique and reversible functional relationships between firm size and unit sales promotion costs—available alike to all firms—probably do not exist in most industries.

Three general findings concerning scale curves have emerged from this sort of study. First, in the usual industry, economies of large scale are realized as the firm expands from miniscule size to some identifiable minimal optimal scale, but not beyond that scale. Second, unit costs tend to remain constant at the optimal level as the firm grows still larger, and diseconomies of very large scale ordinarily do not seem to be encountered. Third, most of the scale economies observed are economies of the large-scale plant. Although these findings apply specifically to scale curves measuring only production and distribution costs, they are roughly sustained when sales promotion costs are included, except that in some product-differentiated industries smaller firms seem to encounter diseconomies of very large-scale sales promotion.

Reprinted from *American Economic Review,* 59 (Proceedings), May 1969, pp. 99-104, courtesy of the American Economic Association.

Three other connected findings also deserve mention. First, in the great majority of industries, a firm of minimum optimal scale, or of a smaller scale not involving significantly higher unit costs, would supply an appreciable but distinctly minor fraction of the output of its industry. Second, in most industries, the largest firms are from several to many times larger than minimum optimal scale. Finally—and for purposes of the ensuing argument most important—a significant minor proportion of industry output—in one sample of industries from 10 to 30 percent—is generally supplied by a fringe of small firms that suffer significantly from diseconomies of small scale (primarily of small-scale plant). And these fringes of inefficient one-plant firms appear to survive over considerable periods of time—perhaps indefinitely.

STIGLER'S POSITION

This last is a tentative finding of some theoretical interest and policy importance. Yet before it was developed, George Stigler, writing in 1949, advanced a proposition that might appear to contradict the finding and to deprecate the research effort underlying it. Let me quote him as follows:[1]

> The comparative private costs of firms of various sizes can be measured in only one way: by ascertaining whether firms of the various sizes can survive in the industry. Survival is the only test of a firm's ability to cope with all the problems: buying inputs, soothing laborers, finding customers, introducing new products and techniques, coping with fluctuations, evading regulations, etc. A cross-sectional study of the costs of inputs per unit of output in a given period measures only one facet of the firm's efficiency and yields no conclusion on efficiency in the large .... If a firm of a given size survives, we may infer that its costs are equal to those of other sizes of firms .... [However,] the equality of private costs carries no implication that social costs of firms of different sizes are equal.

He also implicitly suggested as a tentative indicator of "survival" of firms of a given size class whether or not they were maintaining or increasing their relative numbers in the industry.

Given this seeming disagreement between empirical findings and a priori doctrine, two related questions arise. First, is there a genuine contradiction or conflict between the two? Yes or maybe. There is definitely a conflict between the criteria of efficiency reflected respectively in the findings and in Stigler's doctrine. The findings refer to the comparative efficiency of firms of different size as measured approximately in terms of social costs (neglecting externalities generated by firms), whereas Stigler clearly espouses private costs as a criterion of efficiency. This choice of criterion, moreover, is not simply a neutral matter of taste. Conclusions referring to interfirm differences in social costs have a clear

[1]George J. Stigler, "Monopoly and Oligopoly by Merger," *American Economic Review*, XL, May 1950, pp. 23-24.

normative content; those emphasizing only private costs have at best a descriptive one. From a normative standpoint, moreover, one might object to Stigler's terminology when he asserts that a firm's advantage derived from such things as buying factors at lower prices and evading regulations improve its "efficiency in the large."

On the other hand, the empirical findings in question and Stigler's proposition are not of necessity contradictory on a technical level. Because they rest on significantly different definitions of cost, both could be correct simultaneously, at some level of probability. But if there is, as seems plausible, a fairly high degree of correlation between social and private costs, the presence of some contradiction seems on balance likely.

This leads us to our second question: In his proposition was Stigler probably correct on his own ground—that where only private costs matter? Unfortunately, we cannot dismiss the matter by observing that his proposition is tautologically true and not subject to confrontation with evidence, simply because he has arbitrarily defined efficiency as survival-ability. He has precluded us from this by holding that all surviving firms in an industry, regardless of size, have equal private average costs. To deal with the issue, we must examine the sources of the survival power of socially inefficient firms on which Stigler expressly or implicitly had to rest his case, and judge to what extent these sources are likely to give all surviving firms equality in private costs. We thus inquire generally as follows. Why can smaller firms in an industry that are comparatively inefficient in terms of social unit costs survive persistently or for appreciable periods of time?

WHY SMALL FIRMS SURVIVE

Before turning directly to the question, let us note that there are some instances in which small survivors are actually not surviving in the same industry as the larger firms with which they are compared, because of misleading Census or other groupings. They are supplying essentially different products than those large firms, and products which are distant substitutes to any common group of buyers. The simultaneous survival, for example, of Ferrari and Aston-Martin, on the one hand, and General Motors and Fiat, on the other, has about as much to do with comparative efficiency as the simultaneous survival of General Foods and National Steel. The first and second pairs of auto firms mentioned have different production functions, are on different scale curves, and are essentially noncompeting. A comparison of their unit costs (as well as of their survival-ability) would be meaningless.

In the same vein, let us also note that small surviving firms in some industries, in spite of evident diseconomies of small-scale production, may not actually be less efficient, socially or privately, when all costs are taken into account. The best examples of this phenomenon are perhaps found in some industries where the larger firms are localized to a few geographical points (possibly to minimize assembly costs of raw materials) and where the product has high outshipment costs relative to selling price. Then, small firms may be able to locate in and supply geographically remote local markets, offsetting diseconomies of small-scale production with reduced costs of delivery. The American steel industry, for one, appears to fit this mold fairly well, as does the petroleum refining industry. In such cases, of course, the smaller firms are probably surviving because of equivalent social efficiency, and not in spite of comparative inefficiency.

To these examples we might add (with some misgivings about including selling costs in measures of efficiency) examples of small surviving firms that systematically offset diseconomies of small-scale production with sales promotion costs per unit of output lower than those of their larger rivals. This strategy, which may put the smaller firms in some sense on the same level of social efficiency as that of the larger ones, is not conducive to large or growing market shares for the small firms. But it may suffice to maintain them with small capacities that are suboptimal from the standpoint of production costs. I am hard put to identify any "pure" examples of the phenomenon in question, but it would appear to have been alloyed with other considerations; for example, in the shoe industry and the petroleum refining industry.

With these and similar false or misleading examples of survival with inferior social efficiency out of the way, let us turn to some valid grounds for such survival. The following explanations of the phenomenon seem particularly important in the light of empirical observation:

1. *Living under a Price Umbrella.* Consider industries with market structures featuring a rather concentrated oligopolistic core of a few large firms, together with a competitive fringe of smaller firms that are clearly less efficient by either social or private criteria. In a number of these it has been observed that the dominant firms establish prices noticeably in excess of their own average costs, but roughly equal to the average costs of their smaller rivals. This policy, in addition to yielding excess profits to the larger firms, allows the smaller firms to survive with low or normal profits, and perhaps keeps them hungry enough to discourage their expansion. Such a structional situation, featuring the persistent survival of a group of relatively inefficient small firms, may be reasonably stable over time because of product-differentiation disadvantages of the small firms and of other intra-industry barriers to their expansion.

Supposing that it is, it is important to note that the large and small firms are generally—unless other factors intrude—surviving at distinctly different levels of affluence (e.g., different private rates of excess profits on sales). And equal survival-ability at quite different levels of affluence definitely does not itself imply equal private costs, nor equal social costs. This phenomenon will probably not explain a majority of the cases we are interested in, but it does not seem to be especially rare.

In some product-differentiated industries, of course, it is possible that some small sellers with both social and private inefficiency do not need a price umbrella in order to survive. Without the benefit of having the product prices of their major rivals held above average costs, they can or could command minor market shares at superior selling prices sufficiently high to offset their diseconomies of small scale. To the extent that such sellers could survive in this way, they might be considered to have at least adequate allocational efficiency, by virtue of supplying the wants of buyer minorities with distinctive products which would otherwise be unavailable. But "pure" cases of this phenomenon, unalloyed with price umbrellas, are hard to find.

2. *Surviving with the Support of Large Rivals.* In some very highly concentrated oligopolies, there has been evidence that the dominant firms have pursued policies designed to support the survival or avert the disappearance of their few relatively inefficient small rivals, generally in order to preserve the appearance of competition and thus avoid antitrust charges of joint monopolization. One such policy of course involves holding a price umbrella. But others include supplying the small rivals with materials on favored terms, giving them access to controlled distributive outlets, etc. This phenomenon is unquestionably rarer than the first mentioned, but it has been evident, for example, in the automobile industry, wherein the Big Two or Three evidently made efforts to keep Kaiser from going under after its entry to the industry, and where the failure of American Motors would be a minor disaster to the principal firms. Small firm survival secured by this route may reduce small firm private costs, but seems in general unlikely to equalize them with those of larger firms.

3. *Securing Hired Productive Factors at Lower Money Prices.* There are evidently a number of industries in which small firms, that are definitely less efficient than larger rivals in terms of real factor inputs, partly or wholly offset their virtual cost disadvantage by securing labor and other factors at lower prices than the large firms do. In some cases this is done by exploiting the geographical and possible occupational immobility of the labor force in a declining area. (It is not a sign of an offsetting social efficiency unless labor mobility is strictly not a viable alternative.) In some cases it is accomplished through favored treatment by unions or through locating so as to use nonunion labor. In all these cases—and kindred ones as they may affect other productive factors—the attainment of or approach to equality in private costs by socially inefficient small firms is possible. Of course, this fails to erase the fact that these firms have found a way to survive in spite of inferior real efficiency. The shoe industry of New England appears to have offered a good case in point.

4. *Entrepreneurial Absorption of Losses.* In a number of industries—generally of only moderate concentration but very easy entry—we have observed that a persistent survival of numerous small firms with definite diseconomies of small scale has been made possible mainly by one fact. That is, owner-entrepreneurs are persistently willing to accept profits yielding subnormal returns or no returns on their investments, or imputed wages below their market value in other employment, or both. In some instances, the same inefficient firms survive for long periods of time. In others, such firms periodically go bankrupt, but their plants remain in operation as another wave of entrepreneurial cannon fodder assumes ownership with the same odds against it. In either event, we may find persistent survival or its equivalent in spite of clear social inefficiency, based on a

reduction of private costs. This source of survival power may frequently be coupled with monetary advantages in securing hired factors.

This phenomenon has persisted for a long time in the New England region of the shoe industry. It has been continually observed in gasoline retailing, where the owner-operators of small-volume service stations stay in business in return for total monthly personal earnings approximately equal to the market rental values of the self-owned lands on which their stations are situated.

5. *Favored Treatment or Subsidy by Governmental Bodies.* It is a well-known fact that small corporations and other small firms receive favored treatment in the matter of federal income taxes and that they may condone survival by reducing private costs in spite of comparative inefficiency. It is also known that numerous local or state governmental bodies have offered tax remissions to new firms in order to attract industry. Such remissions may of course favor large and small firms alike, but there is some probability that they may serve to keep inefficiently small firms alive.

6. *Holding a Market Through Unfair Trade Practices.* Among the ways of surviving other than being as efficient as your competitors are those of deception of consumers, design piracy, commercial bribery, and so forth. The considerable evidence of such practices encouraged the passage of Section 5 of the Federal Trade Commission Act, and in particular of the Wheeler-Lea amendment thereto, in 1937. An aim of this legislation was to establish a "plane of fair competition" on which efficient firms would prosper and given which less efficient firms could not prosper or survive through various forms of "cheating."

Yet unfair competition does persist, and though large as well as small firms may play the game, it appears in a number of industries that small firms of inferior social efficiency do survive mainly by engaging in deception of consumers and other unfair trade practices. Instances in which this is true are perhaps not extremely numerous, but segments of the pharmaceutical and cosmetic industries would seem to offer fair examples. In some cases, such use of unfair trade practices may support small-firm survival by allowing them to reduce their private costs to a level competitive with those of larger rivals. In others, it may simply enable them to elevate their selling prices, neither private nor social costs being reduced.

The preceding list of sources of survival power of socially inefficient firms is of course not exhaustive, but are there any generally important sources we have omitted? In his 1949 article, Stigler mentioned as advantages of small firms which might let them secure competitive private costs in spite of inefficient scales the following: buying inputs, soothing laborers, evading regulations, finding customers, introducing new products and techniques, and coping with fluctuations. The first three of these are essentially covered under points 3 and 6 above. It is not appararent that small firms systematically or usually have significant off-setting advantages in the latter three respects, and we will not consider them here.

We may now return to the magnum question which led us into an exploration of the main sources of survival-ability of socially inefficient small firms. That is, to what extent was Stigler correct in holding that small firms with survival power have private costs (though not necessarily social costs that are equal to those of larger surviving firms. In view of the preceding argument, it seems that he was possibly correct so far as the bases of small-firm survival ability—other than equal social costs—are lower money factor prices, entrepreneurial absorption of losses, favored treatment by governments, some unfair trade practices, and some sorts of artificial respiration administered by large rivals. Yet it is not apparent on a priori grounds or from observation that these sources of survival-ability must operate to give smaller firms full equality in private costs. This might be required in some models of atomistic competition, but not in actual markets.

Correspondingly, he was incorrect to the extent that the survival-ability of small firms depends on their living under price umbrellas held by large rivals or on some varieties of unfair trade practices. To this extent, his original proposition should be amended.

How serious is this amendment likely to be? The answer lies in factual information that has not been adequately developed and analyzed, but I would hazard a few guesses on the basis of accumulated observation. First, within the competitive fringes of firms of inefficiently small scale, which in most industries appear to supply from 10 to 30 per cent of industry outputs, an appreciable minority do not deserve to be designated as socially or privately inefficient. This is either because they have been grouped for comparison with larger firms in different theoretical industries, or because some of their compensating real advantages have been neglected. Second, a clear majority of these fringe firms are socially inefficient, all things considered. Third, within this latter group, survival-ability depends wholly or in part on things other than equality in private costs—mainly on living under price umbrellas—in a substantial minority of cases. A close scrutiny of a sample of twenty manufacturing industries with which I have previously worked suggests that price umbrellas contribute strongly to small-firm survival-ability in about 40 per cent of the cases. The indicated amendment to Stigler's proposition thus appears to be more than trivial.

THE "SURVIVOR" TECHNIQUE

In conclusion, what of the so-called "survivor" technique? This of course embodies a sort of reverse-English application of Stigler's proposition by trying to identify which size classes of plants or firms in Census industries have minimal private costs by determining which size classes survive the best, in terms of holding of increasing either their comparative populations or their shares of industry value added over selected time intervals. (It should be noted that even when the focus is nominally on optimal plant sizes, firm sizes are also involved because in the bulk of industries plants in the smaller size classes are predominantly held by one-plant firms.) I will not attempt an appraisal and critique of this novel sort of numerical exercise here, deferring to W. G. Shepherd's masterful review of issues in his recent article in the *Southern*

Economic Journal.[2] But I will note that the economic arguments outlined above suggest that the survivor technique among other things rests on shaky conceptual foundations, as applied either to firms or to plants. All things considered, survival-ability is an uncertain and perhaps treacherous indicator of even private efficiency.

[2]William G. Shepherd, "What Does the Survivor Technique Show About Economies of Scale?" *Southern Economic Journal,* XXXIV, July 1967, pp. 113-22.

Chapter Twelve

The Comparative Stability of Market Structures

During the last twenty years, and especially in the latter part of the 1960's, a considerable number of economists have published the results of statistical tests–referring to private industries, markets, and even individual firms–for the association of market structure and market performance. Single-equation multiple regressions have typically been employed, most frequently with some measure of profit as the dependent variable and with some set of aspects of market structure, or proxies therefor, as the independent variables. Results have varied; but the preponderance of statistical experiments has found significant, though often weak, associations of structure and performance, as opposed to "no significant association." One typical, if not universal, characteristic of the a priori hypotheses tested in these experiments is that the dominant attributes of market structure used as independent variables are viewed as being, over substantial time periods, "comparatively immutable" determinants of market performance.

The general purpose of this essay is to appraise, from an a priori standpoint and empirically, the comparative stability over time of market structures, and then to consider the effects of any instability in market structures on experiments that test for structure-performance relations. First, however, it seems advisable to "clear the underbrush" of two fundamental issues involving a priori hypotheses to be tested–issues frequently left unresolved as econometric work proceeds.

CLEARING SOME UNDERBRUSH

Mason's Hypothesis

The major impetus to the statistical experiments mentioned above seems to have come from the germinal work of Edward S. Mason, who during the 1930's in his classes, and in print in 1939,[1] advanced the general proposition that the performance of a firm was largely explained by the structure of the market in which it operated–and in fact that there was something like a deterministic association between market structure and performance. A little later I shall say more concerning the details of this proposition.

Debate over Mason's Hypothesis

The first piece of "underbrush" to be considered is whether or not a deterministic association between market structure and performance is to be expected a priori. On this point, Mason encountered a forceful opponent in the person of Edwin G. Nourse, who had been approaching the question of the determinants of market performance from quite a different angle.[2] It was one of Nourse's contentions that there was, or should be, substantially no deterministic association between market structure and performance. Rather, the idiosyncrasies of managers or managements were the dominant determinants of performance, regardless of market structures. Nourse went on to suggest that the idiosyncrasies of managers were systematically linked with their earlier occupational experiences. For example, Wall Street bankers would tend to follow quite different, and more conservative, price and related policies than would managers who had risen from production lines in manufacturing. This formulation further implied that there was more than one solution to a profit-maximizing problem, depending on the risk-aversion propensities of individual managers, and that the variance in solutions potentially overwhelmed associations of performance with market structure. Concerning the alleged attitudes of the manager who rose from the production line, we also seem to find the first seeds of the sales-maximization hypothesis.

Some debate between Mason and Nourse over the issue described above (the content of which is firmly imbedded in my notes of the time) is recalled by one of the principals thereto, but I have been unable to discover it in print. In any event, nobody won the debate, largely because it was on an a priori level and about ten years before the first statistical test of Mason's hypothesis appeared. In retrospect, we can say first that, if Nourse had been absolutely right, a lot of subsequent econometric experiments would have been conducted substantially to no point. Second, Mason's basic hypothesis has been confirmed to a considerable extent by such experiments. Third, if Mason and Nourse were both partly right–if, for example, there were a systematic and significant, but not strictly deterministic, association between structure and performance and if managerial idiosyncrasy also played quite a role–this circumstance would help explain the large amount of "statistical static" typically encountered in experiments relating structure to performance.

[1]E. S. Mason, "Price and Production Policies of Large-Scale Enterprise," American Economic Review, XXXIX, Suppl., March 1939, pp. 61-74. Reprinted in American Economic Association, *Readings in Industrial Organization and Public Policy,* ed. Heflebower and Stocking, 1958, pp. 190-204.

[2]See especially E. G. Nourse and H. B. Drury, *Industrial Price Policies and Economic Progress,* Washington, 1938, and E. G. Nourse, *Price Making in a Democracy,* Washington, 1944.

The Possibility of Applying Statistical Tests to Mason's Hypothesis

The second piece of "underbrush," not wholly unrelated to the first, is the issue of whether or not the attributes of market structure that in Mason's system supposedly influence or determine market performance are few enough to make Mason's original hypothesis conceivably susceptible to statistical test—as in a cross-sectional analysis of industries. If, after all, the number of attributes of market structure is very large for any firm, statistical testing goes out the window. Nearly every industry or class of firms is then structurally unique in some respect (has a distinctive "mix" of significant structural attributes) and cross-sectional testing becomes unproductive. Every individual firm or industry becomes a case automatically self-explained by its singular total market structure or environment. In this event, the explanation of performances in terms of structures becomes at best an heuristic exercise, industry by industry, with no generalizations really in sight. That the original Mason hypothesis should have begun with this hidden blight is probably attributable to the fact that, when he propounded it, research in the nascent field of industrial organization centered on studying individual industries rather than on cross-sectional econometric experiments.

To trace the progress of the germinal Masonian doctrine, let us cite a few quotations. In his 1939 article, mentioned above,[3] when referring to the Chamberlain model, he commented that

> . . . The only part of that foundation which is likely to be found useable is composed of the ascertainable facts of numbers of sellers (and buyers) and product differentiation.[4]

To which he added:

> At least in the industrial area, the market, and market structure, must be defined with reference to the position of a single seller or buyer. *The structure of a seller's market, then, includes all those considerations which he takes into account in determining his business policies and practices. His market includes all buyers and sellers, of whatever produce, whose action he considers to influence his volume of sales.*[5]

And finally:

> The classification of market structures on the seller's side consists, then, in grouping together those firms, in whatever industry, which operate under the same or similar objective conditions. Among these conditions are the economic characteristics of the product; is it a producers or consumers good, is it durable or non-durable, is the product of an individual seller differentiated with respect to the

[3]Mason, op. cit., p. 195 in *Readings.*
[4]Ibid., p. 195.
[5]Ibid., p. 198. Italics added.

> products of other sellers in the same market or is it standardized? Another group of conditions relate to the cost and production of characteristics of the firm's operation. The ratio of overhead to variable costs at given volumes of output and for given variations in volume of output, the flexibility of costs, locational factors, and existence of joint costs are all important. A third class of considerations has to do with the numbers and relative sizes of buyers and sellers of whose action our given seller has to take account and with the relative ease of entry for new firms. Among the demand conditions which are empirically determinable may be mentioned the trend of sales, seasonal and cyclical fluctuations in sales, and roughly, the knowledge possessed by buyers with respect to the quality and characteristics of the product. Differences in distribution channels provide another set of conditions of great importance for the policies and practices of a firm. The accurate specification and measurement of these and other market conditions with respect to an individual firm admittedly presents great, but not insuperable, difficulties. Properly used the available data should permit of an illuminating grouping of firms into classes exhibiting roughly the same type of market conditions. Under similar market conditions may not firms be expected to pursue similar policies and practices? A careful study of the empirically determinable differences in market structure may go far in explaining observable differences in policy and practice.[6]

This formulation of the Mason hypothesis was, and is, both stimulating and thought-provoking, however much tied to a view that research in the newly created field of industrial organization should center on individual firms or classes thereof. Regarding Mason's suggested grouping of firms into classes with roughly the same type of market structure, we tend to stumble on the same rock mentioned above . . . . If we introduce into our classificatory system a large number of attributes of market structure, we rapidly approach the limit where there are only one or two instances of each "class"–especially given the reduction of the size of the sample for various extraneous reasons–and where statistical testing is fruitless. Despite this difficulty with too many independent variables, Mason's suggestion of a market-classification approach stands as a tall landmark in the development of a new field of industrial organization. The writer endorsed the original Masonian view for a number of years, as indicated in the following excerpt from a book published in 1944:

> A considerable acquaintance with the population of sellers and buyers in a market, with the source of the materials and the character of their productive techniques, with the geography of the market, and with the framework of law surrounding it is a prerequisite to the effective study of competition and price behavior within the market. This is true for both the author and the reader. The merits of such an analysis should not be confined, however, to

[6]Ibid., p. 198-199.

> its service as a preface to further work. A description, from the vantage point of economic analysis, of the environment of a principal industrial market may prove useful and perhaps illuminating to the economist and the general reader alike. It may further acquaintance with the extremely complex character of business institutions in the modern world, and may suggest hypotheses for investigation in the immediate or other industries.[7]

Even in the early 1960's, I endorsed the comparable views of my co-authors of a book, though in the special context of an exploratory study of structure-performance relations in a single public-enterprise industry, as follows:

> "Market structure" encompasses those elements of the common environment of firms in a market which theoretical reasoning identifies as having a possible significant influence on their behavior. Elements of market structure that are customarily identified as theoretically significant include the number and size distribution of buyers and sellers in the market, the extent of barriers to the entry of new buyers and sellers, the presence or absence of product differentiation, the magnitude of fixed costs in the short run, the rate of growth of demand, and the presence of any special governmental regulations affecting the behavior of firms in the industry.[8]

By this time, however, I had certainly changed my mind about the original Mason hypothesis, and along the following line. First, if one poured into market structure as determinants of performance "everything but the kitchen sink," we were left with an hypothesis irrefutable a priori and not subject to statistical test, because we were approaching the limit at which nearly every industry was in a very significant degree structurally unique, in a different "class." And an hypothesis that is not conceivably susceptible to empirical refutation is not much of an hypothesis at all.

Second, the only way out of this trap—if one were to test for structure-performance relations—was to specify a very few, supposedly leading, structural variables that should be primarily associated with market performance—few enough to make cross-sectional testing meaningful. This would involve some revision, but no destruction, of the original Masonian hypothesis. The revision would simply adapt the hypothesis to a shift from the industry-study to the cross-sectional approach.

This revised approach is indeed not without its difficulties. No one ever supposed that the variance of dependent performance variables, especially within short or medium spans of time, was fully or in large part dependent on any selected few structural variables, whatever their names. In a limited time period, the expectation—as supported by experiment—is that the variance in any

[7] Joe S. Bain, *The Economics of the Pacific Coast Petroleum Industry,* Berkeley, 1944, Part I, p. vii.

[8] Bain, Caves, Margolis, *Northern California's Water Industry,* Baltimore, 1966, p. 5.

dependent performance variable like a profit rate is proportionally much more influenced by "random" independent variables—such as demand variation, windfalls, and the like—than by a few specified structural variables—such as seller concentration and the condition of entry. Thus, in any experiment relating a few specified structural variables to performance, we encounter a great deal of "statistical static," or, in other words a large proportion of variance in the dependent performance variable not accounted for by the few specified structural variables. Hence enters first the dependence on statistical significance tests. And we find disappointingly low coefficients relating dependent to selected independent variables, and relatively low values of correlation coefficients.

Thus, we get into a box from which it is hard to escape. Being in this box is a price paid for trying to confirm a Masonian hypothesis with cross-sectional experiments. Either recognizing the dimensions of the box or just charging ahead without much thought, nearly all practitioners in the area of econometric tests of structure-performance relations have opted for specifying very few structural independent variables and then put the experiment in the "computer mill" to see what would fall out. Most interpretations of results have reflected a fairly sophisticated appreciation of the basic hypothesis and of the statistical problems involved. If we are interested in cross-sectional testing of the Masonian hypothesis, the counsel of wisdom seems to be that we should specify on a priori grounds or from experience a very few independent structural variables and deal with our statistical problems as they arise. One note might be added. In a more or less standard single-equation multiple regression (and elsewhere), every time we add an additional independent structural variable, we tend to enhance the problem of collinearity of independent variables—a result not generally to be desired.

THE COMPARATIVE STABILITY OF MARKET STRUCTURES

We now return to the main theme by inquiring into the comparative stability of market structure—and particularly into the stability of those few dimensions of structure usually emphasized in the sort of econometric tests referred to above. In these dimensions, I would include especially, but not exclusively, seller concentration, product differentiation, and the condition of entry. Some proxies for the preceding—such as ratios of selling cost to sales for product-differentiation barriers to entry or such as measures of plant concentration for plant scale economies and resulting barriers to entry—might be used.

The issue of structural stability is indeed crucial to any meaningful test of the central Masonian hypothesis, which rests fundamentally on the postulate that independent structural variables are comparatively immutable variables determining in the long run the values of dependent performance variables. If, after all, attributes of market structure were will-o'-the wisps that moved quite significantly with the tides or seasons, there would not be much left to test, except in some very mechanical econometric context in which a number is just a number. Thus, we do need to inquire into comparative structural stability.

Not enough attention has been given to the issue for us to suggest conclusive answers, but we can offer some relevant a priori indications and evidence. As regards seller concentration, we might expect it to change at least slowly over time as surrounding circumstances vary. The record shows that *on the average* such concentration within industries has changed little for quite a while; for example, one Census publication indicates that from 1935 to 1947, with respect to 103 comparably defined 4-digit manufacturing industries, concentration as measured by the 4-firm concentration ratio increased perceptibly in 33 cases, decreased perceptibly in 34 cases, and was substantially unchanged in 36 cases. Subsequent studies, carrying us to 1958 or beyond, have revealed a similar sluggishness in the average of individual-industry concentration ratios. Still, there is evidently an appreciable variance in seller concentration within many individual industries, so that we cannot assume, for purposes of statistical testing, that individual-industry concentrations are in general practically immutable for periods as long as a decade.

It should be added to the preceding that, for a number of industries in this country, the actual degree of seller concentration has at once been overstated and made deceptively to appear stable because Census concentration data systematically disregard shipments or sales of foreign imports. After the period of postwar reconstruction, tariff reductions and comparable measures passed before World War II "took hold," thereby encouraging appreciable increases in foreign imports of a number of goods—for instance, steel, automobiles—with the result that actual seller concentration in the United States market moved more than Census statistics indicate.

What of the condition of entry? My observations suggest that, on the average among industries, the condition of entry tends to be comparatively stable over time, but it is a bit more of a will-o'-the-wisp than sellers' concentration, though selectively among industries. As regards absolute-cost barriers to entry, we need mainly note that patent expirations—or destruction of patent protection by antitrust decrees—sporadically lower such barriers significantly or even radically. As regards product-differentiation barriers to entry, we may note that in some significant cases—distilled liquors, for instance—relatively rapid shifts in consumer preferences, like that away from bourbon whiskey, have radically reduced entry barriers in less than a decade, as have product innovations in other cases. But the proportion of manufacturing industries appreciably affected is relatively small. As regards scale-economies barriers to entry, growth of the size of the market regularly reduces their impact; otherwise, there is relative stability. We must note, however, that scale-economy barriers in the United States market for a product may be significantly eroded if a foreign producer with a world market can exploit all scale economies while still exporting to the United States a minor fraction of his output. Think of the Volkswagen. Although this phenomenon is a long way from being ubiquitous, it must be taken into account.

Product differentiation within industries is sometimes fairly stable over time, but I conclude from observation that it is probably the least stable of the principal structural attributes of markets considered—this mainly of course with regard to consumer-good industries. Examples of instability in this regard include sellers of fountain pens, portable transistorized radios, typewriters, distilled liquor, and soft drinks. Here we seem to have a structural variable which often is disturbingly unstable over time.

My overall impression (very much of a guess-estimate) is that seller concentration is a variable which, on the average, is fairly stable over time, but not nearly as stable as we would like in order to get a very clear test of the central Masonian hypothesis. The condition of entry in general seems to have a roughly comparable stability. The stability of intraindustry product differentiation is probably a bit less.

These observations raise some serious statistical problems for cross-sectional testing of the hypothesis concerning the relation of structure to performance—problems that are not destructive but disturbing. Let us turn to some parts of these problems.

STRUCTURAL INSTABILITY AND TESTING OF HYPOTHESES

The basic hypothesis to be tested is that comparatively immutable dimensions of market structure have a *long-run* association with market performance. If we are really going to test this hypothesis, the market-structure variables ought to "hold still," or pretty still, for at least medium terms of time. For example, if at the one extreme the market-structure variables should be highly unstable from year to year, we could not test the hypothesis successfully, mainly because its a priori foundations would have been undercut rather thoroughly. Fortunately, we do not seem to be in this extreme situation.

But suppose that one or more of three or four basic structural variables are sufficiently unstable over time that we can only associate structure with performance for a succession of quite short-term periods—such as periods of three or four years. (Stigler, for example, apparently wary of the variability of his own dubiously devised concentration ratios, chopped the period 1938 to 1957 into six separate periods, each separately tested.[9] Waiving the temptation to dissect Stigler's data and methodology in detail, I only point out that chopping up tests into three- or four-year intervals is almost as good as throwing the experiment away. Whatever is ostensibly picked up in statistical degrees of freedom is much more than cancelled by the very strong influence on the dependent performance variable—here profit rates—of short-run nonstructural influences on these rates, influences that are mostly unregistered in the formal statistical tests. From the standpoint of the basic hypothesis, "statistical static"

[9]See George J. Stigler, *Capital and Rates of Return in Manufacturing Industries*, Princeton, 1963. See especially p. 68.

tends to become so dominant that it is terribly difficult to ascertain any medium- or long-term associations of structure with performance.

More generally, where are we left in conducting experiments testing the long-run relation of structure to performance under conditions where the independent structural variables are appreciably mutable over time, even if not as mutable as Stigler might have suggested? In view of this mutability, it seems first that we need to look for the longest time period during which structural mutation has not been very large–I like about ten years on the average.

Having selected such a time period, the prevailing practice of assigning to each industry or firm a single measure of each structural variable, to be used as applicable to the whole test period, seems undesirable if the structural variable is appreciably mutable. This is because the statistically determined association of structure with performance will then be more or less arbitrarily weakened. It would be somewhat more desirable in a regression to use for each independent structural variable for every case a mean of the beginning and ending values of the variable. Greater statistical sins have been committed. One might also, in every case, complement the selected measure of each mutable structural characteristic with a matching independent variable that denotes roughly the direction and degree of structural change over the period of the statistical test. Use of these or comparably sensible statistical devices might help resolve some of the numerical difficulties that have been encountered in past experiments. As we continue to test the adapted Masonian hypothesis, this approach seems like a possibly rewarding track.

Chapter Thirteen

Changes in Concentration in Manufacturing Industries in the United States, 1954-1966: Trends and Relationships to the Levels of 1954 Concentration

This presentation of descriptive statistics is designed to explore two main questions concerning changes in seller concentration in American manufacturing industries from 1954 to 1966:

1. Over this period, was there any significant upward or downward trend in individual-industry concentration ratios, as indicated both by the frequencies of positive and negative concentration changes, and by the size distributions of these changes? (And, as a sub-question, were there any significant shifts between 1963 and 1966?)

2. Was there, over the period in question, any systematic relationship between the directions and sizes of concentration changes in individual industries and their concentration ratios in 1954?[1]

Reprinted from *The Review of Economics and Statistics,* 52, November 1970, pp. 411-416, courtesy of the publisher.

[1]We will not pursue further here various explorations into the relationship of changes in industry concentration to market growth, product differentiation and durability, changes in minimum optimal plant scale, height of barriers to entry, etc. (See, e.g., Ralph S. Nelson, "Market Growth, Company Diversification, and Product Concentration, 1947-1954," *Journal of the American Statistical Association,* LV (Dec. 1960), pp. 640-649; Leonard W. Weiss, "Factors in Changing Concentration," *Review of Economics and Statistics,* XLV (Feb. 1963), pp. 70-77; William G. Shepherd, "Trends of Concentration in American Manufacturing Industries," *Review of Economics and Statistics,* XLVI (May 1964), pp. 200-212; David R. Kamerschen, "Market Growth and Industry Concentration," *Journal of the American Statistical Association,* LXIII (Mar. 1968), pp. 228-241.) Initial level of industry concentration, here emphasized, appears to be at best a weak proxy for any of the other "determinants" of concentration mentioned (serious collinearity problems are not expected).

We pose the first question because we would like to know to what extent individual-industry concentration has been responsive since 1954 to increases in the shares of all manufacturing activity controlled by the largest 50, 100, and 200 manufacturing firms, and to the considerable number of large manufacturing mergers.

Statistics prepared by the Bureau of Census show a large increase from 1947 to 1954 in the share of total value added by manufacture accounted for by the largest manufacturing firms, and a smaller increase from 1958 to 1963 (Table 13.1).[2] Although the increase in the share of all manufacturing value of shipments made by the largest firms was evidently smaller than the corresponding increase in the share of all value added, an appreciable increase in the value of shipments share evidently took place.[3] At the same time, changes in individual-industry concentration did not display a comparable trend from 1947 to 1954. Over this period, for 367 comparably defined manufacturing industries, 41.4 per cent showed increases in their 4-firm concentration ratios (based on value of shipments) of 2 percentage points or more, 38.9 per cent decreases of 2 percentage points or more, and 19.7 per cent concentration changes less than 2 percentage points. More significantly, perhaps, of 161 comparably defined industries that showed increases or decreases in their concentration ratios of 5 percentage points or more from 1947 to 1954, 50.3 per cent showed increases and 40.7 per cent showed decreases.[4] It should be interesting to know if this high degree of stability of individual-industry concentration ratios persisted in subsequent years.

Table 13.1 Share of Total Value Added by Manufacture Accounted for by Largest Firms

Year	*Largest 50 firms*	*Largest 100 firms*	*Largest 200 firms*
1947	17	23	30
1954	23	30	37
1958	23	30	38
1963	25	33	41

In its analysis of mergers in manufacturing and mining from 1951 to 1966, the Federal Trade Commission has identified 923 "large" mergers (those wherein the

[2]U.S. Senate, Subcommittee on Antitrust and Monopoly, Committee on the Judiciary, 89th Congress, 2nd Session, *Concentration Ratios in Manufacturing Industry, 1963* (Report prepared by the Bureau of the Census), part I, p. 2, table 1A. Washington, 1966.

[3]Ralph S. Nelson, in his *Concentration in the Manufacturing Industries of the United States* (New Haven, 1963, p. 13) found that the change from 1947 to 1954 in the share of all manufacturing value of shipments made by the 50 largest firms was only from 22.6 to 24.8 per cent, and attributed the difference between this change and the larger one measured for value added in part to increased vertical integration by the largest firms, and in part to the transitory effect on the 1954 value-added shares of some increase in the profit margins of the largest firms from 1947 to 1954.

[4]U.S. Senate, Subcommittee on Antitrust and Monopoly, Committee on the Judiciary, 85th Congress, 1st Session, *Concentration in American Industry* (Report prepared by the Bureau of the Census), p. 25, table 19. Washington, 1957.

acquired or minor company had assets of $10 million or more), and of these 241 were either of the "horizontal" (combining directly competing firms) or geographical "market extension" types—both of which would tend directly to increase individual industry concentration ratios as reported by the Census. Although 60 of these 241 mergers were challenged by the Federal Trade Commission or the Antitrust Division of the Justice Department (in a great majority of cases successfully challenged), there were enough large horizontal and market extension mergers successfully consummated that we might expect, ceteris paribus, some modest trend toward increasing individual-industry concentration from 1954 to 1966.[5]

The second question is raised because of curiosity as to whether or not, from 1954 to 1963 or 1966, there was an appreciable systematic tendency for individual industries with initially rather low concentration to experience significantly more numerous and larger increases in concentration than decreases, and conversely for individual industries with initially rather high concentration to experience more numerous and larger decreases in concentration than increases. Was there a centripetal tendency affecting concentration ratios in individual industries, such as would bring them closer together over time?

THE DATA USED

The data used in seeking answers to the questions posed above were drawn from Bureau of Census publications containing comparisons of 4-digit Census industry concentration ratios (based on value of shipments) for 1954 and 1963 and for 1954 and 1966. Inter-year comparisons were necessarily limited to industries which were comparably defined in the years being compared. Because there was a substantial revision in the Standard Industrial Classification used by the Bureau of Census between 1954 and 1963, the samples of comparably defined industries are substantially smaller than the corresponding total populations.

For the comparison of 4-digit industry concentration ratios of 1954 and 1963, the sample of comparably defined industries numbered 212, as compared to 417 such industries in 1963—or about half of the total population (Table 13.2). The sample is reasonably representative of the total population with respect to the concentration classes within which the industries fell, as indicated by the following tabulation, where concentration refers to share of industry value of shipments supplied by the four largest firms.

The sample is also reasonably representative of the total population with respect to the average size (in terms of value of shipments) of the industries included, although it does include a somewhat larger proportion of smaller industries than the total population, as indicated by Table 13.3. It is not clear that such sample bias as exists should significantly affect our findings.

[5]U.S. House of Representatives, Antitrust Subcommittee, Committee on the Judiciary, 90th Congress, 1st Session, *The Celler-Kefauver Act: Sixteen Years of Enforcement,* by Willard F. Mueller, Director, Bureau of Economics, Federal Trade Commission, p. 7, table 5. Washington, 1967.

Table 13.2 Industry Concentration Ratio Comparisons

Total population[a] *1963 (n = 417)*		*Sample population*[b] *1963 (n = 212)*	
1954 concentration class	*Percentage of* n	*1954 concentration class*	*Percentage of* n
0-19	22	1-20	26
20-39	39	21-40	30
40-59	22	41-60	23
60-79	11	61-80	15
80-100	6	81-100	6
	100		100

[a]U.S. Senate, Subcommittee on Antitrust and Monopoly, Committee on the Judiciary, 90th Congress, 1st Session, *Concentration Ratios in Manufacturing Industry, 1963* (Report prepared by the Bureau of the Census), part II, p. 259, table 5.

[b]See Table 13.4 below.

Table 13.3 Percentages of Industries in 1963 Value-of-Shipments Class[a]

Value of 1963 industry shipments	*Sample number industries*	*Industries not in sample*
Under 1 billion	78	71
1 to 2 1/2 billion	16	22
2 1/2 to 5 billion	4	6
Over 5 billion	2	1

[a]U.S. Senate, Subcommittee on Antitrust and Monopoly, Committee on the Judiciary, 89th Congress, 2nd Session, *Concentration Ratios in Manufacturing Industry,* 1963 (Report prepared by the Bureau of the Census), part I, pp. 6-37, table 2.

In the comparison of 4-digit industry concentration ratios of 1954 and 1966, the sample of comparably defined industries numbered 195. It was the same sample used for 1963, reduced by the omission of 18 industries for which 1966 data were not available, and augmented by the addition of one industry for which data were available for 1966 but not for 1963. Fifteen of the 18 omissions fell in the 1954 concentration class (four largest firms) of 1 to 40.

In all cases we have accepted Census concentration ratios and thus Census industry definitions as given, making no attempt to rectify them. We are well aware of the fact that Census industries, and thus the concentration ratios computed for them, are in a very substantial proportion of cases quite poor approximations to "theoretical industries" or to theoretically meaningful concentration ratios. For our purposes here, however, where we are comparing concentration within more or less identically defined groups for two or more time periods, the biases in Census concentration ratios should not invalidate the results of our experiment.

STATISTICAL FINDINGS

The statistical findings relating to the questions posed are summarized below in four tables, referring to the numbers, directions, and average sizes of changes in 4-firm concentration ratios of sample industries: Table 13.4, for 4-digit

Table 13.4 Changes in 4-Firm Concentration Ratios for 212 Comparably Defined 4-Digit Census Industries, 1954-1963, Classified by 1954 Concentration

A. Number of positive, negative, and zero concentration changes.

1954 concentration class (four-firm ratios)	*0-20*	*21-40*	*41-60*	*61-80*	*81-100*	*Total*
No. of positive changes	35	37	19	10	4	105
No. of negative changes	17	25	26	18	7	93
No. of zero changes	5	1	4	3	1	14

B. Average per industry percentage-point changes in concentration.

1954 concentration class (four-firm ratios)	*0-20*	*21-40*	*41-60*	*61-80*	*81-100*	*Total*
For positive changes	5.1	6.1	8.2	6.3	4.0	6.0
For negative changes	3.5	4.1	6.4	6.4	4.7	5.2
For zero changes	0	0	0	0	0	0

Source: U.S. Senate, Subcommittee on Antitrust and Monopoly, Committee on the Judiciary, 89th Congress, 2nd Session, *Concentration Ratios in Manufacturing Industry, 1963.* (Report prepared by the Bureau of the Census.) Derived from part I, table 2 therein, pp. 6-37. Washington, 1966.

Table 13.5 Changes in 4-Firm Concentration Ratios for 212 Comparably Defined 4-Digit Census Industries, 1954-1963, Classified by 1954 Concentration, and Grouped into "Large" Positive, "Large" Negative, and "Small" Changes

A. Number of "large" positive, "large" negative and "small" concentration changes.

1954 concentration class (four-firm ratios)	*0-20*	*21-40*	*41-60*	*61-80*	*81-100*	*Total*
No. of "large"[a] positive changes	13	19	12	5	1	50
No. of "large"[a] negative changes	5	9	15	13	3	45
No. of "small"[b] changes	39	35	22	13	8	117

B. Average per industry percentage-point changes in concentration.

1954 concentration class (four-firm ratios)	*0-20*	*21-40*	*41-60*	*61-80*	*81-100*	*Total*
For "large"[a] positive changes	9.6	9.6	11.1	10.6	6.0	10.0
For "large"[a] negative changes	5.8	7.1	9.5	7.6	8.3	8.4
For "small"[b] changes	2.2	2.2	3.6	2.0	2.3	2.5

Source: Same as Table 13.4.
[a]"Large" refers to percentage-point concentration changes of 5 or more.
[b]"Small" refers to percentage-point concentration changes of 4 or less.

industries, 1954-1963, all positive, negative, and zero changes listed; Table 13.5, for the same industries and time period, with changes grouped as "large" positive, "large" negative, and "small"; Table 13.6, the same as Table 13.4, but referring to 1954-1966 changes; and Table 13.7, the same as Table 13.5, but referring to 1954-1966 changes. All concentration ratios are based on value of shipments.

Indications concerning any possible trends in individual industry concentration from 1954 to 1963 or 1966 are contained in the "Total" columns of Tables 13.4 through 13.7. From 1954 to 1963, omitting 14 industries with zero changes in concentration (or 6.6 per cent of a total of 212 industries), 53 per cent of the industries showing changes had increases in concentration, and 47 per cent had decreases. Moreover, the mean change for industries with increasing concentration was 6.0 percentage points, as contrasted with 5.2 percentage points for industries with decreasing concentrations (Table 13.4). From 1954 to 1966, again omitting a few industries with zero concentration changes, 54.3 per cent of industries showing changes had increases in concentration, and 45.7 per cent had decreases. The mean change for industries with increasing concentration was 7.5 percentage points, as against 4.9 percentage points for industries with decreasing concentration (Table 13.6). The preceding suggests an appreciable though moderate trend toward increasing industry concentration from 1954 to 1963, and a continuation and acceleration of this upward trend from 1963 to 1966.

Let us now focus attention on relatively "large" increases and decreases in industry concentration, of 5 percentage points or more, eliminating "small" changes, of 4 percentage points or less, over the same time periods. (This results in eliminating 117 observations, or about 55 per cent of the total in the 1954-1963 comparison, and 96 observations, or about 49 per cent of the total in the 1954-1966 comparison.) Of "large" changes only, between 1954 and 1963, increases accounted for 52.6 per cent and decreases for 47.4 per cent—about the same ratio observed for all positive and negative changes over this period. Similarly, the mean of "large" positive changes was 10.0 percentage points, compared with a mean of 8.4 percentage points for "large" negative changes (Table 13.5). But from 1954 to 1966, "large" increases in concentration accounted for 65.7 per cent of the total of "large" changes, and "large" decreases for only 34.3 per cent. The disparity in mean percentage point changes between "large" increases and decreases, however, was only that between 10.2 and 9.1 (Table 13.7). In the net, nonetheless, there is further indication that the moderate trend toward increasing industry concentration from 1954 to 1963 was continued and accelerated from 1963 to 1966.

We now turn to our second question, concerning possible relationships of the directions and sizes of concentration changes in individual industries after 1954 to their concentration ratios in 1954. Inspection of "A" parts of Tables 13.4 through 13.7 suggests that increases in concentration were appreciably more frequent than decreases in industries with 1954 concentration ratios from 1 to 40, whereas decreases in concentration appreciably outweighed increases in industries with 1954 concentration ratios from 61 to 100. Inspecting all four

Table 13.6 Changes in 4-Firm Concentration Ratios for 195 Comparably Defined 4-Digit Census Industries, 1954-1966, Classified by 1954 Concentration

A. Number of positive, negative, and zero concentration changes.

1954 concentration class (four-firm ratios)	*0-20*	*21-40*	*41-60*	*61-80*	*81-100*	*Total*
No. of positive changes	33	29	22	11	7	102
No. of negative changes	13	26	23	19	5	86
No. of zero changes	3	1	2	0	1	7

B. Average per industry percentage-point changes in concentration.

1954 concentration class (four-firm ratios)	*0-20*	*21-40*	*41-60*	*61-80*	*81-100*	*Total*
For positive changes	6.3	8.3	9.8	6.3	4.0	7.5
For negative changes	3.5	3.6	6.2	6.3	5.6	4.9
For zero changes	0	0	0	0	0	0

Source: U.S. Department of Commerce, Bureau of the Census, *Annual Survey of Manufactures, 1966: Value-of-Shipment Concentration Ratios by Industry*. Derived from table therein, pp. 3-29. Washington, 1968.

Table 13.7 Changes in 4-Firm Concentration Ratios for 195 Comparably Defined 4-Digit Census Industries, 1954-1966, Classified by 1954 Concentration, and Grouped into "Large" Positive, "Large" Negative, and "Small" Changes

A. Number of "large" positive, "large" negative, and "small" concentration changes.

1954 concentration class (four-firm ratios)	*0-20*	*21-40*	*41-60*	*61-80*	*81-100*	*Total*
No. of "large"[a] positive changes	22	18	15	7	3	65
No. of "large"[a] negative changes	4	6	11	11	2	34
No. of "small"[b] changes	23	32	21	12	8	96

B. Average per industry percentage-point changes in concentration.

1954 concentration class (four-firm ratios)	*0-20*	*21-40*	*41-60*	*61-80*	*81-100*	*Total*
For "large"[a] positive changes	8.1	11.7	13.1	8.7	6.0	10.2
For "large"[a] negative changes	6.3	8.3	10.8	8.4	11.0	9.1
For "small"[b] changes	2.2	2.3	2.0	2.9	2.0	2.2

Source: Same as Table 13.6.
[a]"Large" refers to percentage-point concentration changes of 5 or more.
[b]"Small" refers to percentage-point concentration changes of 4 or less.

tabulations, increases and decreases were roughly in balance for industries with 1954 concentration ratios from 41 to 60.

Thus, of all positive and negative concentration changes from 1954 to 1963 (omitting zero changes) for industries with 1954 concentration ratios from 1 to 40, 63.2 per cent were increases and 36.8 were decreases. In the same sample for industries with 1954 concentration ratios from 61 to 100, 35.9 per cent of concentration changes were increases and 64.1 per cent decreases (Table 13.4). The same comparison for 1954 to 1966 changes yields corresponding increase and decrease percentages of 61.4 and 38.6 for industries with 1954 concentration ratios of 40 or below, and 42.9 and 57.1 for industries with 1954 concentration ratios of 61 or above (Table 13.6).

Similar comparisons referring only to "large" positive and negative changes in concentration show that from 1954 to 1963 "large" increases comprised 69.6 per cent of "large" concentration changes for industries with 1954 concentration ratios from 1 to 40, and that for industries with 1954 concentration ratios of 61 to 100, "large" decreases constituted 72.7 per cent of "large" changes (Table 13.5). The corresponding percentages of "large" changes between 1954 and 1966 are 80 per cent increases for industries with 1954 concentration ratios of 40 or below, and 56.5 per cent decreases for industries with 1954 concentration of 61 or above (Table 13.7). Generally, these findings referring to "large" concentration changes tend to reinforce the hypothesis that increases in industry concentration after 1954 appreciably outweighed decreases for industries with comparatively low 1954 concentration, and that decreases similarly outweighed increases for industries with comparatively high 1954 concentration.

Considering all four tables, there was not a comparably distinct tendency for the average percentage-point sizes of positive and negative changes to bear relationships similar to those found for numbers of positive and negative changes in the 40-or-below and 61-or-above 1954 concentration groups of industries. A comparable relationship (average size of increase greater than average size of decrease) is observed for industries with 1954 concentration of 40-or-below for all comparisons (1954-1963 and 1954-1966, all changes and "large" changes only), but the relationship is weak and inconsistent for industries with 1954 concentration ratios of 61 or greater. This finding, however, does not significantly undermine the overall findings based on numbers of concentration increases and decreases in various 1954 concentration classes.

In interpreting our findings concerning the relationships of directions of industry concentration changes since 1954 to the industries' initial concentration ratios, some allowance should perhaps be made for the fact that industries with relatively low concentration have relatively more "room" for concentration increases than decreases, and vice-versa for industries with relatively high concentration. Without the aid of a detailed and implausible ceteris paribus clause, however, this hardly translates into the proposition that, on strictly statistical grounds, a preponderance of concentration increases is significantly more probable in the low-concentration sector of industries, and a preponderance of concentration decreases significantly more probable in the high-concentration sector.

We also analyzed concentration changes from 1954 to 1963 for 446 comparably defined 5-digit product groups (a sample equalling about 30 per cent of the total population) in a manner identical to that followed for 4-digit industries in Tables 13.4 and 13.5[6]. The resulting tabulations are not presented here but the findings were generally consistent with those already described.

CONCLUSIONS

We have arrived at two tentative conclusions, which are subject to check by somewhat more sophisticated statistical analysis. The first is that from 1954 to 1963 there was a moderate trend toward increasing concentration in individual manufacturing industries—as indicated both by the relative frequency of increases and decreases in concentration and by the relative average sizes of increases and decreases—and that this trend continued and accelerated from 1963 to 1966. The second is that over the period 1954 to 1966 there was an appreciable relationship between the relative frequencies of increases and decreases of the concentration ratios of industries on the one hand, and the level of concentration of the industries in 1954 on the other. The relationship was such that concentration increases appreciably outweighed decreases for industries with 1954 concentration ratios from 1 to 40, whereas decreases outweigh increases for industries with 1954 ratios of 61 to 100. This suggests some modest centripetal tendency for individual-industry concentration ratios to become more similar or less disparate over the time period in question. The first finding is not unexpected in view of merger activity and increasing concentration in the manufacturing sector as a whole. We leave it to the reader to select a theory or conduct a further experiment to explain the second finding.

[6]The analysis was derived from U.S. Senate, Subcommittee on Antitrust and Monopoly, Committee on the Judiciary, *Concentration Ratios in Manufacturing Industry, 1963* (Report prepared by the Bureau of the Census), part I, table 4, pp. 137-242, Washington, 1966.

Chapter Fourteen

Chamberlin's Impact on Microeconomic Theory

Anyone setting out to appraise the impact of Chamberlin's major work on "microeconomic theory" may quickly regret that the infelicitous terms "micro" and "macro" have been coined to dichotomize economic theory and have gained nearly universal acceptance. The terrain of economic theory is thus divided into two parts, although the subterritories of microstatics, microdynamics, macrostatics, and macrodynamics are also recognized. And the part that could reasonably be viewed as "micro" is very large. Theories of consumer behavior, of the firm, and of both commodity and factor markets should be included offhand, bringing with them a part of capital theory, much of the theory of international trade, and the neoclassical theory of general equilibrium.

A comprehensive evaluation of the influence of *The Theory of Monopolistic Competition* (hereafter referred to as *Monopolistic Competition*) on contemporary microeconomic theory should not neglect any of these broad segments, but in this essay some arbitrary limits have been self-imposed. Because other contributors assess the impact of *Monopolistic Competition* on several designated areas of microeconomic theory and because it has had only a minor impact on some others, this essay considers only the influence of Chamberlin's work on the central system of microstatic theory that embraces the interrelated theories of the consumer, of the firm, and of individual commodity markets–on "price theory" thus construed.

THE GENERAL IMPORTANCE OF THE IMPACT

What are the major impacts of *Monopolistic Competition* on this corpus of economic theory? Before trying to answer this question in detail, we should recognize the broader issue of whether it has had a major impact at all, for at present different economists or schools thereof evaluate the general importance

Reprinted from *Monopolistic Competition Theory: Studies in Impact,* edited by R. E. Kuenne, pp. 147-176, courtesy of John Wiley & Sons, Inc.

of Chamberlin's work quite differently. At the negative extreme, we find the opinion that *Monopolistic Competition* and subsequent theory in its tradition have added little of importance to microstatic theory. This view has several evident wellsprings aside from laziness, a nostalgia for things past, or a disrespect for any theory that isn't mathematically formulated. Most vigorously asserted is the belief that the systematic deviations from purely competitive market behavior that Chamberlin predicted for oligopolistic and product-differentiated markets *in fact* do not significantly affect the allocative efficiency of the actual price system, technical efficiency in production, or income distribution. These deviations are in this view sufficiently unimportant that his theory explains the working of a market-controlled economy no better than a simpler theory of pure competition (supplemented by a theory of pure monopoly to take care of pathological situations). A sophisticated version of Marshall and Walras will do nicely. Right or wrong, this belief evidently rests on the ultimate in casual empiricism, as well as an odd standard of empirical relevance.

A related basis for discounting the importance of *Monopolistic Competition* is a genuine lack of interest in the empirical relevance of price theory, matched by a preoccupation with the refinement for its own sake of the theory of a purely competitive economy. For economists of this persuasion, microeconomic theory appears to be a logician's or mathematician's game, most readily played with a bare minimum of assumptions and of variables. Modern scholastic theorists simply aren't very interested, when considering microstatics, in Chamberlinian theory.

Another evident ground for neglecting Chamberlin's work also deserves mention. This is the fact that the centrally important Chamberlinian model of ologipoly does not generate unique general predictions of market performance. Unique predictions may be wrested from it only by introducing special institutional assumptions; otherwise, even a sophisticated theory of oligopoly at best yields probability judgments. To some theorists this "deficiency" is fatal because the incorporation of oligopolistic markets into a system of microstatic theory precludes the deduction from very general assumptions of uniquely determined equilibria not only for one class of markets but also for the economy as a whole. Embracing the theory of oligopoly would frustrate the fulfillment of what they view as the essential purposes of a system of microstatic theory.

Those among contemporary price theorists who disparage or neglect the Chamberlinian type of theory are not a small minority, though their numerical importance is hard to judge. Price theory in general and microstatics in particular have not been the major preoccupation of economic theorists for some time, whereas a great deal of attention was given to price theory in the 1920's before Chamberlin's and Joan Robinson's works were published, and their books engendered a great flurry of writing in the two succeeding decades. The more recent comparative neglect of price theory seems attributable in large part to the well-known shifting of fads or fashions in economics, which frequently sets off mass migrations to new territories before those recently occupied have been thoroughly explored, and in lesser part to the fact that after the easy gold in the vein opened by *Monopolistic Competition* had been panned, most theorists abandoned the mine. Nonetheless, the considerable number of contemporary theorists who are detractors of Chamberlinian theory, who would like to forget about it, or who have never really studied it, clearly poses an issue concerning its ultimate importance in the system of price theory.

A probable majority of theorists still accords to *Monopolistic Competition* and subsequent literature in its tradition a major role in the development of modern microstatic economic theory. It has been held that in *Monopolistic Competition* Chamberlin really introduced a new price theory with a vastly greater empirical relevance than that of pre-existing theory and with an immensely increased immediate or latent power to generate hypotheses concerning enterprise behavior in the actual economy. As an advocate of this general view, I have put the case as follows in an earlier brief essay on *Monopolistic Competition:*

> This work simultaneously did two very important things. It advanced expressly—really for the first time—the major and crucial theoretical construct in which an economy of enterprises was viewed as being made up of industries having a variety of distinctly different market structures, with market conduct and performance tending to differ significantly with differences in structure. And it implemented this construct by developing an uncomplicated but actually quite sophisticated classification of market structures. This classification reflected a remarkable insight into what in the world of markets was empirically relevant to price theory, was the evident parent of substantially all more elaborate market classifications which have been subsequently suggested, and provided the basic skeleton for all of them which have had appreciable merit. . . . Further, [its] identification of dimensions of market performance in addition to those involving price, production cost, and output—that is, selling cost and product quality and variety—suggested an expanded range of matters deserving empirical [and, we might add here, theoretical] study within the sort of theoretical framework . . . established.[1]

This view places major emphasis on Chamberlin's introduction into microstatic theory of an empirically relevant theory of markets, via the primary route of innovating an empirically relevant set of assumptions concerning varieties of market structures and the secondary route of recognizing some empirically important additional decision variables. In retrospect, this important global contribution clearly overshadows Chamberlin's accomplishments in "grinding the deductive mill" to arrive at group equilibria, and also his specific predictions of market performance associated with various market structures and combinations of variables. For although *Monopolistic Competition* displayed considerable technical virtuosity for its time, it ran toward special rather than general solutions, failed to explore many significant implications of its general

[1] J. S. Bain, "*The Theory of Monopolistic Competition* after Thirty Years: The Impact on Industrial Organization," *American Economic Review, Papers and Proceedings,* LIV (May 1964), pp 28-32.

assumptions, and generated only qualitatively ambiguous predictions concerning some sorts of equilibria in which ambiguity is not intrinsic.

Its detractors have made the most of these shortcomings, at the same time endeavoring to prove by vigorous assertion that the empirical relevance of the assumptions of a theory—and in particular a theory of pure competition—does not matter much as long as that theory generates (as it is held to do) reasonably accurate predictions concerning selected economic phenomena. There are two main objections to this position. First, it remains to be demonstrated on general grounds that a theory based on assumptions that are patently and significantly at odds with the relevant facts is likely, except by accident, to generate satisfactorily accurate predictions. Second, the predictive power of a Marshallian or other purely competitive theory has been alleged to be confirmed by empirical evidence generally by persons who exhibit a slight familiarity with and thoroughgoing disrespect for the mass of relevant evidence, or who in a purely ex parte spirit casually adduce selected scraps of evidence in support of their positions.[2] The major defense of Chamberlin's principal contribution rests on the methodologically sound proposition that an economic theory can only be as good as its assumptions, and on the observation that Chamberlin in his theory of markets replaced unrealistic with empirically relevant assumptions concerning both market structures and the number of evidently important decision variables.

Logically, the next issue in this overview of the importance of *Monopolistic Competition* for microstatic theory concerns the over-all significance of theorizing evidently engendered or inspired by Chamberlin's major work and extending its tradition. It seems appropriate, however, to withhold any initial broad statements on this question in order to turn at once to a more detailed consideration of the post-Chamberlinian literature, as the main question really is what and how much others have made of what Chamberlin began (through elaboration, extension, and revision) in striving for a more satisfactory price theory. This is a pressing question because although Chamberlin pointed the way to a revolutionary change in price theory and drew its broad outlines, he did not himself fully exploit the implications of his major conceptual discoveries. Although *Monopolistic Competition* made an unshakable major contribution to price theory, it left an immense amount of work to be done if its potential were to be realized. Correspondingly, an assessment of microstatic theorizing inspired by Chamberlin necessarily involves considering criticism of his work and revisionism as well as simple elaboration or gap-filling.

The succeeding pages consider several sorts of development of price theory that have extended or been inspired by Chamberlin's work and identify some

[2]Koopmans states a related but more general objection to the methodological position, well summarized in the following remark: "To state a set of postulates, and then to exempt a subclass of their implications from verification is a curiously roundabout way of specifying the content of a theory that is regarded as open to empirical refutation. It leaves one without an understanding of the reasons for the exemptions." T.C. Koopmans, *Three Essays on the State of Economic Science,* McGraw-Hill, New York, 1957, p. 139 (see also pp. 132-142).

potentially fruitful lines of theorizing that were suggested by *Monopolistic Competition* but have not been adequately explored. Considered successively are: (1) market classifications and the industry concept; (2) monopoly power under monopolistic competition; (3) the theory of oligopoly; and (4) equilibria involving product determination and selling costs.

MARKET CLASSIFICATION AND THE INDUSTRY CONCEPT

In *Monopolistic Competition* Chamberlin began by asserting that the assumption of nearly universal pure competition was unrealistic. He set out to repair things by assuming product differentiation to be pervasive, by resuscitating and reformulating a theory of oligopoly, and by developing or suggesting market equilibria especially for monopolistic competition (the large group with product differentiation) and also for oligopoly without and with product differentiation. The ink on the first edition was only well dried when a number of people realized that Chamberlin had suggested (deliberately or inadvertently) a system of price theory based on a classification of markets or industries in terms of market structures. This was discussed in print early in a short article by Machlup,[3] but the idea was in circulation before this presentation.

The rudimentary Chamberlinian classification, distinguishing markets according to number of sellers and whether or not their products were differentiated, naturally took the familiar form:

1. Markets with many sellers
   a. Pure competition
   b. Monopolistic competition
2. Markets with few sellers
   a. Pure oligopoly
   b. Heterogeneous oligopoly
3. Single-firm monopoly

In recognizing this express or implied classification it was possible to grasp the systematic implications of Chamberlin's work and to see the possibility of exploiting them to revise and elaborate Marshallian particular equilibrium analysis as applied to industries. Also apparent was the intriguing possibility of generating empirically testable hypotheses concerning the relationships of the structure of industries to their market performance.

But had a classification of "industries" really been suggested, and if it had been, was it theoretically valid and useful? Could or should Chamberlinian theory be used to rebuild a Marshallian particular equilibrium theory based on the industry as a unit? Chamberlin himself, intent on discrediting the unrealistic Marshallian concept of a world of isolated industries each with a homogeneous

[3]F. Machlup, "Monopoly and Competition: a Classification," *American Economic Review,* XXXVII (September 1937), pp. 445 ff.

product that was a very distant substitute for every other product, had shied away from calling his competing or rivalrous groups of sellers "industries." He emphasized that "groups" of close-but-imperfect substitute products might and probably would overlap, the product groups being only more distant substitutes inter se. Triffin,[4] in 1940, holding that Chamberlin had nonetheless retained the industry concept, felt it improper for purposes of formal theorizing to accept both the assumption of pervasive and complex product differentiation and the concept of the industry at the same time, although he readily conceded that the industry was a valid and powerful organizing concept in applied price analysis. He therefore suggested the abandonment of particular-equilibrium price theory and called for but did not develop—nor has anyone since—a general-equilibrium theory incorporating Chamberlinian concepts. Heeding his counsel would evidently have insured the relegation of Chamberlinian theory to the category of a major curiosity, and aborted any major exploitation of its potential.

The "Chicago school" still holds a view akin to Triffin's. Even in recent literature we find it popping away at Chamberlinian theory on the grounds that in employing such concepts as "close substitutes" and "substantial gaps in cross-elasticities" it "introduces fuzziness and indefinable terms *into the abstract model where they have no place,* and serves only to make the theory analytically meaningless."[5] This stand is transparently ludicrous. It is argued that a price theory must be kept pristine and simple at any cost, even if empirically relevant assumptions won't let it stay that way. And it is by implication held that a modest and approximately accurate simplifying assumption—that firms in an admittedly product-differentiated economy are grouped into industries that are held together by close substitutability and separated by distant substitutability of their products—should be rejected in favor of the heroically and destructively unrealistic assumption that industries are as Marshall had them, purely competitive and isolated. An unrealistic assumption is involved in either case, but why stretch for the ultimate in unrealism, if assumptions are after all only the empirical generalizations from which a theory begins? We also wonder why Triffin could at once recognize the industry as a powerful organizing concept in applied Chamberlinian price theory and fail to perceive that it was an equally potent concept in a "pure" Chamberlinian theory.

Triffin and Chicago notwithstanding, Chamberlinian theory has proved formally satisfactory, tractable, and productive of meaningful hypotheses precisely when it has been adapted to particular-equilibrium analysis by assuming explicitly that the enterprise economy is made up of industries that are identified and separated by the value of cross-elasticities of demand among products, and by then classifying such industries according to their market structures. This assumption would have produced an unrealistic version of neo-Marshallian price theory if it had not indeed been true that in the real world

[4]R. Triffin, *Monopolistic Competition and General Equilibrium Theory,* Harvard University Press, Cambridge, Mass., 1940, pp. 88-89.

[5]M. Friedman, "More on Archibald versus Chicago," *Review of Economic Studies,* XXX (1961), p. 66. Italics added.

products were clustered in close-substitute groups with gaps of distant substitution among them (intergroup cross-elasticities of demand being negligible or approaching zero), and if instead there were a single tangled mass of products related substitutionwise in a fashion so complex that industries could not be readily identified or separated. But the former and not the latter appears to be empirically the case, whatever may be the abstract possibilities, and this being so a Chamberlinian particular equilibrium theory is analytically meaningful, far more than the Marshallian one.

Flippant examples purportedly destructive of the industry concept in a product-differentiated economy (such as the alleged close substitution of nightclub admissions, pleasure cruises, and cold showers) are not persuasive; for each of these there can be twenty queries such as those concerning the evident degree of substitutability between cigarettes and kitchen sinks, automobiles and roller skates, or concrete and gunpowder. A little serious endeavor to couple our powers of observation with our knowledge of the concept of cross-elasticity of demand might have shut off a great deal of pseudomethodological quibbling over the acceptability and validity of the industry concept in a price theory that deals with a product-differentiated economy.

The Classification of Industries

Having incorporated the industry concept into a particular-equilibrium version of Chamberlinian theory, let us return to the classification of industries. Chamberlin did not build his market classification from a foundation of assumptions concerning cross-elasticities of demand between different products or sellers, and thus whatever he was effectively assuming concerning cross-elasticities was implicit rather than expressed. This omission on his part was the source of some of the earliest criticism of his model of group equilibrium in monopolistic competition, centered on the proposition that the monopoly power of the individual seller should fade toward the vanishing point as the number of sellers in the group increased, presuming that the cross-elasticity of demand as among pairs of products did not change or increased.[6] Discussion of this and related matters is reserved for the succeeding section, in which monopoly power under monopolistic competition is considered.

This sort of criticism engendered systematic attempts to define in terms of cross-elasticities of demand the rudimentary market classes suggested by Chamberlin. Triffin did an initially quite satisfactory job,[7] the only evident flaw in which seems attributable to a slip or a typographical error. Some subsequent literature tended to obscure the issue because of mathematical misunderstandings until Bishop[8] and Heiser[9] analyzed the definitional matter adequately and

[6]See, e.g., N. Kaldor, "Monopolistic Competition and Excess Capacity," *Economica,* New Series, II (1935), pp. 33 ff.

[7]Triffin, op. cit., pp. 98-112.

[8]R. L. Bishop, "Elasticities, Cross-Elasticities, and Market Relationships," *American Economic Review,* XLII (December 1952), pp. 781-803.

[9]R. Heiser, "Elasticities, Cross-Elasticities, and Market Relationships: Comment," *American Economic Review,* XLV (June 1955), pp. 373-382; and R. Bishop, "Reply," *American Economic Review,* XLV (June 1955), pp. 382-386.

smoked out in the course of journal controversy[10] a special Chamberlinian assumption concerning the responsiveness of cross-elasticities between individual products to the number of products in a group or industry. Without reviewing the controversy, but taking sides to some extent (with the *general* position of Triffin, Bishop, and Heiser), I suggest that the following propositions have emerged:

1. A formal classification of markets requires reference both to a conventional price cross-elasticity, $(\delta q_j / \delta p_i) \cdot (p_i / q_j)$ (designated by Bishop as E_{ji}) as a substitutability-of-products criterion, and either to an unconventional quantity cross-elasticity, $(\delta p_j / \delta q_i) \cdot (q_i / p_j)$ (designated by Bishop as e_{ji}), or to some alternative measure, as a number-of-sellers or interdependence criterion.
2. Perfect substitutability of products in a market, regardless of the number of products or sellers in it, is denoted by the price cross-elasticity between every pair of products (E_{ji}) approaching infinity; "symmetrical" product differentiation[11] in a market is denoted by E_{ji} for every pair being finite; and E_{ji} between products that are in different markets, industries, or groups will approach zero.
3. A large number of small sellers in a market, with or without product differentiation, is denoted (under symmetry assumptions) by a quantity cross-elasticity between every pair of sellers (e_{ji}) approaching zero; oligopolistic interdependence between any pair of sellers in a market is reflected in e_{ji} being finite.[12] In simple oligopoly (each of the few sellers having circular interdependence with all the others), e_{ji} will be finite for all pairs.
4. A market classification of the rudimentary Chamberlinian type can then under symmetry assumptions be described in cross-elasticity terms as seen in Table 14.1. A single-firm monopolist would simply have an E_{ji} that approached zero with respect to every product in the economy.[13]

This classification seems formally unassailable unless the notion of an infinite number of sellers in a competitive market is introduced (a mathematical possibility that is axiomatically excluded,[14] in which case some cross-elasticity terms would become indeterminate and a more complex system of formal criteria would be needed. Neglecting this possibility, we see that one really

[10]W. Fellner, "Elasticities, Cross-Elasticities, and Market Relationships: Comment," *American Economic Review,* XLIII (December 1953), pp. 898-910; E. H. Chamberlin, "Elasticities, Cross-Elasticities, and Market Relationships: Comment," *American Economic Review,* XLIII (December 1953), pp. 910-916; R. Bishop, "Reply," *American Economic Review,* XLIII (December 1953), pp. 916-924.

[11]That is, product differentiation such that every product has the same degree of substitutability for every other product in the group (all intrapair substitutabilities thus being the same, and no pair of products being distant substitutes).

[12]Except in the limiting case in which the own-price elasticity of the industry or group demand function is zero or nearly so.

[13]This definitional system fails to provide a distinction between single-firm monopoly and monopolistic competition in the event that the latter is construed as potentially incorporating values of E_{ji} which, though finite, approach zero. If it is so construed, then an added criterion referring to the own-price elasticities of the sales curves in the two situations must be introduced to distinguish pure monopoly.

[14]In any real economy it is axiomatic that all populations (of persons, firms, etc.) are finite in number.

Table 14.1 A Market Classification Under Symmetry Assumptions

Market type	Cross-elasticities between each pair of members of the market	
	E_{ji}	e_{ji}
Pure competition	$\rightarrow\infty$	$\rightarrow 0$
Monopolistic competition	Finite	$\rightarrow 0$
Pure oligopoly	$\rightarrow\infty$	Finite
Heterogeneous oligopoly	Finite	Finite

controversial issue has remained: whether additional attributes of monopolistic competition are (1) that the finite value of E_{ji} between every pair of products is small enough to insure that the own-price elasticity of demand of the individual seller $(\delta q_i / \delta p_i) \cdot (p_i / q_i)$, or E_{ii} in the symmetrical case is not extremely large (its sales curve is not approximately horizontal), and (2) that as the number of sellers or products in a market becomes larger, the value of E_{ji} between every pair of products inevitably becomes proportionally smaller.

If E_{ji} is not small enough, the sloping ceteris paribus sales curve of the seller in monopolistic competition, which Chamberlin derived intuitively from product differentiation cum large numbers, will actually tend toward horizontality. If E_{ji} does not decrease or decreases less than proportionally as the number of sellers increase, E_{ii} tends to approach perfect elasticity with such an increase. These propositions are quickly evident in a simple model of fully symmetrical monopolistic competition (with all sellers producing equal outputs at the same price, and the value of E_{ji} the same for every pair of sellers), where obviously $E_{ii} = E_{ji}\ (n - 1)$, when n is the number of sellers. They are capable of extension to more general cases.[15]

Alerted to these logical possibilities, Chamberlin[16] has elected to defend the slope of the seller's demand curve in monopolistic competition by insisting that E_{ji} must be "small enough" and must fall as n increases.[17] The validity or invalidity of these propositions, like that of the equally plausible counterpropositions that the finite value of E_{ji} might just as well be larger and in particular remain unchanged as n increases, cannot be proved on a priori grounds (unless we adopt as axiomatic the noticeable slope of Chamberlin's little dd' in

[15]The two putative attributes of monopolistic competition (E_{ji} quite small and declining proportionally with increases in n) might be considered as formally interrelated and together require that with the smallest group (symmetrical heterogeneous duopoly) E_{ji} which would equal E_{ii} for each duopolist, does not exceed a critical value associated with a significantly sloping sales curve, and that with increases in the number of sellers in the group, from two through few to many, E_{ji} declines proportionally to maintain E_{ii} for each seller unchanged at the initial value.

[16]See Chamberlin, "Comment," in Footnote 10 above.

[17]And others (e.g., Bishop) have held that as a definitional matter monopolistic competition must have these properties, for otherwise the case would be indistinguishable from pure competition. The latter may be denied on the ground that monopolistic competition with approximately horizontal sales curves is not the equivilant of pure competition if selling costs and product determination are incorporated into the model.

monopolistic competition, and this is really not an axiom). Whether or to what extent the rejection of Chamberlin's postulates concerning the size of E_{ji} and its interaction with n deprives the large-group case of all novelty is considered below. Here two things may be simply noted. There is no good evident reason, logical or empirical, for believing that Chamberlin's postulates to support the slope of dd' in monopolistic competition must be valid ones.[18] And a generalized approach to his basic market classification via the route of cross-elasticities of demand, possibly backed by some propositions concerning the underlying consumer indifference maps, at once suggests the possibility of an elaborated variety of solutions for Chamberlin's product-differentiated market categories.[19]

Although the formal definition of the categories in Chamberlin's rudimentary market classification turns out to have more than a taxonomic importance, a more substantive issue has been whether the connected theory of markets could be improved by introducing initially a finer subclassification of markets. This may be done by employing as principles of classification added attributes of market structure other than number of sellers and degree of product differentiation, and also by recognizing with respect to some attributes more than a dichotomous distinction such as that between "many" and "few" sellers. If the theory is to be improved in this way, the addition of principles of classification and of market categories must be quite limited, because the primary function of an a priori theory—to produce generalizations—would not be fulfilled if a classification including very numerous market categories were employed. Nonetheless, some elaboration of the original Chamberlinian classification has seemed promising.

[18]First, the finite value of E_{ji} found with some minimal number of sellers sufficient to qualify as a "large group" can clearly be at once small enough to indicate that all pairs of products are distinctly imperfect substitutes and large enough that $E_{ji}(n-1) = E_{ii}$ is extremely large for each seller. Second, though some decline of E_{ji} with increases in n may seem plausible, there is no particular reason to suppose that any such decline of E_{ji} need be great enough to keep E_{ii} from increasing with n, in the event that there was a significant departure from perfect elasticity for the sales curve before n increased. Chamberlin effectively argues as if, in the fully symmetrical case, $E_{ji} = k/(n-1)$, where k is a constant with a relatively small absolute value, as suggested in Footnote 5 above. This is clearly a special and arbitrary assumption.

[19]It may be noted that Bishop, fearful of the pitfalls inherent in assumptions of infinite numbers and of industry demands with own-price elasticities of zero (which we reject or neglect here), hedged in his own final market classification along the following lines:

	$-E_{ii}$	$-E_{ii}E_{ji}$
Near-pure competition	$\to\infty$	Large
Significantly differentiated competition or pure monopoly	$< \infty$	Large
Near-pure oligopoly	$\to\infty$	Small
Significantly differentiated oligopoly	$< \infty$	Small

This end result does not fit well with his incisive exposition of classification principles in 20 preceding pages of his major article (op. cit. in Footnote 8, above). Heiser (op. cit. in Footnote 9, above) effectively criticizes Bishop's final retreat from a fully interpreted Triffin criterion.

Elaboration of the Chamberlinian market classification by recognizing more than a dichotomous distinction with respect to seller concentration seems clearly indicated within the magnum category of oligopoly. In an empirically relevant theory, oligopoly broadly construed embraces not only industries populated by "a few sellers, all large," with circular interdependence for every pair, but also any industry in which at least one pair of sellers has such circular interdependence, even though it includes other smaller sellers having circular interdependence neither inter se nor with their large rivals. Furthermore, fewness of sellers is both a broad and a loose concept, so that oligopoly defined in general terms embraces both industries with very high seller concentration in which the strength of recognized interdependence might be expected to be dominant, and industries with only moderate seller concentration in which such interdependence, though present, is relatively weak. The writer has thus previously suggested a slightly elaborated market classification that not only distinguishes pure and heterogeneous oligopolies but also subclassifies each of these types according to degree of seller concentration and presence or absence of a competitive fringe of small sellers.[20] The theoretical rationale of this subclassification of oligopoly, and its potential as a basis for a more adequate theory, are discussed below in the consideration of the theory of oligopoly.

I have also suggested that the Chamberlinian market classification may be fruitfully elaborated by introducing a third principle of classification—the condition of entry to an industry. It is notable that Chamberlin generally assumed both free entry (except for exact imitation of differentiated products) and the neglect by established sellers of the threat of entry, even for the market category of oligopoly, thus incidentally arriving at some implausible equilibrium solutions. Repair of this theory through elaboration of assumptions requires initially subclassifying oligopolies and single-firm monopolies according to the heights of barriers to the entry of additional sellers.[21] The exploitation of the implications of the added assumptions, involving an additional theorem, is also discussed in the subsequent section of the theory of oligopoly. Let us turn first, however, to issues concerning the extent of monopoly power under monopolistic competition.

MARKET POWER UNDER MONOPOLISTIC COMPETITION

Chamberlin assumed as a central market model a large group of small sellers purveying differentiated products (relatively close but not perfect substitutes to buyers) and then intuitively concluded that the ceteris paribus demand curves of individual sellers would be negatively sloping with a price elasticity that, though relatively high, would not approach infinity. He also assumed that these *dd'*

[20]See, e.g., J. S. Bain, *Price Theory,* Holt, New York, 1952, pp. 268-270.

[21]J. S. Bain, "Conditions of Entry and the Emergence of Monopoly," *Monopoly and Competition and Their Regulation,* E. H. Chamberlin, ed., St. Martin's, New York, 1954, pp. 215-241 (Ch. 6, this book).

demand curves would slope smoothly, no kinks occurring at the going or any other output, and that their price elasticities would not increase as the number of sellers increased. Given these assumptions plus those of U-shaped cost curves, of his version of free entry, and of "symmetry" of position as among all sellers, he derived his famous long-run group equilibrium for the "large-group case" as an alternative to purely competitive long-run equilibrium. His novel conclusions under these assumptions were that a long-run equilibrium would be reached with no excess profits, with all sellers operating slightly below optimal scale, and with every seller continuing to exercise a modest degree of monopoly power. He put his major emphasis on this model and these conclusions, and in consequence his theory at first came to be identified mainly with them.

In retrospect this is unfortunate, for his reformulated theory of oligopoly, on which he spent much less time, had greater empirical relevance and more revolutionary implications for price theory, whereas his theory of large-number monopolistic competition was undermined by implicit assumptions concerning consumer preference patterns even more than by his special symmetry assumptions, and was open to attack from numerous directions.

As seen above, a significantly sloping *dd'* for the individual seller cannot be unequivocally deduced from the assumption of a large number of symmetrical sellers of products that are close but imperfect substitutes (have finite price cross-elasticities). If the number of sellers is absolutely large (let us say 100 or more), it is additionally required that all price cross-elasticities be very small. Then, in one sense at least, the various products are individually quite poor substitutes for each other, pair by pair, and, moreover, the cross-elasticities must become smaller as the number of sellers increases. These were implicit assumptions in *Monopolistic Competition,* made explicit by Chamberlin only after others brought them to light. If we reject them, the general structural definition of monopolistic competition is consistent with ceteris paribus sales curves that are price elastic enough that the difference from infinite price elasticity is negligible. Then in monopolistic competition individual sellers would not necessarily have monopoly power, and the long-run group equilibrium would appear—*until product variation and selling costs are brought into play*—potentially to resemble very closely that of pure competition. When nonprice competition through product variation and sales promotion are recognized and incorporated into the theory, however, predicted market performance in monopolistic competition remains potentially distinctive even if individual sellers are essentially devoid of conventional monopoly power.

The preceding, moreover, suggests only one of the bases for revising Chamberlin's formulation of the individual seller's demand curve in monopolistic competition. In a notable article[22] Nicols went behind the sorts of cross-elasticities of demand that Chamberlin had implicitly assumed for the large-group case, to uncover what had also been implicitly assumed concerning

[22] A. Nicols, "The Rehabilitation of Pure Competition," *Quarterly Journal of Economics,* LXII (November 1947), pp. 31-63.

the maze of individual buyer preferences among the numerous differentiated products assumed to be offered. His most important expressed suggestion was that in order for individual sellers to have ceteris paribus sales curves that were both negatively and smoothly sloping (devoid of kinks) over any relevant interval, they would have to be supplying "scale-of-preference" buyers each of whom ranked all available products in some particular way (from most to least preferred), and that in addition different buyers or subgroups thereof would need to assign a reasonably full variety of different preference rankings to the various products.

One revealing corollary of the existence of a mixed lot of scale-of-preference buyers may be illustrated as follows. Suppose 101 sellers from a group, each with a differentiated product and each with 500 buyers when the sellers are charging equal prices. The scale-of-preference conditions would require that if any seller *A* raised his price by say one percent (equivalent to all other sellers lowering their prices by approximately one percent) he would have 100 buyers who would shift to other sellers, with one of these 100 shifting to each of the other sellers, because each shifting buyer had a different "next-best" product on his preference scale, and these 100 were the most easily detached of his 500. Then seller *A*'s cross-elasticity of demand with respect to every other seller for his price increase would be 0.2, and his own elasticity of demand for his price increase would be –20. Conversely, if seller *A* cut his price by one percent, each of his 100 competitors would have one most-easily detached buyer who put *A*'s product "next-best" on his list, so that by cutting his price *A* would gain one buyer from each of his 100 competitors, and would have the same cross-elasticity of demand (0.2) with respect to every other seller, and the same own-price elasticity of demand (–20) for his price decrease as for his price increase. Thus *A*'s dd' curve would have a continuous slope at the ruling output, as Chamberlin had it. As further successive price increases or decreases by any one seller were considered, comparable scale-of-preference properties of buyers' interproduct preference patterns would be required to secure the continuity of slope of any sellers' demand curve.

As Nicols suggested, this implicit assumption concerning a complex combination of scale-of-preference buyers is on a priori grounds, and apparently in terms of empirical relevance, a special assumption that we would not in general expect to be fulfilled. If it is not, alternative buyer-preference patterns could lead to individual sellers' demand curves being "obtusely kinked," or more elastic beyond going output than short of it. To take an extreme case, suppose in the preceding example that all of the buyers from any one seller preferred his product to all those of all competing sellers, though some preferred it more strongly than others and could thus be detached only by larger price difference; but that all such buyers were indifferent as to their choice among the other 100 products, viewing them effectively as perfect substitutes. (Each buyer would be a one-product man with weaker or stronger loyalty, and all other competing products would be indifferent choices inter se to him.) Then, assuming symmetry, if a one percent decrease by any one seller *A* would attract one "most detachable" buyer from each of 100 competitors, he would encounter a cross-elasticity with each competitor again of 0.2 and an own-elasticity of demand of –20, *for his price decrease.* But if *A* raised his price by one percent (equivalent to all his competitors lowering their prices by about one percent) he would lose only his one "most detachable" buyer to some competitor, and his own-elasticity of demand *for his price increase* would be only –0.2. (His "average" cross-elasticity of demand with the other 100 sellers would be 0.002). Then his ceteris paribus demand curve would clearly have an obtuse kink at his going output. Moreover, if somewhat higher values of cross-elasticity of demand are assumed (e.g., 2.0 instead of 0.2 for *A*'s price decrease, and an "average" of 0.02 for his price increase) his own demand curve would approach perfect elasticity for his output increases (–200 in this example), whereas it would be substantially less elastic for his output decreases (–2 in this case). Here Nicols obtained a very elastic seller's *dd'* by familiar reasoning concerning cross-elasticities and numbers, but obtained it only for output increases (price decreases) as he abandoned the scale-of-preference assumptions implicit in Chamberlin's model.

Nicols' suggestions were significant for several reasons. First, he revealed clearly that Chamberlin really failed to explore formally the implications of his theory on the level of the theory of consumer choice, and thus neglected to forge an analytical system incorporating product differentiation that led logically forward from the theory of consumer behavior through the theory of the firm and to his theory of the market in monopolistic competition. In making this revelation, Nicols suggested the importance of "completing" the Chamberlinian theory by building it from an adequate foundation theory of consumer behavior in the context of differentiated products. (Nicols himself merely scouted this territory.) Second, he properly identified the Chamberlinian solution for the large-group case as a distinctly special one and suggested the existence of a variety of equally plausible alternative solutions that might profitably be explored. Third, in introducing the notion that with some sorts of buyer-preference patterns (such as that featuring buyers each of whom views one product as superior and all others as indifferent choices) sellers in monopolistic competition may face ceteris paribus demand curves that are obtusely kinked at going output and very elastic beyond it, he suggested a model for monopolistic competition in which dynamically unstable prices within some equilibrium range may readily be deduced (as elementary experimentation will show), thus generating an interesting new hypothesis concerning long-run equilibrium tendencies in monopolistic competition.[23]

A full reconsideration of Chamberlin's model of and solution for the large-group case suggests: (1) that the model and the solution are special rather

[23]Nicols' own special case of a monopolistic competition in which a significant fraction of buyers are totally unattached (view all projects as perfect substitutes) and in which, therefore, each seller faces a perfectly elastic demand curve in the relevant range of output (any kinks being displaced to occur at smaller than going outputs) indeed gives purely competitive results, but the case is as uninteresting as it is special.

than general, mainly because they rest on special implicit assumptions concerning consumer behavior, his symmetry assumptions representing a lesser, if superficially more obvious, departure from generality; (2) that in the general case the existence of significant degrees of monopoly power should not characterize such monopolistic competition; and (3) that its distinctive features emerge when selling costs and product variation are incorporated into the model. Manipulation of these decision variables clearly opens the probability (if the symmetry assumption is abandoned or collapses) of equilibria with systematic price, product, and selling-cost differences among sellers even though none has perceptible monopoly power. It is possible, however, that buyer-preference patterns may be such in some instances that the seller possesses monopoly power for price increases but not for price decreases, in which case a price "yo-yo" effect is suggested.

THE THEORY OF OLIGOPOLY

The Chamberlinian contribution that was individually most important in implementing and giving vitality to his classification of markets was his discovery and formulation of a sophisticated theory of oligopoly. Cournot and others had played about with the model of duopoly as a theoretical curiosity, under assumptions that were internally inconsistent with the definition of the model. Chamberlin recognized oligopoly as a significant broad category of markets, introduced alternative assumptions that were implicit in the definition of the model, and drew the main outlines of a theory of oligopoly resting on these assumptions.

His most important assumption, of course, was that of "mutual dependence recognized" (or "circular interdependence" as others have called it) among the sellers in an oligopolistic industry. Chamberlin was quick to see that, given such interdependence plus a sort of comprehensive symmetry in rival sellers' situations and a complete absence of time lags in every seller's response to the price or output changes of the others, the member firms of an oligopoly should move inevitably to a joint monopoly price. (Specific conditions necessary to validate this conclusion include, in addition to instantaneous responses, identical market shares that cannot be influenced by price cuts or otherwise, and identical cost functions—all generally implied or expressed by Chamberlin.) He completed the blocking out of an elementary theory by suggesting that nonfulfillment of one or more of the necessary conditions for a joint monopoly solution for oligopoly could lead to any of a range of price outcomes between the joint monopoly and competitive limits—in either pure or heterogeneous oligopoly.

It must be recognized that Chamberlin did not develop a complete and fully articulated theory of oligopoly (in part because he held himself forever bound by symmetry assumptions). Only about 20 of the 176 text pages of the first edition of *Monopolistic Competition* were devoted to his own theory of oligopoly, and many of them were discursive. But he revealed the need for a complete theory of oligopoly, demonstrated the crucial importance in such theory of his own concept of circular interdependence, and suggested the critical structural characteristics of oligopolies (other than fewness of sellers) that would have to be formally recognized in a more complete theory. At the same time, he left a great deal of work to be done by other theorists.

Reactions in subsequent years to Chamberlin's innovation have been varied. There was some initial tendency to consign the theory of oligopoly to an early limbo on the ground that in the *general* case all that was to be found was a maze of interdependent conjectures about rivals' reactions and an indeterminate equilibrium solution. Others chose to develop a theory for oligopoly only under special institutional assumptions such as that a cartel or a viable and well-observed price or market-sharing agreement existed, and to neglect the rest. This pursuit was not entirely fruitless, for the exploration of the theory of oligopoly with express agreements revealed some fundamental tendencies within oligopolies that a more generalized theory would have to recognize and account for.[24] Much later, various attempts were made to arrive at a general theory of oligopoly through the application of the theory of games. To date these have not proved very successful (the n-person nonzero-sum game with coalitions admitted seems to be the appropriate general model) but they have shown us how to reach a Cournot duopoly solution the hard way.

Others have attempted positive elaborations of a general theory of oligopoly along the line that Chamberlin's work suggested, by exploring the internal logic of the oligopolistic situation and, without reliance on special institutional assumptions, tracing the implications of an added range of empirical generalizations that may be incorporated into the theory as assumptions. Perhaps the most significant general work in this tradition is William Fellner's *Competition among the Few,*[25] which incorporates a brilliant and lucid general statement of the logic of oligopoly in its first chapter and then proceeds to develop a theory of qualified or limited joint-profit maximization. Fellner's general theorem is that within any oligopoly there are likely to be conditions and motives present that oppose or mitigate the intrinsic drive toward joint-profit maximization and engender a market performance that, although not competitive, falls short of or deviates from monopolistic performance. Although he properly notes as relevant conditions such things as incompleteness of coordination in the nonprice dimensions of seller decisions and safety-margin considerations in the presence of uncertainty, he strikes at the heart of the problem when he notes that only qualified joint-profit maximization and quasi-agreements are generally possible because of the unwillingness of the individual oligopolist to yield up his sovereignty at all fully for the sake of joint-profit maximization, except in exceptional circumstances.

Fellner specifically emphasizes this reluctance as a pervasive deterrent to the emergence of perfect cartels (in which firms would pool their resources and

[24]This quality is particularly apparent in D. Patinkin, "Multi-Plant Firms, Cartels, and Imperfect Competition," *Quarterly Journal of Economics,* LXI (February 1947), pp. 173-205.
[25]Knopf, New York, 1949.

earnings and agree on interfirm compensations) whenever cost functions are nonhorizontal or differ among firms or when product differentiation is present. But the thesis is readily generalized and extended (1) to identify comparable deterrents within oligopolies that forestall agreements to charge an approximately monopolistic price, and (2) to explain difficulties that make several sorts of imperfect collusion (e.g., collusion at a submonopoly level of price, imperfectly observed collusion, collusion on price cum rivalry for market shares) predictable possibilities or probabilities. Fellner recognizes this in a general way, but does not pursue the point very far.

A generalization of Fellner's thesis might take the following form: if an oligopoly is defined as being composed of several independently owned and controlled firms, its members intrinsically have two or three conflicting motives. One is the motive for joint profit maximization (most probably long-run maximization), because all would like to divide the largest profit pie. Such joint maximization is exactly obtainable via a perfect cartel, or, if that is barred by law, attainable to a reasonable approximation through price and kindred agreements that may be reached tacitly by nothing more than "implicit bargaining," for example as offers to agree are made and accepted or rejected through press releases. Another motive, however, is present because of the fundamental antagonism of interests of separately owned entities: each oligopolist would also like to increase his share of joint profits at the expense of his rivals, and is willing to do so even if his action reduces joint profits, provided that the absolute amount of his separate long-run profit is increased. This motive does not vanish simply because there is also a mutual interest in maximum joint profits, and because it does not, the movement by oligopolists toward joint-profit maximization (even of the approximate sort attainable without perfect cartels) is not a foregone conclusion. A motive corollary to the general antagonism of interest among rival oligopolists is that of each to protect his sovereignty; this deters him from exposing himself to loss through agreements or treaties comprehensive enough that his rivals can hurt him without hurting themselves by failing to observe or abrogating the treaties or agreements. This consideration places a definite constraint on the probable scope and content of tacit or express agreements, and even on the degree to which they represent attempts to approach joint monopoly pricing or selling-cost or product policies.

All of the preceding being recognized, pricing and related policies and market performance within oligopolies depend on the relative operational strength of joint-profit maximizing and antagonistic motives in particular situations. This relative strength of motives in turn depends on the specific structural characteristics of the oligopolistic market—characteristics that effectively determine the probability of success of antagonistic pricing and related policies in enhancing the profit positions of individual sellers. If these structural characteristics are such as to render antagonistic policies unprofitable to sellers who undertake them, generally or with respect to certain decision variables (price, product, selling cost), then collusive action for joint-profit maximization generally, or with respect to given variables, is predictable. If these characteristics tend to render antagonistic actions profitable to some or all of the rival sellers, independent profit-maximizing motives come into at least limited play. Then it is predictable that collusive monopoly outcomes will be whittled away in some degree by independent actions (clandestine price cutting, product competition, etc.); that agreements will initially not aim so high as joint-profit maximization because they would then be too vulnerable to defections; or that agreement with respect to one variable (e.g., price) may be accompanied by limited antagonistic policies with respect to another (e.g., product).

The structural characteristics of oligopolies that seem to be most important in determining the relative importance of joint-profit-maximizing policies and antagonistic policies include, in addition to the state of market information and other considerations affecting the promptness with which rivals can respond to each others' actions: (1) the degree of seller concentration, or more generally the number and size distribution of sellers in the market; and (2) the effective differentiability of the product, which establishes the scope for independent product adjustments or variations that are not readily or rapidly matched by rivals.

The importance of the degree and pattern of seller concentration is obvious as we distinguish oligopolies with only a very few large sellers from those with a somewhat greater number of large sellers, their number being small enough that circular interdependence is still readily inferred. In addition we may distinguish subcategories of each of the preceding classes according to whether or not the oligopolistic industry also includes an appreciable competitive fringe of small sellers who do not have circular interdependence with the large ones. In highly concentrated oligopolies, circular interdependence tends to be so strong (the effect of each seller's price or related adjustments on each of the others so great) that antagonistic actions tend to be rapidly and fully "punished" and thus discouraged; joint-profit-maximizing actions are then likely to be dominant, leading toward monopolistic market performance.

In moderately concentrated or more dilute oligopolies, the self-policing mechanism of circular interdependence, though present, is weaker, encouraging limited antagonistic actions, profitable to those who undertake them, as a pull against joint-profit-maximizing action. (Limited antagonistic action may be expressed through independent clandestine price concessions to individual buyers, leading toward "chaotic" price discrimination, through independent forays in product variation and increases in sales-promotion budgets, etc.) Price, product, or selling policies may then not be held at the joint-profit-maximizing level both because tacit agreements are selectively violated and because the terms of the agreements themselves are adjusted to mitigate destructive violations. A profit-maximizing principle that is a hybrid of joint-profit-maximization and independent-profit-maximization may in effect be the working principle. The probability of this happening is enhanced if the oligopolistic industry is in fact made up of of an oligopolistic core and an appreciable competitive fringe of small firms, for reasons so obvious as not to require discussion. The preceding suggests that an elaborated theory of oligopoly should rest on a structural subclassification of the general oligopoly category to recognize three or four degrees and patterns of seller concentration, and that, at least as probability judgments, different market conduct and performance may be predicted for each subcategory.

Further subclassification is suggested according to the effective differentiability of the product the industry sells. With products having high effective differentiability, limited antagonistic action in the area of product policy and related sales promotion are tentatively predictable even with high seller concentration and even with joint-profit-maximizing collusion on prices; a less restricted antagonistic action is indicated for oligopolies that are moderately concentrated and that have significant competitive fringes of small sellers.

The preceding theory, like Fellner's, is not a "complete" theory of oligopoly according to criteria ordinarily applied, principally because it does not tie its assumptions to its conclusions by a complete process of deductive reasoning that would lead unequivocally to unique predictions of market performance for each of several subcategories of oligopoly. It does provide a framework for a complete theory, the development of which (if possible) would require the introduction of some added concepts and assumptions, among them the values of both price and quantity cross-elasticities, and the "pivot man" or "police man" seller whose policies limit the scope of the antagonistic policies of others. Such a generalized theory may emerge if sufficient time and ability are devoted to the problem. Meanwhile, this quasi-theory is of some value as a source of refutable hypotheses to be tested through empirical studies.

One relatively recent elaboration of the theory of oligopoly (and of monopoly) has involved the introduction of (1) the concept of the condition of entry (or height of barriers to entry) to oligopolistic industries as an added significant dimension of their market structures; (2) the theorem that established firms will tend to recognize threats of entry and deter it by "limit pricing" below the monopoly level if that is more profitable to them in the long run than charging higher prices and inducing entry; and (3) further theorizing concerning the conditions under which they will and will not follow limit-pricing policies.[26] This theory has not yet had its fullest obviously attainable formal development. In its present rudimentary form it proposes a new range of hypotheses concerning the pricing and related policies and the market performance of oligopolists, and suggests the validity for theoretical purposes of further subclassifying oligopolies according to the height of the barriers to entry to them. A notable aspect of this theory is that it finds a new role for product differentiation—namely, as one of the main types of barrier to entry—which might be held to be as important as the role Chamberlin assigned to it. Its full development depends on the application of Chamberlin's novel construct. As far

[26] J. S. Bain, "Conditions of Entry and the Emergence of Monopoly," op. cit., and *Barriers to New Competition,* Harvard University Press, Cambridge, Mass., 1956. One aspect of this theory was independently developed, on somewhat special assumptions, by Sylos-Labini, *Oligopoly and Technical Progress,* Harvard University Press, Cambridge, Mass., 1962 (translated from the original work in Italian published in 1956).

as the genesis of the theory goes, the writer must give further credit to Chamberlin, whose implausible "high-tangency" solution for heterogeneous oligopoly (where all established sellers were supposedly oblivious to threats of entry and to the long-run effects of entry on their profits) fostered a desire to arrive at a more plausible solution.

The consideration of theories involving barriers to entry and limit pricing has suggested incidentally the desirability of extending the theory of long-run equilibria in oligopolistic industries to comprehend the determination of market structures, especially in the dimension of degree and pattern of seller concentration. Such an extension should comprehend among other things the systematic classification of certain models of oligopolistic behavior, such as price warfare to weaken or eliminate rivals, as representing disequilibrium situations and reflecting dynamic processes of market adjustment. Some tentative work has been done on this front, which remains open for exploration.

EQUILIBRIA INVOLVING DETERMINATION AND SELLING COSTS

If Chamberlin's theory of oligopoly was most important in developing the implications of his market classification, second in importance would be his elaboration of price theory by introducing product and selling cost as variables that the firm manipulates along with price, quantity of output, and production cost. Through this elaboration he clearly suggested the possibility and presumptive importance of a multidimensional theory of the firm and of industry equilibrium with greatly enhanced empirical relevance. He also implied the need for developing an elaborated set of criteria of market performance, to include socially optimal product quality and variety and a socially optimal size of selling costs (in addition to "efficiency" criteria referring to marginal cost-price relations, scale of firm, and excess capacity), against which theoretically predicted performance in the dimensions of product and selling cost could be measured.

The major reasons that Chamberlin's innovation in this area has failed to have a vital impact on subsequent theoretical literature seem to be that Chamberlin himself did not develop any normative system to match his predictions concerning market performance in the dimensions of product and selling cost, that these predictions of his were almost devoid of normative content, and that theorists later have conspicuously failed to remedy his omissions by developing a coordinate set of norms. Distinctly secondary reasons for this lack of strong impact would include the facts that, being restricted to formal analysis via two-dimensional geometry, Chamberlin was unable to develop fully the interactions of five variables and larger numbers of intervariable relationships in arriving at equilibria for the firm or industry, and that most of his predictions in this area were so general in character as scarcely to be susceptible to empirical refutation. These latter deficiencies have become readily remediable with advances in related branches of theory and in mathematical economic theory generally.

Chamberlin's own failure to develop or attempt to develop the sort of norms described is consistent with his general disinclination to delve into the theory of consumer behavior, even though the need for the development of some aspects of this theory was clearly implied by his theories of markets and of the firm. This is a disinclination already identified as being responsible for the fact that major parts of his theory rested partly on a foundation of unexplored implicit assumptions and thus ran to special solutions. But he contributed a great deal as it was, and it is puzzling that others have not pursued the theoretical inquiries that he neglected by working over the area of consumer preference theory to provide norms at least for "ideal product."

Norms for selling costs are elusive creatures, because of the direct action of selling costs on consumer preference patterns. However, the road toward developing the concept of buyers' price-quality-quantity preference functions,[27] defining optimal coadjustment of these variables, and deducing the extent to which market performance within each of several market structures tends to diverge from such an optimum is fairly well marked and appears to be passable. The best explanations available for a general failure to push along this road are that it is rough and can be navigated only with quite advanced technical equipment, that many economic theorists have been temporarily beset by a disenchantment with normative economics, and that those with the most adequate technical equipment are more interested in other problems or perhaps never heard of this one. Yet a careful study of Chamberlin's theory of group adjustment including product variation clearly suggests propensities toward product qualities that are "excessive" from the standpoint of buyer welfare, under any of a number of constellations of buyer price-quality preferences, and an analysis of this suggestion at the level of rigorous formal theory would clearly be important.

Chamberlin's own analysis of decision making by the firm and of equilibrium for the group when price, quantity, production cost, selling cost, and product are all variable is well known. He developed partial solutions for various trios of variables, each including production cost and quantity–taking as the third variable successively price, product, and selling cost–and avoided most of the more obvious pitfalls of this procedure through literary interpolations that qualified his partial solutions by considering the coordinate influence of the adjustment of another variable. Then he poured together the partial solutions into a general solution that says nothing more than that the firm will seek a *maximum maximorum* position in which all partial marginal-equality conditions are simultaneously fulfilled, and that the group will do likewise after exit or entry. Insufficient emphasis was perhaps placed on the fact that two of the partial marginal-equality conditions could be fulfilled at points and with intervariable relationships inconsistent with a *maximum maximorum*, and the

[27]These preferences might be reflected, for example, in maps of indifference curves relating price to quality, quantity being given, or quantity to quality, price being given–or in more complex four-variable functional relationships linking price, quality, quantity, and the level of satisfaction.

interplay of all the variables could not be adequately analyzed with the equipment at hand. A conspicuous omission from relevant empirical generalizations entered as assumptions in Chamberlin's theory was one concerning the relation of the demand for a seller's output (represented by price, quantity being given, or by quantity, price being given) to increase in product quality. A related omission was the failure to distinguish markets in which all buyers have identical price-quality or quantity-quality indifference maps from those in which buyers differ systematically in this regard—and thereafter to explore the relevance of this distinction.

Chamberlin's theoretical models involving selling cost and product were thus not productive of many formal hypotheses that were meaningful in the sense that they were conceivably susceptible of empirical refutation. If there is product differentiation, selling costs will be incurred and be covered by price. With respect to the outcome of group product adjustment, "the most that can be said is that it [the exact point of equilibrium] will be characterized by (1) the equation of cost and price, and (2) the impossibility of a 'product' adjustment by anyone which would increase his profits."[28] The equilibrium product under monopolistic competition is inevitably "inferior" because of sellers' monopoly power, but this really turns out to mean only that product quality is slightly lower than if we had monopolistic competition without such monopoly power, so that the term "inferior" is devoid of normative connotations. About the most that is made of selling costs is Chamberlin's deduction (to abbreviate a prolonged argument) that the competitive use of selling costs will virtually enlarge the markets of individual sellers by concentrating a given industry demand in the hands of fewer sellers (and perhaps by enlarging industry demand), that this virtual increase will not be fully offset by consequent price increases, and that firms undertaking selling costs will thus operate at larger scales than otherwise. This is a conclusion that if generally supportable is of much interest mainly in the context of the inefficiently small scales or excess capacity that Chamberlin's rather special solutions for monopolistic competition and oligopoly predict.

The foregoing might be construed as expressing a dim view of Chamberlin's contribution so far as it introduced selling costs and product variation into the theories of the firm and of markets. It is really dim, however, only with respect to Chamberlin's formal exploitation of the constructs he introduced, and to the inadequate underpinning of his argument in the area of the theory of consumer choice. A consistent positive view is that he opened up a fruitful territory for theorizing that should by now have been explored far more thoroughly than it has, because of both its policy implications and its general theoretical interest. His formal models, together with his literary commentary on them, are a rich source of informal and implied hypotheses concerning market performance in the dimensions of product and selling cost that clearly invite formal development, just as the need for feeding much more normative content into his models is implied.

[28]Chamberlin, *The Theory of Monopolistic Competition,* p. 97.

However, the payoff from his crucial constructs and derived rudimentary models in this area has been slow in coming—much slower than that from his innovation of the theory of oligopoly. Properly neglected are miscellaneous regurgitations and reformulations of Chamberlin's three-variable partial solutions (mostly emphasizing selling costs as the more quantifiable of the added variables), because by and large they added nothing to and sometimes subtracted from what we already had. Abbott[29] made a valiant effort to develop the theory of product determination. Although he contributed significantly to the theory of the "horizontal" equilibrium of products (degree of differentiation,[30] in dealing with "vertical" product equilibrium (level of quality of all products in a group) he succeeded mainly in demonstrating unmistakably that on an inflexible price-is-given assumption it is possible to reach nonsense conclusions concerning both the level of product quality a market will reach and the positions of firms via-à-vis exploitation of scale economies—albeit displaying considerable technical ingenuity en route.[31] In subsequent argument he unfortunately failed to eradicate this blight or to arrive to an improved general solution for product determination where price is also variable.

At present, the blueprint for the development of the product and selling-cost phases of Chamberlin's theory calls for many additional building blocks; without these blocks the full potential impact of his pioneering work in the area of multivariate analysis on the theories of the firm and of the industry remains largely unrealized. Correspondingly, its major impact has so far been registered on the conceptual structure of empirical work in the field of industrial organization.

CONCLUSION

A concluding synopsis of the foregoing may be omitted in favor of some general remarks about Chamberlin's broad contribution to microeconomic theory and subsequent contributions that his work has inspired or should inspire.

Chamberlin's *Monopolistic Competition* had its wellsprings in the brilliance, originality, breadth of view, and rigor of intellect of its author. His most important contribution to price theory was one of broad conceptualization and of organization or reorganization of ideas. In this function he stands preeminent as an original architect of a new system of price theory. He has been perhaps less outstanding, though indubitably competent, as a "construction man" who followed his own blueprints, in that he has built only pilot models on selected assumptions (being a bit unwary about implied assumptions), but he certainly has built enough to point the way to the fulfillment of his master architectural plan. He has been perhaps least outstanding as a self-critic. In 30 years of active work following the initial publication *Monopolistic Competition*, he did not really revise it although it remained his major interest and went through eight

[29] L. Abbott, *Quality and Competition,* Columbia University Press, New York, 1955.
[30] Ibid., pp. 143-152.
[31] Ibid., pp. 152-170.

editions. He has tended to resist rather than accept and benefit from numerous criticisms and suggestions, and has been curiously reluctant to go on with the main construction job he began on completing the manuscript first published in 1933.

Examination of his main contributions would suggest that he contributed most importantly to the theory of markets by introducing the construct of a market classification based on distinctions among market structures and on a brilliant identification of those dimensions of market structure that provided the most significant principles of classification. Of substantially equivalent importance were his contributions to the theories of the firm and of markets, through his innovation of "mutual dependence recognized" for firms in oligopoly and through his introduction of a multivariate theory of the firm's market policy and of market equilibrium. He contributed very little, however, to the theory of consumer choice, even though his theories of the firm and of markets cried out for such a contribution. Partly in consequence, the notable deficiency of these theories was their comparative lack of normative content.

Thus Chamberlin passed on to theorists both an enormous opportunity and an exciting challenge to implement his broad architectural plans and to explore the *terra nolum cognita* he had viewed from a distance. What has been the quality of the response to this opportunity and challenge, within the general confines of a priori microeconomic theory, and where have there been conspicuous failures to respond?

First, his taxonomy of market structures has been systematized and regularized on a formal level, and also deliberately elaborated as logic and observation have dictated, with resultant improvement, albeit at the cost of questioning certain of his primary deductions concerning the sufficient conditions for the existence of monopoly power. Tentative advances along this line, however, have been marred generally by a failure to refer back at all sufficiently to the theory of consumer choice.

Second, much less has been done in developing his model of large-numbers monopolistic competition. Retrospective evaluation of his original work has suggested that this Chamberlinian model was a much less important novelty than his theory of oligopoly, at any rate except so far as it incorporated selling cost and product as decision variables. That the seller in such monopolistic competition should be viewed as possessing significant monopoly power remains seriously in doubt—a doubt that arises only in very diminished degree with respect to the oligopolist. Moreover, oligopolistic markets seem empirically more important than those that combine atomism with product differentiation. Given this doubt, theoretical progress has nonetheless been made toward recognizing that large-numbers monopolistic competition may generate a variety of special and distinctive types of market performance, of which the original Chamberlinian type was only one.

Third, exploitation or development of Chamberlin's germinal theory of the firm and industry in situations where selling costs and products as well as price and output are variable has been quite limited. This seems explicable in part by a passing shift of economists' interests to other matters (or to types of national economies in which allocation of resources among different sorts and qualities of consumer goods is hardly the central problem), and in part by their failures to recognize (here Chamberlin did not explicitly draw a road map) the need for a correlative probing of the theory of consumer choice—and to probe it.

Finally, perhaps the most fruitful effort devoted to exploiting the potential of Chamberlinian theory has centered on the theory of oligopoly, and not improperly so if empirical relevance is introduced as a criterion. Some successes have been scored in this area, resulting from endeavors that would probably not have been launched lacking a *Monopolistic Competition.* That this should be the main area of successful efforts to advance Chamberlinian theory matches well with the fact that Chamberlin wrote mostly of the theory of markets, and implies some things about the habits and limitations of most economic theorists. Yet in spite of comparative success in exploiting the potential of Chamberlin's ideas in this area, both generally and with regard to the analysis of conditions of entry, we still have something resembling fuller architectural plans much more than completed theories.

From this we might infer a dismal fate for sophisticated price theory, but of necessity only if fads and fancies continue to tempt theorists always to abandon the half-explored claim in order to join a new gold rush. A resurgence of interest in the actual allocation problems of an affluent enterprise economy, as distinct from its growth problems, may engender the development of a much more adequate neo-Chamberlinian microeconomic theory than we now have.

Chapter Fifteen

On Distributing Income in Terms of Specific Goods

As good a way as any of opening this topic may be to quote from a piece by E. B. White entitled, "The Morning of the Day They Did It." By way of explanation, "they" were a couple of astronauts patrolling the earth on an orbiting space platform armed with a sufficiency of nuclear warheads, and what they did was to get a bit space-happy and lob their weapons just about everywhere. Wherefore, Mr. White reflects on the human estate just prior to the last days of the planet earth, as he imagines it, and in part as follows:

> In many respects mine was a good job. It paid two hundred and twenty-five dollars a week, of which two hundred and ten was withheld. I should have felt well satisfied. Almost everything in the way of social benefits was provided by the government–medical care, hospitalization, education for the children, accident insurance, fire and theft, old-age retirement, tri-D shots, vacation expense, amusement and recreation, welfare and well-being, Christmas and good will, rainy-day resource, staples and supplies, beverages and special occasions, babysitzfund–it had all been worked out. Any man who kept careful account of his pin money could get along all right, and I guess I should have been happy. Ann never complained much, except about one thing. She found that no matter how we saved and planned, we never could afford to buy flowers. One day, when she was a bit lathered up over household problems, she screamed: "God damn it, I'd rather live dangerously and have one dozen yellow freesias." It seemed to prey on her mind.[1]

This carries the distribution of income in terms of specific goods about to the limit, but if we are going to consider this medicine, we might as well

This is a slightly revised version of a paper read to a seminar at Harvard University, November 1967.

[1]Excerpt from pp. 58-59 of "The Morning of the Day They Did It–February 25, 1950," in *The Second Tree from the Corner* by E. B. White. Copyright © 1947 by E. B. White, Hamish Hamilton, London. Copyright 1950 by E. B. White. Reprinted by permission.

contemplate the full dose before building up a tolerance by taking it in small but increasing amounts. In any event, I want to talk about redistributing income in terms of specific goods—taxing those with higher incomes in order to dispense specified goods to those with lesser ones—and also about just distributing some substantial part of income to everyone in terms of specified goods, financing it by proportional taxation.

In this distribution or redistribution, two sorts of goods are involved: first, ordinary private goods, the consumption of which by a person or household precludes consumption by others; and second, goods that have at least in part the attributes of public goods, and that usually cannot be efficiently supplied by private markets. We are already of course distributing or redistributing income in terms of specified goods of both types. The most obvious pure public good that comes to mind is euphemistically referred to as *national defense.* Included among quasi-public goods that we dispense are fire and police departments, preservation or development of recreation areas, and some aesthetic amenities. Essentially private goods so far subjected to this treatment include medical care (for the aged or indigent at home, for all some places abroad); some subsidized low-cost housing for low-income groups; school lunches; relief payments in the form of food stamps; and of course education. (Of these only education, up to a point, is also now a compulsory good.)

But the path is open. We could distribute or redistribute much more income in terms of quasi-public goods, and also in terms of many more private goods—for example, food to fulfill minimal dietary standards, shelter to meet minimal housing standards, clothing, even leisure. Food, clothing, and shelter may seem to bring us to an apparently obvious cut-off point in private goods, but remember that the definition of a necessity is elastic over time.

So far, of course, we have only walked a short distance down this path, but it is time to look at present and future alternatives. Do we stop with status quo; do we go farther; if so, how much farther—both in redistribution and plain old distribution in terms of specific goods?

THE CONSUMER SOVEREIGNTY ISSUE

Let me put aside public and quasi-public goods for the moment, and consider the alternatives with respect to private goods. The decision here might turn largely though not entirely on the comparative reliability of consumer sovereignty as a guide to resource allocation. Correspondingly, the strongest implicit support among economists for the specific goods approach to income distribution comes from those who have lost faith in this sovereignty. So we might begin by considering the related arguments of John Kenneth Galbraith[2] and Tibor Scitovsky.[3]

[2] *The Affluent Society*, Boston, 1958, and *The New Industrial State,* Boston, 1967, Chaps. 30, 31.

[3] *Papers on Welfare and Economic Growth,* Stanford, Calif., 1964, Chap. 15, "On the Principle of Consumers' Sovereignty."

The Galbraith argument or creed, as I read it in brief, rests mainly on these propositions: (1) There is really a difference, that does not change elastically over time, between necessities and luxuries, or between urgent and frivolous goods. (2) Producers, by making ever greater numbers of frivolous goods available, make it possible for consumers to want them. (3) The consumer's judgment as to what he ought to have has been dangerously impaired by the nefarious process of multiplying the frivolities that are available for him to demand, by informing him of their availability, and by persuading him.

We should note, of course, not only that all this is argued mainly in support of a heavy sales tax to be used to divert resources from frivolities to "public production," but also that it incidentally provides a basis for supporting other programs for governmental distribution of income in terms of specific goods.

The Scitovsky argument (again condensed and again deferring consideration of public production) is a bit fancier, offers a larger target, and is about as follows: (1) Consumer preferences are unreliable as data for guiding resource allocation, because they are so malleable by advertising. (2) The crux of the matter, however, is that the exploitation of scale economies in production forestalls the supply of a sufficient *variety* of products to cater to *minority* tastes concerning the character and design of goods. (3) Further, the neglected minority generally embraces those with "informed tastes"–including, first, experts in judging specific goods and, second, "generally educated people," who know how to inform themselves and know of a wider range of consumption alternatives than uneducated people do. (4) Therefore, the uneducated or unwashed miss the precious opportunity of being able to emulate the minority elite in setting their preference patterns, and thus make poor choices, or accept inferior alternatives when they are offered.

But there is more, as Scitovsky has other strings for his bow. (1) Again because of the exigencies of scale economies, private producers are deterred from risking "imaginative innovations," and rely instead on market research into consumers' unfulfilled desires. (2) This either slows down genuine progress and innovation, or, worse yet, leads to a serious misreading of public tastes. On the latter point, Detroit's prolonged failure to find out that people wanted little cars, and Hollywood's failure to find out that people wanted sophisticated movies, are cited.

Before going further, let us note that Scitovsky derives no strong policy proposals from this analysis, but that his general argument could support at least control of product designs by boards of experts or holders of advanced degrees. And, having done so, let us consider these mazes of assertions.

CRITIQUE OF GALBRAITH AND SCITOVSKY

Galbraith simply reads the facts differently than I do and advances judgments I would not accept. Among other things, I see no clear line between urgent and frivolous goods, if it is satisfaction and not mere survival we are talking about.

Admitting that consumers are subjected to many conflicting as well as complementary persuasions, I do not perceive that they have been hornswoggled or brainwashed. And I would consider it arrogant to tell a random housewife that she was dumb to want a seven-phase clothes washer, a three-phase dryer, and a self-cleaning electric oven instead of something I picked out.

I have some complaints about Scitovsky that are more specific. First, the constraints of scale economies on product variety seem much exaggerated, as does the alleged suppression of variety. In this connection, incidentally, if the market doesn't supply the variety of alternatives the elite would prefer, where did they acquire their superior knowledge of the better alternatives? Second, the technical excellence and custom building that experts and educated people might prefer would or does usually cost enough more so that the majority of consumers would prefer a lower and perhaps more standardized quality at a lower price, given the choice. Or, aren't the informed tastes of the elite on the average expensive tastes, so that their transference to the masses would be blocked by income distribution?

Third, I wonder how much better highly educated people inform themselves of the relative merits (cost considered) of alternative products than do high-school graduates. My own experience with academic Ph.D.'s is discouraging. Further, there is some question about the disposition of the unwashed mass consumer to heed the advice of diet experts, housing experts, or even the medical profession when he goes to market, and it is not axiomatic that he is always wrong. Finally, I wonder if market research is really a less reliable guide than an epicure's taste to what else the consumer wants or should have, or if misreading of the true consumers' tastes is common. In this connection, Scitovsky's automobile and movie examples belie themselves—the *full* markets, including imports, offered the missing alternatives about as soon as they were sorely missed.

In sum, I do not feel that a case has been made for the distribution of income in terms of specified private goods—made, that is, on the basis of the unreliability of consumer sovereignty or the unresponsiveness of private producers. In any event, the alternatives to consumer sovereignty are discouraging. Consider the caprice, bias, and general unreliability of "experts" in housing, diet, clothing, transportation, and so forth, not to mention the prospective fallibilities of a select panel of mature, experienced educators in the sciences or humanities.

And even if in some sense the experts were "right" about what products people should have, it doesn't necessarily follow that they should be virtually forced to take them. A dietary expert can specify the ingredients and cost of an optimal diet for good health, or a housing expert can specify the minimum necessary amount of floor and window space and sanitary plumbing per square individual, but should any household be forced or financially induced to take the specified goods before he buys a frivolity? If some critics hold that existing consumer preferences are unreliable data for guiding the allocation of resources, one very reliable datum is that at least 80 per cent of our adult population would vehemently reject the distribution of any significant part of their incomes in terms of goods specified by any panel of experts or any elite.

Turning specifically to the *redistribution* of incomes in terms of specific goods, the relatively poor are ill-equipped to strike back when they are offered a choice between specified goods and nothing at all. But it is not self-evident that a borderline-poor family is made better off by a $50 per month rent subsidy that moves it from substandard to "acceptable" housing, than it would be by a $50 cash subsidy per month–spend it as you will. Most recipients could probably get on a higher indifference curve if you gave them the cash. There are evidently many households in our society which would accept the dissatisfaction of queues at the bathroom, or of someone sleeping on the living room sofa, in return for an automobile, or a better automobile, or a television set. And are they wrong? I once knew a linotyper who in the prime of his years quit whatever job he had every June 15 to go fishing for three months. Otherwise he did not live well, but he seemed well-balanced to me, and was by far the best fly fisherman I ever saw.

Thus I reject the idea that the unreliability of consumer preference patterns per se–or, in other terms, that human improvidence, ignorance, and gullibility per se–provide adequate support for programs of distributing or redistributing private production in terms of specified goods.

Correspondingly, the valid occasions for such distribution or redistribution arise mainly from other circumstances, including: (1) *External benefits* accruing to society from induced individual consumption of some things–for example, education, regular and competent medical care, possibly adequate diet. But we should be careful not to overextend this list; it is very stretchable. Perhaps even Franklin Roosevelt went too far or not far enough in stressing that a third of the nation was ill-fed, ill-clothed, and ill-housed. Practically everyone had shelter and functional clothing; the incidence of diseases of malnutrition was low; and much of the nation was ill-automobiled, non-televisioned, under-travelled, and awfully short of original oil paintings. (2) *External disbenefits* to society accruing from the use of certain goods, or designs of goods. It looks, for example, that the air pollution stemming from the contemporary use of automobiles provides a basis for direct or indirect governmental control of engine designs, sizes, exhaust systems, and other design features, aimed at eliminating air-pollution emissions from motor vehicles. Or, the waste disposal and litter problem may quickly become acute enough to justify public insistence on the sole use of quickly destructible (burnable or rustable or biodegradable) containers, or of returnable and returned glass containers, for just about everything. (3) *Genuine market failure* (outside the realm of public and quasi-public goods, which I will consider shortly). Often cited here are the housing industry and medical care. Having mentioned this as a ground for direct distribution of goods, I must question it. Suppose that there is an undersupply of doctors, associated with unduly high fees and rationing, or an intractable building industry that won't build low-cost housing when it could, or can't because of slum owners. The direct distribution method is one way out. But a better ultimate way out is probably to work on the industry, improve its market, and then, if some poor are still shut out, redistribute money income. Personally, I would justify direct distribution of medical care mainly on the basis of external economies to society, and not accept or plead market failure as being in the long run inescapable. And I would note that the governmental supply of low-cost housing has done little to reform the building industry or ease the binds on land.

In this connection, I question Scitovsky's proposition that direct distribution of some goods is needed because their relative prices are so high as to cause them to be distributed too inequitably for public tolerance. If this is a market failure argument, I question it on grounds just stated. If it is a general argument, let us note that there are a lot of things that are too expensive for at least a big minority of the population to have at all or to have as much of as they want—including quasi-urgencies as well as frivolities. And public tolerance, like consumer preference, is a sometime thing, and also one which Madison Avenue could shape about as well. Moreover, any time that Scitovsky can find an indispensable or very urgent good that is actually priced out of the reach of a great many people, he should look for a way to get the cost down, because the indicated redistribution of income is probably going to be unmanageable.

ALLOCATION BETWEEN PRIVATE AND PUBLIC GOODS

I will consider more briefly the allocation of resources between private goods and quasi-public goods. To get back to my mentors, Galbraith holds that overall satisfaction would be increased by expanding public production at the expense of private production foregone, but that people are unwilling to vote the necessary funds because the private sector offers more and more goods and because they are hypnotized by Madison Avenue. The public production he mentions includes education, medicine, recreation areas, aesthetic services, and waste disposal—to which we might add "anti-production" in protecting the natural environment. He would like to have a pro-rata share of income automatically go, via a sales tax, to public authorities, whose problem would then be to allocate this fund according to needs. About all that Scitovsky adds here is that society has not developed adequate mechanisms for expressing public preferences as between public and private goods, and that this is increasingly distressing as previously free quasi-public goods become scarce as population grows.

The major issues as I see them are: (1) Would we indeed get greater overall satisfaction if private consumption were reduced in favor of supplying more quasi-public goods? (2) Do we really lack adequate mechanisms for expressing public preference on this point? (3) Supposing we had a steady flow of tax revenues earmarked for public goods, are there any serious intrinsic problems we haven't been told about?

As to whether we would get closer to a Pareto-optimal position by following the Galbraith-Scitovsky road, about all I would care to say is first that it is possible but not axiomatic, and second that they haven't proved it. A good deal would depend on whether and how we counted and weighted the essentially unavoidable income-redistribution effects, and a great deal on the actual composition of public output. The latter problem seems to belong under the heading of unrevealed intrinsic problems.

As to mechanisms for expressing public preferences, there seems to be no physical shortage of them, though the complaint might be made that they are unduly crude and also of varying effectiveness as related to different public goods. There aren't many difficulties in getting school-bond issues on ballots, but just in getting them passed. Federal and state legislatures that are reasonably responsive to their constituencies continually ponder on how and where to spend money. But those preferring some public goods—e.g., recreation areas or concerts in the park—are less readily organized and represented than some others, unless perhaps they can grab a spectacular issue, like preserving the Grand Canyon of the Colorado. However, the reasons for the ineffectiveness of known mechanisms may be strongly interlinked with some intrinsic problems in determining the composition and quality of bundles of quasi-public goods. (These problems, incidentally, would become more acute if public authorities were endowed with an earmarked annual flow of tax revenues for public production.)

One of the buried problems is that the direction of public expenditures has long been strongly influenced by particular pressure groups, that special minorities rather than majorities are frequently the beneficiaries, and that many citizens are aware of this. Consider the rural component of the Interstate Highway System, which seems to have flunked a benefit-cost test but is an indubitable gift to the trucking industry. More generally, citizens lack assurance that enlarged public expenditures won't have a dominant commercial bias. Just enlarging them solves nothing.

A related problem is the dissatisfaction of many citizens, based on experience, with the performance of public enterprises. I will single out just two sources of dissatisfaction. One is the propensity of public agencies systemically to underestimate the costs of projects, so that tax costs turn out to be substantially greater than predicted. In the San Francisco Bay Area, for example, a progressive disenchantment with rapid transit has set in as the authority that is building the system periodically reveals that it has underestimated costs by progressively larger amounts, inflationary effects aside. The public voted a large bond issue to finance a system that they knew was going to be heavily tax-subsidized, but they resent the prospect of doubling the taxes.

A second source of dissatisfaction stems from the fact that various specific public-enterprise bodies become dominated by bureaucracies with rigid ideas, commercial biases, and low sensitivity to the desires of the general citizenry. For example, urban freeway programs, including those tied into the Interstate Highway System, have been a source of much public dissatisfaction because of the bias of many highway engineers toward the straight line as the shortest distance between two points, and away from aesthetic amenities and preservation of environments—often in the teeth of organized civic opposition. It is trite but true that one difficulty with public enterprises is that, once financed and launched on their journeys, they generally don't live or die according to the judgment of any real market.

A further difficulty of a perhaps more intrinsic sort is that expenditures on quasi-public goods, when they are not catering to specific commercial interests, understandably tend to cater to majority or mass tastes, and relatively to neglect an assortment of minority tastes. Consider the provision of recreational facilities, as in national or state parks or as adjuncts to water projects. The emphasis is on fast and ready access by paved roads, camping facilities adapted to stopping in or next to the motor vehicle, boat-launching ramps leading to reservoirs for water-skiing or sit-down fishing, put-and-take stocking of fish, and accommodations for large crowds in limited areas (the last no doubt linked to the mass preference never to leave a crowd). Preservation of wilderness areas or any areas that take some effort to reach, of wild rivers, or of native runs of anadromous fish are disadvantaged competitors for public funds. Thus the majority, or very possibly only the plurality, of recreation-seekers get what they want, whereas an assortment of minorities who may even add up to a majority are rather poorly served. And the argument is not confined to recreation.

In this respect, governments as purveyors of quasi-public goods do not seem to perform as well in providing an optimal variety and mix of goods as does the private sector, Madison Avenue and all. Getting back to mechanisms, it could in fact be argued than an outstanding failure of public enterprises is found in their generally neglecting to provide ways for the individual citizen to vote his preferences for what public goods he wants, just as he votes his dollars for private goods. (Such voting, of course, should be conducted with the understanding that majority rule is abandoned in favor of what we might call *proportional allocation.*)

The preceding is meant to suggest that before we get into a greatly enlarged provision of quasi-public goods, we need to improve the habits of public enterprises, and also do some serious planning as to how best to determine the allocation of public expenditure. In summary, it appears that Galbraith has made his grand plan sound much simpler than it would be. Without a thorough reorientation and reorganization of the control of public enterprise, we might grow a Big Brother we really didn't like.

Chapter Sixteen

Technostructure, Revised Sequences, and the Locus of Power

Since 1950, the most prominent and no doubt the most widely read author of popular books on economics for the layman has been that eminent public servant and economist, John Kenneth Galbraith. Possibly to be sure, and certainly for those who have written the dust-jacket copy for his latest major work, he has had an important influence on the general public's thinking about economic problems, altering their view of economic life. Some testimony to this accomplishment is that he has assertedly enriched the vernacular language such phrases as "countervailing power," "affluence," and "the conventional wisdom."

Professional economists in general have perhaps been less enthusiastic about his accomplishments. This could, of course, be attributed dually to jealousy and to pique. In the first place, practically none of them could approach Galbraith's facility and style in writing popular books. In the second place, the typical Galbraith take-off point for an argument has been a deprecation of the intelligence and perspicacity of nearly all of his academic contemporaries, whose errors he is about to set right. And even though he generally manages this by attributing to them outmoded theories and views which most have not espoused for twenty or thirty years, and thus running his lance through a straw man, his tactics can be a little annoying.

But the disenchantment of the "establishment" of professional economists with his principal books really has had a professional rather than a personal basis. His modus operandi has been to choose a simple and perhaps topical issue concerning the working of the economy and, after attacking what he alleges to be the relevant views of his professional contempories, to present his supposedly novel view, and then hammer it home at length. These contemporaries, or some of them, have had several objections.

First, the true novelty of many of his arguments is seriously in question. The notion of "countervailing power" that he introduced in *American Capitalism,*[1]

This is a slightly revised version of a lecture delivered at Boston College, November 1967.
[1]Boston, 1952.

for example, seems mainly to revive and rehash the theory of bilateral monopoly or bilateral oligopoly, which is then pasted on the whole industrial economy. Or, there is precious little that surprises one in *The Affluent Society,*[2] unless it is a proposal for more public goods financed by sales taxes.

Second and more important, he has tended to attach an exaggerated importance to his novel explanations of how things really work. Bilateral monopolies are asserted to have replaced competitive or oligopolistic markets rather generally in the American economy, but–labor markets aside–the serious student of industrial organization would be hard-pressed to identify 25 per cent of the national output of goods and services as changing hands in situations of countervailing power. And the role of Madison Avenue in our economic affairs seems to have been inflated out of any reasonable proportion. To borrow a phrase from a venerated colleague: "These arguments are all right as far as they go; the only trouble is that they go too far."

Finally–and perhaps this sums up a good deal–Galbraith seems to be straining a bit too hard and obviously to be today's Thorstein Veblen–to introduce a revolutionary change in our whole view of economic society. In the process flamboyancy supersedes accuracy, and anything goes. Galbraith's contemporaries in his profession have in general not been converted so far.

"THE NEW INDUSTRIAL STATE"

This brings me to Galbraith's most recent major book in economics, *The New Industrial State.*[3] It has received a lot of publicity, and I propose to consider it seriously. Serious consideration is indicated because the work is his most ambitious so far, because it integrates and extends his previous lines of thought, and because in its substance it is by far the most controversial of all his works. It is also indicated because this time Galbraith certainly feels that he has written a major work and wants to be taken seriously. In his Introduction he says: "This book had its origins alongside *The Affluent Society.* It stands in relation to that book as a house to a window. This is the structure; the earlier book allowed the first glimpse inside."

What does this edifice look like? Except for the very peculiar way its heating plant runs, it looks quite familiar to any student of industrial organization. As a matter of fact, it embodies much more that is old and familiar than is new and surprising. But the surprising part is sufficiently incredible to require discussion of the whole thing. Perhaps I can best analyze the structure or argument by considering in turn his recitation of the familiar and obvious; some familiar but debatable or ambiguous propositions; the crucial assertion of a revolutionary theory of how the economy works, which would essentially put the most modern and sophisticated price theory on the scrap heap; and related observations and asides.

[2]Boston, 1958.
[3]Boston, 1967.

RESURRECTION OF THE FAMILIAR

Among the things that Galbraith tells us as background that have been known, digested, and reflected on by economists for a long time, and about which there is no particular debate, are the following:

1. That in that the last seventy years we have seen the ascendancy of the modern corporation, separation of ownership from control of large corporations, a growing share of government in economic activity, Keynesian fiscal policies, the rise of Madison Avenue, and affluence.
2. That the consequences of modern industrial technology include a long period of capital-intensive production, comparative inflexibility of capital commitments, the importance of administrative organizations, and the need for much advance planning by corporate enterprise. Incidentally, the pivot of economic power has thus shifted from *land* to *capital* since the eighteenth century.
3. Given the modern corporation and modern technology, we arrive at *group decision-making* in big corporations, as distinct from one-man decision-making. So the importance of the individual entrepreneur has declined. The organized decision-making group, or group of groups, is designated as the *Technostructure.* Technostructure seems to consist of corporate management as usually understood, including influential specialists and technicians.

In all fairness, it must be said that Galbraith neither claims nor disclaims discovery rights to any of this except Technostructure, which appears to represent mainly a terminological innovation.

ESPOUSAL OF THE DEBATABLE

So much for the unquestionable; let us turn to the debatable. Most but not all this involves Galbraith's embracement of or flirtation with Organization Theory (ala Simon, Cyert, and March) and a type of Sales Maximization Hypothesis. But there are some added starters that we might consider first.

One is the undocumented observation that planning by large corporations has superseded markets, and that this has been done by vertical integration, by long-term contracting, and by big firms "controlling" markets. It would be interesting to see someone try to document this claim. Granted the effect of integration and contracting in reducing the number and frequency of buyer-seller transactions, it would still appear that some multiple noticeably greater than one of the value of the net national output of goods and services, or of manufacturing output alone, passes through buyer-seller transactions in what the average economist would call a *market.*

Another observation, also undocumented, is that private corporations, as an incident of their planning the economy, control the supply of savings—largely, it would appear, through reinvesting profits and other quasi-rents. So the money market really doesn't matter. This assertion should surprise quite a few people.

Back now to Organization Theory and Sales Maximization. This argument, or series of assertions, is a little confusing. The opening proposition is that large corporations in concentrated markets don't try to maximize profits (if they do, they are not in concentrated markets). This is because profit maximization is inconsistent with the Technostructure. Its real goals are *compensation* plus *compulsion* plus *identification* plus *adaptation*, which added together equal *the motivating system*. In the inner circle of Technostructure, *identification* and *adaptation* dominate, with the result that profit maximization is superseded by the pursuit of "the goals of society" (which must be consistent with the goals of individuals), or with "goals that appear to have social purpose." The only constraint is that corporations make "satisfactory earnings" in order to preserve the autonomy of the Technostructure.

Up to this point, Galbraith like his mentors seems to have said almost nothing at all. In any event, the cutting edge of any motivational pattern is not revealed or described. What policies identification and adaptation lead decision-making groups to pursue is more or less left up to their own judgment.

We are rescued in the nick of time, however, by the revelation that, given minimal satisfactory earnings, the real goals of technostructured corporate managements turn out to be mainly (1) a maximal rate of corporate sales growth, and (2) technical virtuosity. At least the first of these possible goals is familiar from the literature, but I cannot ascertain that they are in any way deduced from or obviously follow from Galbraith's motivating system. His propositions concerning the motivations of corporate management are proved, if at all, only by vigorous assertion.

It is worth notice in passing that at this juncture the theory of oligopolistic pricing (the existence of which theory Galbraith this time recognizes) is cryptically labelled and characterized as more or less of a hoax, presumably because of its qualified dependence on profit-maximizing assumptions, which we have just been told are false. Price theory is also charged with a paradox for saying that oligopoly is inefficient but that a system containing oligopolies is efficient. The absence of the paradox is of course apparent as soon as we recognize that some allocational inefficiency can go hand in hand with considerable technical efficiency.

"THE REVISED SEQUENCE"

We arrive now at the revolutionary proposition about how the economy works—honored by a newly coined term, *The Revised Sequence.* The assertion is really as simple as it is incredible: In the New Industrial State, the producers of the Technostructure plan and determine the volume and composition of total output—allocation of resources among uses—and then control or manage the demands for goods by advertising and related sales promotion so that what they have decided to produce is bought. That is, producers more or less autonomously determine what goods are to be produced and how much of each of them, and manipulate buyer demands to match their production plans. The pattern of buyer demands is not something that producers respond or adapt to, but something they propagate. So the traditional sequence is reversed, as producer sovereignty has replaced consumer sovereignty.

Galbraith does not suggest, moreover, that this magnum planning of production and manipulation of demand is accomplished by any corporate superstate or comprehensive conspiracy that might coordinate and reconcile the individual plans and advertising campaigns of a large absolute number of huge corporations. Apparently the independent plans of each of them magically emerge as somehow mutually compatible and consistent, with no central planning. Yet it seems that he would not have widened the credibility gap and might even have narrowed it if he had conjured up some super cartel.

This then is what is inside the edifice to which *The Affluent Society* was a window—a workable system of decentralized private planning of the volume and composition of total output, linked with a decentralized system of manipulating demands to correspond to what is produced. Price theory in general as we have known it—as well as nearly all the extensive literature of industrial organization related to it—is not just mistaken on some matters; it is in its entirety dead wrong.

Having made his major claim, of course, Galbraith backs and fills a little bit. That is, the revised sequence doesn't apply to unconcentrated industries. But it does apply to the huge corporations, guided by the Technostructure, that supply much or most of the national output of goods and services, and is thus the dominant motif in our economy.

ANALYSIS OF "THE REVISED SEQUENCE"

Where do we begin in analyzing his amazing proposition? To begin somewhere, it is worth noting that it is really nothing more than a bald assertion. It is not proven by logic. It is absolutely unsupported by any evidence presented. It does not follow in any visible way from Galbraith's preceding recital of well-known facts, or from his arguments and conclusions concerning corporate motivation, or both. Therefore, we have no particular reason for believing it at all.

Even if the revised sequence did operate for the sphere of very large corporations located in concentrated industries, and not elsewhere, we would hardly have discovered a motif for much or most of our economic activity. Galbraith has more or less glossed over the fact that a substantial majority of all goods and services produced and sold in the United States are supplied by industries of relatively low concentration, in which relatively small firms account for a major share of output. If consumer sovereignty has waned, has it waned generally, or just mostly for soap and cigarettes and toothpaste and automobiles?

Also, what about producer goods and the firms that buy them? It is well-known that a majority of the value of shipments of manufactured output that passes through purchase-sale transactions consists of producer goods and is bought by producer-buyers. It is equally well established by observation that the great bulk of producer-buyers are notably insensitive to advertising and other sales-promotion appeals, and buy what they want when they need it and in amounts that they determine. Granted that the demands of consumer buyers for some consumer goods are somewhat malleable in the hands of Madison Avenue, would Galbraith have us believe that the suppliers of producer goods control the demands for their outputs? I am sure, for example, that the assertion that they do would come as a surprise to the United States Steel Corporation or the member firms of the steel industry generally, and similarly to the member firms of dozens of concentrated producer-goods industries. To arrive at this conclusion, moreover, I do not need to read the minds of the corporate managements involved, but only observe how unstable and market-sensitive are the demands for many of their outputs. If the steel industry autonomously plans its output rate and manipulates the demand for steel to match, why has it repeatedly permitted its output rate and sales to change upward or downward by 25 to 30 per cent between adjacent years, when the level of general business activity moved only slightly over the same span of time? The notion that markets and buyer sovereignty are inoperative in producer-goods markets is belied by an overwhelming mass of comparable evidence.

Finally, what about consumer goods, Galbraith's heartland? As already suggested, he ultimately does not claim them all for the revised sequence, as he surrenders relatively unconcentrated industries to the old-fashioned realm of markets. In so doing, moreover, he concedes a great deal at once—for example, most food processing and distribution, the garment industries in general, the housebuilding industry—or, roughly, enough food, clothing, and shelter to account for about half of all personal consumption expenditures.

This leaves us with relatively concentrated consumer-good industries, and incidentally most of the big advertisers. Even if Galbraith's grand edifice is already tottering, let us center attention on them.

In this realm, which includes automobiles and refrigerators and television sets and liquor and cosmetics, to name a few, is production planned and consumer demand correspondingly regulated by the Technostructure? Granted the power of advertising and related product policies, we must recognize that there is a long distance between influencing consumer demands with varying degrees of success, and controlling or determining them. And the great body of casual evidence at our disposal suggests two things.

First, about the most that the dominant firms in concentrated-good industries usually succeed in doing—or hope to do—is to influence consumer demands in their favor, and possibly increase or sustain their sales volumes. Second, most of their selling campaigns do not appear to be pieces in a grand design to match up consumer demands with planned outputs. They seem mainly to implement rivalries among firms for larger shares of consumer expenditures—including rivalries among companies in the same industry for larger shares of the same market, and rivalries among industries for bigger shares of the consumer's dollar. If this is the case, markets for consumer goods are very much alive, even if they are heterogeneous oligopolistic markets, and we do not have producer sovereignty. In other words, the varying and limited sensitivity of the preference patterns of consumers to advertising appeals does not signify that consumer sovereignty is moribund. Consumers are influenced but not brainwashed.

I suggest this in part because the construct of producer sovereignty, even in concentrated consumer-good industries, comports poorly with verifiable facts. If producers control demand, why has the automobile industry permitted its sales to fall from about 7 million to 5 million units annually from one year to the next; when nothing much else was happening? Why was the Ford Motor Company unable to make people buy Edsels, but sold two or three times more Mustangs than it thought possible? Why did the industry producing color television sets get at least five years behind its own schedule for penetrating the market? How could the Big Four in the distilled liquor industry have been so stupid since 1952 as to allow consumer tastes to shift away from American whiskey (and to gin, vodka, and Scotch whiskey) sufficiently that their combined market share for all liquor has dropped from 75 to 58 per cent, and that their profit rates were almost cut in half? And so forth. Any unbiased observer with all the relevant advertising and sales data for the last twenty years before him would almost have to conclude that oligopolistic consumer-good suppliers are unable to control the demands for their outputs, but can only with highly variable success influence them. The indication then is that Galbraith's revised sequence should be almost entirely rejected.

SOME OTHER ISSUES

Much of the rest of what Galbraith has to say in *The New Industrial Estate* is anticlimactic or not very interesting, and I will comment on only a small part of it. His observation that the Technostructure is increasingly dependent on what he chooses to call *The Educational and Scientific Estate,* but that there is latent conflict between the two, is hardly surprising. Nor is it news that our industrial system is remiss in giving enough attention to health services, care of the aged, poverty relief, recreation areas, aesthetic services, waste disposal, and the external disbenefits it generates. But the observation that public enterprises fail to fill these gaps mainly because we are all quite confused in thinking we have a market system in the private sector is debatable and apparently a non sequitur.

In his remarks on the interrelationship between the industrial system and the government, Galbraith seems to be on somewhat firmer, though sometimes controverted, ground. Without accepting the revised sequence for an instant, for example, most of us would agree with him that the Technostructure must depend on the government to stabilize the level of aggregate demand through taxing and spending policies. And it may be that the industrial system has devised more effective and complicated means of influencing governmental policy than buying senators.

His most provocative thesis concerning business and the state, however, concerns government spending—that the industrial system, depending heavily on government purchases for its sustenance, has contrived and promoted images of the needs and dangers of the state which induce the government to continue a high volume of purchases. Thus, it more or less manages government demand for industrial output in much the same way as it allegedly manages private demand. He offers two examples of its commercially oriented image-building: its preservation of the cold war image for twenty years, and its later participation in the promotion of the space race.

Now this hypothesis has at least a certain superficial plausibility, and is certainly more plausible than the one about the revised sequence. But it must be quite a bit oversimplified, and perhaps enough so that the overall picture is obscured. There are, after all, buyers as well as sellers of munitions and space hardware, and the immediate customers are located in or closely associated with the armed services and the Congress. This being so, a legitimate first question concerns what parties are mostly or primarily responsible for generating governmental demands for the goods in question. Does the industrial system take the lead in creating a climate of opinion that results in the purchases, or does the military, or do Congressmen who want defense or space facilities in their states or districts? Or is this a sort of shared responsibility, and if so, what are the shares?

I am not in a position to give definite answers to these questions, but I am reasonably sure the industrial system or its Technostructure does not play the only important role. And this brings me, its errors aside, to a striking lacuna in the general content of Galbraith's argument. He has, after all, set himself the task of presenting a general explanation of how our economy and society really work, and in particular of where economic and social power are located and how they are exercised. In performing it he has identified and given capital-letter names to principal loci of power, including The Industrial System, the Technostructure, and the Educational and Scientific Estate. But somehow, in his analysis of the distribution of power today, Galbraith has failed to single out, in either lower-case or capital letters, The Military Establishment. This seems to be more than a trivial oversight if the locus of power is at issue.

Joseph Schumpeter, whom Galbraith recognizes only in an inconsequential footnote, worried at length in 1942 in his famous *Capitalism, Socialism, and Democracy,*[4] about who would assume the reins of power that were being dropped by the vanishing entrepreneur. He foresaw a power vacuum that would have to be filled in some way, but was ambivalent in predicting who would fill it and how. Now, twenty-five years later, Galbraith is abreast with Schumpeter in recognizing the demise of the entrepreneur, and implicitly in recognizing the power vacuum. But he sees this vacuum filled, and power seized, only by a bloodless thicket of committees called Technostructure. Shouldn't he have given a chance to The Military Establishment? Or to something else a little more tangible than the Technostructure? We are left with the feeling that the problem of the locus of power remains at best partly solved.

And finally as to the noxious uses of Madison Avenue, it is possible that the

[4]New York, 1942.

emphasis has been misplaced. It seems less distressing that the fraternity in question is able to overpersuade the consumer of toothpaste, than that it employs the same techniques to persuade the "consumer in politics" concerning both national policies and political candidates. The most dangerous power of Madison Avenue expertise might well be found in its developing ability to sell worn-out movie stars as political leaders supposedly worthy of election to positions of frightening responsibility.